BUILDING A STRONGER ECONOMIC FUTURE FOR BRITAIN

Economic and Fiscal Strategy Report and
Financial Statement and Budget Report
March 1999

Return to an Order of the House of Commons dated 9 March 1999.

Copy of Economic and Fiscal Strategy Report and Financial Statement and Budget Report – March 1999 as laid before the House of Commons by the Chancellor of the Exchequer when opening the Budget.

Barbara Roche
Her Majesty's Treasury
9 March 1999

Ordered by the House of Commons to be printed 9 March 1999

LONDON: THE STATIONERY OFFICE
£28

House of Commons No. 298

The Economic and Fiscal Strategy Report and Financial Statement and Budget Report contain the Government's assessment of the medium-term economic and budgetary position. They set out the Government's tax and spending plans, including those for public investment, in the context of its overall approach to social, economic and environmental objectives. After approval by Parliament for the purposes of Section 5 of the European Communities (Amendment) Act 1993, these reports will form the basis of submissions to the European Commission under Articles 103 and 104c of the Treaty establishing the European Union.

This document can be accessed from the Treasury's Internet site: http://www.hm-treasury.gov.uk

CONTENTS

Economic and Fiscal Strategy Report

Page

Financial Statement and Budget Report

1 OVERVIEW

1.1   The Government's central economic objective is to achieve high and stable levels of growth and employment. This Budget will help build a stronger economic future for Britain through reforms that will put work, enterprise and families first. By protecting the environment and ensuring that growth is sustainable, this Budget will also ensure a better quality of life today and for future generations.

1.2   The key elements of the Government's strategy are:

- locking in economic stability as a platform for long-term sustainable growth;

- raising productivity through promoting enterprise and investment;

- increasing employment opportunity with a better deal for working families; and

- building a fairer society, with a better deal for families and children.

1.3   The Pre-Budget Report (PBR), published in November, set out the direction of Government policy and measures under consideration to deliver this strategy. A series of regional roadshows has subsequently widened the debate on how to rise to the productivity challenge and secure high and stable levels of growth and employment.

> **This document – Budget 99: Building a Stronger Economic Future for Britain – represents the next stage. It contains two reports. The Economic and Fiscal Strategy Report (EFSR), the first published since the House of Commons approved the Code for Fiscal Stability, sets out:**
>
> - **a coherent framework and strategy to achieve the Government's objectives;**
>
> - **a progress report on steps that have been taken so far; and**
>
> - **how Budget 99 measures will contribute to each element of the strategy.**
>
> **The Financial Statement and Budget Report (FSBR) provides:**
>
> - **a summary of each of the Budget measures; and**
>
> - **a full analysis of the economic and public finance forecasts.**

MACROECONOMIC STRATEGY AND PROSPECTS

1.4   Chapter 2 of the EFSR sets out the Government's macroeconomic strategy and the prospects for the UK's economy and public finances.

The new framework 1.5   In the past, Britain has suffered greater volatility in output and inflation than most other major industrial countries. Such volatility imposed both social and economic costs. On coming into office, the Government therefore introduced a new framework for monetary and fiscal policy to promote economic stability, while ensuring that macroeconomic policy responds sensibly to economic shocks:

- **a new monetary framework** to deliver low and stable inflation: the Bank of England's Monetary Policy Committee has been given operational independence to set interest rates to deliver the Government's inflation target;

- a **new fiscal framework,** including two strict fiscal rules – the golden rule and the sustainable investment rule – to get the public finances under control. Borrowing has been reduced by a cumulative £29 billion over the last two years and tight control has been maintained over public expenditure; and

- a **new public expenditure regime** which together with new three year spending plans, will provide greater certainty and encourage longer-term planning.

The forecast 1.6 The rewards of the new framework are already evident. Inflation is close to target. Interest rates peaked at $7^{1}/_{2}$ per cent last year, half their peak level in the last cycle. Debt interest payments are falling. And employment is up by more than 400,000 since May 1997; long-term and youth unemployment have fallen by 50 per cent. The Budget 99 forecast, summarised in Table 1.1, confirms that:

- **RPIX inflation** is forecast to remain at the target level of $2^{1}/_{2}$ per cent; and

- **growth** will be lower this year than last, following the global slowdown. However, the economy is well placed for stronger growth into 2000, in line with independent forecasters. This means that this cycle is set to be much more moderate than those in recent decades.

Table 1.1: Summary of the economic forecast

	1998	1999	Forecast 2000	2001
GDP growth (per cent)	$2^{1}/_{4}$	1 to $1^{1}/_{2}$	$2^{1}/_{4}$ to $2^{3}/_{4}$	$2^{3}/_{4}$ to $3^{1}/_{4}$
RPIX inflation (per cent, Q4)	$2^{1}/_{2}$	$2^{1}/_{2}$	$2^{1}/_{2}$	$2^{1}/_{2}$

The fiscal rules 1.7 Budget 99 locks in the economic stability that the new framework has delivered. As a result of the strengthening underlying fiscal positon, the fiscal rules are still met while the new Budget measures provide an extra £6 billion support over the next three years to boost the economy during the period when output is below its trend level. The public finances forecast – summarised in Table 1.2 – shows that:

- the **surplus on current budget** is projected to average 0·4 per cent of GDP over the current economic cycle; and

- **net public debt is projected to decline significantly** as a proportion of GDP, to below 35 per cent by 2003–04.

Table 1.2: Meeting the fiscal rules

	Outturn 1997–98	Estimate 1998–99	Projections 1999–00	2000–01	2001–02	2002–03	2003–04
Per cent of GDP							
Surplus on current budget[1]	–0·6	0·5	0·3	0·4	0·8	0·9	1·0
Average Surplus since 1997–98[1]	–0·6	–0·1	0·0	0·1	0·3	0·4	0·5
Public sector net borrowing[1]	1·1	–0·1	0·3	0·4	0·1	0·3	0·4
Public sector net debt	42·5	40·6	39·4	38·2	36·8	35·6	34·6
£ billion							
Surplus on current budget[1]	–5·1	4·1	2	4	8	9	11
Public sector net borrowing[1]	9·1	–1·0	3	3	1	3	4

[1] Excluding windfall tax receipts and associated spending.

1.8 Meeting these rules will allow the UK to:

- maintain high quality public services and deliver the spending commitments – including £40 billion additional investment in education and health over the next three years – announced in the Comprehensive Spending Review (CSR); and

- ensure the overall position of the public finances remains sound. As both rules are set over the economic cycle, they will also allow the automatic stabilisers to play their part so that fiscal policy continues to support monetary policy in the next phase of the cycle.

1.9 In addition, illustrative baseline projections for the next 30 years set out in Annex A of the EFSR indicate a sustainable fiscal position, capable of delivering equitable outcomes for future generations.

1.10 The Government is taking further steps to raise the sustainable rate of growth by tackling the underlying structural weaknesses in the economy. These are explored in Chapters 3-5 of the EFSR.

RAISING PRODUCTIVITY

1.11 Chapter 3 sets out the Government's strategy for raising productivity through a better deal for enterprise and investment.

The productivity gap **1.12** The UK produces less per person than other major economies. The **productivity gap** of 40 per cent with the US and over 20 per cent with France and Germany reflects long-standing weaknesses in the economy:

- the UK has invested less in **Research and Development** (R&D): the US invests 50 per cent more, as a share of GDP, in business enterprise R&D;

- for every £100 per worker invested in **new capital equipment** in the UK during the last economic cycle, the US and Germany invested £140; and

- fewer people have **basic skill levels**: 22 per cent of adults in the UK have poor literacy skills, 50 per cent more than in Germany.

Measures so far **1.13** The Government has already introduced – in the 1997 and 1998 Budgets and CSR – a number of microeconomic reforms targeted on the five key drivers of productivity growth:

- **investment:** corporation tax has been reduced to its lowest ever level and tax measures introduced to encourage investment for the long-term;

- **innovation and enterprise:** £1.4 billion additional investment in science will promote high quality research and innovation;

- **education and skills:** an extra £19 billion will be invested over the next three years in raising achievement and improving skill levels;

- **competition:** new competition laws will increase efficiency and deliver a better deal for consumers; and

- **public sector efficiency:** setting challenging performance targets.

New measures **1.14** Budget 99 builds on this start through a further package of measures including:

- a new **10p corporation tax** rate for small companies and extension of **40 per cent capital allowances** for small and medium enterprises (SME) businesses to encourage entrepreneurial activity and innovative investment;

- a new **£20 million venture capital challenge** to finance early stage high-technology businesses;

- a new **Research and Development tax credit** in 2000 to encourage small businesses investment in R&D;

- an additional **£100 million for basic science infrastructure** to help provide a modern research base;

- a new **Employee Share Ownership** scheme in 2000 to encourage employees to take a stake in the success of their companies;

- a new **Small Business Service** to deliver services to small firms, including a new Automatic Payroll Service;

- from 2000, setting an 80 per cent discount for key courses such as computer literacy, funded through **Individual Learning Accounts.**

1.15   The Secretary of State for Trade and Industry will be making further announcements after the Budget, taking forward the competitiveness agenda.

INCREASING EMPLOYMENT OPPORTUNITY

1.16   Chapter 4 focuses on the Government's strategy of promoting employment opportunities for all – the modern definition of full employment for the 21st century. It sets out how the Government intends to build a stronger economy by providing a better deal for working people.

Changes in the labour market   1.17   The strategy takes account of major changes in the labour market over the last two or three decades, including:

- growing structural unemployment and rising inactivity amongst certain groups,

- an increase in the number of women in work and part-time jobs; and

- a tax and benefit system which has trapped many families into poverty and unemployment.

Measures so far   1.18   Major reforms were introduced in the 1997 and 1998 Budgets and the CSR to take forward the Government's employment strategy based on helping people from welfare to work, and making work pay. For example:

- the **Welfare to Work** initiative, funded through a £5.2 billion Windfall Tax on the excess profits of the privatised utilities, has already benefited over 350,000 people through the New Deal;

- tax and benefit reforms: the **Working Families Tax Credit** (WFTC) will be introduced in October 1999 providing extra help for 1.4 million working families;

- a **National Minimum Wage** will be introduced in April 1999;

- **national insurance contributions (NICs) reform:** removing the burdens on the low paid; and

- a **New Deal for Communities** and **Employment Zones** will tackle pockets of persistent high unemployment.

New measures   1.19   Budget 99 will build on these measures by:

Delivering Welfare to Work

- providing extra help for young people on the New Deal to ensure there is no option of simply staying on benefit;

- providing personalised support to help **people over 50** move back to work; and

- an **Income Support run-on** to ease the transition into work for lone parents.

Making work pay

- from October 1999, a **minimum income guarantee of £200 per week** for full-time working families;

- **no family will pay net income tax until they earn more than £235** (over £12,000 a year);

- **eliminating the NICs bill for about 900,000 people** earning too little even to pay income tax;

- a **cut in the NICs bill for low earning self-employed people** from April 2000;

- a new **10p rate of income tax** from April 1999 which halves the tax bill for 1.8 million taxpayers; and

- a cut in the **basic rate of income tax to 22p** from April 2000 to reward work and ensure working families are better off.

BUILDING A FAIRER SOCIETY

1.20   Chapter 5 outlines the Government's strategy for building a fairer society in which everyone has the opportunity to fulfil their potential. Economic growth, opportunity and fairness go hand in hand: an economy in which a significant proportion of the population is unable to fulfill its potential will be poorer and less productive.

1.21   It also ensures that growth takes place in a way that is fair to today's and future generations. The Government will publish later this year its Sustainable Development Strategy: achieving economic growth while protecting and where possible enhancing the environment and making sure that the benefits are available to everyone, not just the few.

A strategy for **1.22**   The Government is therefore committed to:
fairness

- ensuring that everyone has access to **high quality public services,** including decent schools and a modern health service;

- ensuring that **all families with children are supported** through the tax and benefit system;

- targeted support focusing on:

  - **work as the best way out of poverty** (as set out in Chapter 4);

  - **families and children** to ensure that every child can thrive and take advantage of new opportunities;

  - **help for those not in work,** including giving a better deal to **pensioners;**

- ensuring that **growth is sustainable**, respects the environment and is fair to future generations.

Measures so far **1.23**   The CSR focused on how public services could be modernised to meet these goals. For example:

- an extra £40 billion will be invested in modernising health and education over the next three years;

- child benefit will increase by £2.95 a week for the eldest child from April; and

- new targeted initiatives such as the Sure Start programme were set up to ensure that all children are ready to learn when they reach school.

New measures 1.24 Budget 1999 focuses principally on tax and other measures that will increase opportunity and protect the environment:

A better deal for families and children

- the introduction of a **Children's Tax Credit,** replacing the married couples allowance and related allowances, will be worth £416 a year, with increases in the WFTC and Income Support to ensure all children benefit; and

- a 3 per cent real increase in **Child Benefit** to at least £15 and £10 a week from April 2000 for first and subsequent children respectively.

Modernising public services

- a £1.1 billion package of investment from the Capital Modernisation Fund will provide:

  - £470 million to support a national IT strategy;

  - £430 million to modernise Accident and Emergency services and improve access to primary care services; and

  - £170 million to tackle crime.

Pensioners

- a £1 billion package, including a £100 winter allowance, a minimum guarantee on tax and an increased Minimum Income Guarantee.

Charities

- a **Review of Charity Taxation** consultation document which explores how the tax system can encourage more giving to charity.

Tackling tax abuse

- measures designed to ensure individuals and businesses pay their fair share of taxes.

Protecting the environment

- a package of measures aimed at:

  - encouraging energy efficiency and tackling climate change through a new **climate change levy;**

  - improving local air quality and supporting the integrated transport strategy through a major reform of the **company car tax regime**, a **reduction to £100 in vehicle excise duty rates for cars with the smallest engines**, tax measures to promote **environmentally friendly commuting** and increases in **road fuel duties**; and

  - encouraging sustainable waste management through increases in the rate of the **landfill tax.**

IMPACT OF BUDGET MEASURES ON HOUSEHOLDS

1.25   Budget 99 will support families with children and reward work.

1.26   Taken together with the measures announced in Budget 98, it will:

make people better off

- over 20 million households gain, of which 7 million are households with children and 7 million are pensioner households;

- on average, households will be £380 a year better off.

support families

- families with children will on average be £740 a year better off;

- poorer families will also benefit: 700,000 children will be taken out of poverty.

reward work

- working households will on average be £450 a year better off;

- the new 10p rate of tax will halve the tax bill for 1.8 million, of whom 1.5 million are low-paid employees;

- the Working Families Tax Credit will on average give low earning families an extra £24 a week, compared with Family Credit.

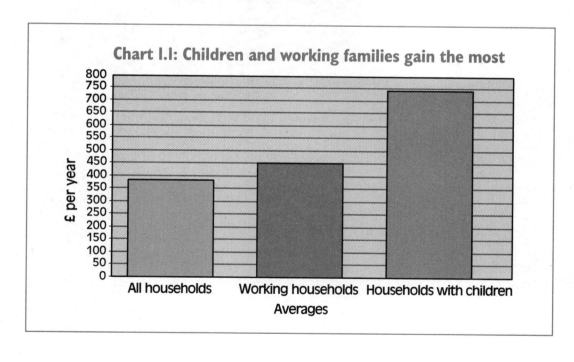

Chart 1.1: Children and working families gain the most

1.28   Charts 1.2 and 1.3 show where taxpayers' money will be spent and where taxes will come from following the Comprehensive Spending Review and Budget 99.

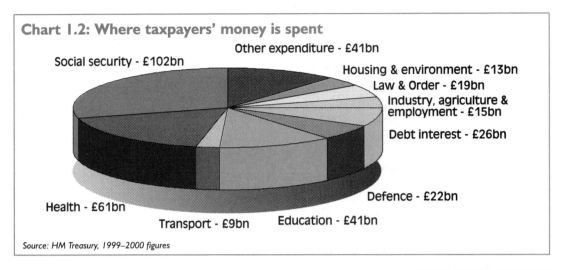

Chart 1.2: Where taxpayers' money is spent

Other expenditure - £41bn
Social security - £102bn
Housing & environment - £13bn
Law & Order - £19bn
Industry, agriculture & employment - £15bn
Debt interest - £26bn
Defence - £22bn
Health - £61bn
Transport - £9bn
Education - £41bn

Source: HM Treasury, 1999–2000 figures

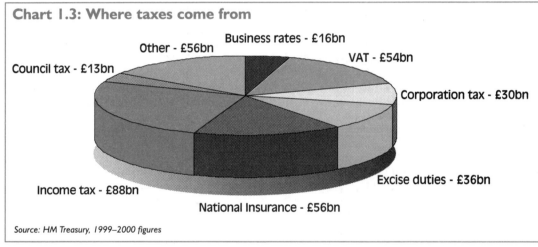

Chart 1.3: Where taxes come from

Business rates - £16bn
Other - £56bn
VAT - £54bn
Council tax - £13bn
Corporation tax - £30bn
Excise duties - £36bn
Income tax - £88bn
National Insurance - £56bn

Source: HM Treasury, 1999–2000 figures

Table 1.3: Budget 99 measures

		(+ve is an Exchequer yield)		£ million
	1999–00 non-indexed	**1999–00 indexed**	**2000–01 indexed**	**2001–02 indexed**
RAISING PRODUCTIVITY				
1 Corporation tax: new 10 per cent rate for the smallest companies from April 2000	0	0	0	–100
2 Extension of first year capital allowances for SMEs at 40 per cent, for one year	*	*	–175	–150
3 Research and development tax credit	0	0	*	–100
4 Tax relief for employer-loaned computers	–5	–5	–15	–30
5 Individual Learning Accounts: making employer contributions to employee ILAs tax and NICs free	0	0	–10	–10
6 Abolition of Vocational Training Relief (VTR)	*	*	+25	+50
INCREASING EMPLOYMENT OPPORTUNITY				
Tax-benefit reform to promote work incentives				
Income tax:				
7 Indexation of most allowances and limits	–1,050	0	0	0
8 New 10 per cent rate from April 1999	–1,600	–1,500	–1,800	–1,800
9 Basic rate reduced to 22 per cent from April 2000	0	0	–2,250	–2,800
National insurance contributions:				
10 Indexation of thresholds	–45	0	0	0
11 Alignment of threshold with income tax personal allowance, in two stages, beginning April 2000	0	0	–850	–1,800
12 Increases to upper earnings limits for employee contributions in April 2000 and April 2001	0	0	+430	+750
13 Reform of self-employment contribution rates and profits limits from April 2000	0	0	+240	+290
14 Reduction in employer contribution rate by 0.5 percentage points from April 2001	0	0	0	–1,700
Benefits:				
15 New Deal package for the over 50s: Employment Credit	–10	–10	–110	–110
16 Income Support: two week extension for lone parents moving into work	–10	–10	–20	–20
BUILDING A FAIRER SOCIETY				
Measures for families with children				
17 Abolition of married couples allowance from April 2000 for those born after 5 April 1935	0	0	+1,600	+2,050
18 Introduction of Children's Tax Credit from April 2001:	0	0	0	–1,400
19 with increases in Income Support child premia	–220	–220	–550	–550
20 and with increases in Working Families Tax Credit and Disabled Person's Tax Credit	–180	–180	–650	–750
21 Child Benefit: indexation of rates and uprating from April 2000 to £15 per week for first child and £10 per week for subsequent children	0	0	–255	–255
22 Sure Start Maternity Grant	0	0	–20	–20
23 Maternity pay reforms	0	0	0	–15
Fairness to pensioners				
24 Increasing personal allowances for older people	–160	–70	–100	–100
25 Increase minimum income guarantee for pensioners	0	0	–220	–220
26 £100 Winter Allowance from 1999	–640	–640	–640	–640
Securing the tax base				
27 Abolition of mortgage interest relief from April 2000	0	0	+1,350	+1,400
28 Countering avoidance in the provision of personal services	0	0	+475	+375
29 Extension of employer national insurance contributions to all benefits in kind which are subject to income tax from April 2000	0	0	+415	+440

Table 1.3: Budget 99 Measures

	(+ve is an Exchequer yield)			£ million
	1999–00 non-indexed	1999–00 indexed	2000–01 indexed	2001–02 indexed
30 Controlled Foreign Companies (CFCs): taxation of dividends	0	0	0	+20
31 Capital gains on sale of companies	+40	+40	+130	+130
32 Stamp duty: compliance	+25	+25	+25	+25
33 VAT: changes to partial exemption rules	+70	+70	+75	+75
34 VAT: group treatment	+5	+5	+10	+10
35 Enlarging of VAT exemption on financing arrangements	+95	+95	+100	+100
36 VAT: bringing supplies by certain organisations in line with trade unions and professional bodies	–10	–10	*	*
37 Taxation of reverse premiums	+20	+20	+50	+50
Environmental measures				
38 Climate change levy	0	0	0	+1,750
39 Energy efficiency measures and support for renewable energy sources	0	0	0	–50
40 Green transport plans	–5	–5	–5	–5
41 Increase in minor oils duties	+30	+25	+55	+90
42 Hydrocarbon oil duty escalator	+1,675	0	0	0
43 Cut in duty on higher octane unleaded petrol	+20	+20	+60	+40
44 Company car taxation: reduction in business mileage discounts from April 1999	+270	+270	+265	+260
45 Landfill tax: introduction of five year escalator	0	0	+45	+85
Vehicle Excise Duty:				
46 Graduated VED – reduction of charge for small cars and indexation for others	+40	–85	0	0
47 New VED for heavy lorries	+45	+45	+40	+35
48 Freeze other lorry VED	–20	–20	–20	–20
Other				
49 Tobacco – aligning escalator with Budget day, freeze handrolled tobacco	+630	+620	+410	+465
50 Alcohol – aligning revalorisation point with Budget day and freeze	0	*	–10	–10
51 Gifts of equipment by businesses to charities	*	*	–5	–10
52 Inheritance tax: index threshold	–30	0	0	0
53 Capital gains tax: rate adjustment	*	*	–10	–15
54 VAT: indexation of registration and deregistration thresholds	–5	0	0	0
55 Football clubs: assistance for transition to new accounting rules	*	*	–45	+20
56 Revised rate of pools betting duty from 26.5 per cent to 17.5 per cent	–30	–30	–20	–15
57 Removing the income tax charge on mobile phones	–25	–25	–30	–35
58 Stamp duty: 2.5 per cent rate for transfer of land and property above £250,000 and 3.5 per cent above £500,000	+270	+270	+310	+340
59 Increase in the rate of insurance premium tax by 1 percentage point (to 5 per cent)	+210	+210	+290	+300
60 VAT: option to tax land and property rules	+30	+30	+30	+30
61 Lloyd's insurance market: simplifying capital gains	*	*	–5	–5
TOTAL	**–570**	**–1,065**	**–1,385**	**–3,555**

* Negligible

2 MACROECONOMIC STRATEGY AND PROSPECTS

This chapter explains how the new framework for macroeconomic policy is continuing to lock in economic stability and helping to deliver high and stable levels of growth and employment. The key points are:

- economic instability has both economic and social costs. The Government moved quickly on coming into office to put in place a new framework for macroeconomic policy that promotes economic stability:

  - the monetary policy framework has been reformed to deliver low inflation. The rewards are already evident: inflation is close to target and expected to remain so, while long-term interest rates are at their lowest level for over 40 years; and

  - the fiscal policy framework has been reformed to deliver sound public finances. The Government has specified two strict fiscal rules: the golden rule and the sustainable investment rule. Both rules are expected to be met over the economic cycle. Even on more cautious forecast assumptions, the rules are still on track to be met.

- the UK is an open economy and is exposed to fluctuations in the world economy. Accordingly, the Government has played a leading role in promoting international economic stability;

- Budget 99 locks in the structural improvement in the public finances that was necessary and which has been achieved. The surplus on current budget is projected to average about ½ per cent of GDP over the economic cycle while net public sector debt as a proportion of GDP is projected to decline to just under 35 per cent by 2003–04. The requirements of the EU's Stability and Growth Pact are met;

- because the public finances are being put on a sound footing, the Budget both continues to lock in the fiscal tightening and can provide discretionary support – some £6 billion – to the economy during the below trend phase of the cycle; and

- the weakness in the world economy means that economic growth is expected to be lower in 1999, in line with the PBR forecast. Thereafter, stronger growth is projected. This reflects a timely monetary policy response, and the support of fiscal policy.

2.1 Over the past three decades, the UK economy has exhibited high volatility in output and inflation. Instability has made it hard for individuals and firms to plan and invest and has damaged the long-term growth of the economy.

2.2 The Government has reformed the framework for macroeconomic policy to promote economic stability. Greater stability will help people and businesses to plan for the long term. This should improve the quantity and quality of long-term investment – both in physical and human capital – and help raise productivity. Making the economy more stable will also raise employment and living standards.

2.3 The Government's reforms to the macroeconomic framework involve both monetary and fiscal policy. These reforms have both domestic and international relevance. The first part of this chapter discusses the reforms; the second part sets out the medium-term outlook for fiscal policy in light of the latest forecast of the UK economy, and illustrates how the framework is delivering sound public finances while supporting monetary policy during the below trend phase of the cycle.

Box 2.1: Sustainable development

Sustainable development is concerned with ensuring a better quality of life for everyone, now and for generations to come. It means achieving economic growth while protecting and, where possible, enhancing the environment and making sure that the benefits are available to all. The Government will shortly publish its Sustainable Development Strategy, taking account of responses to the consultation paper, *Opportunities for Change*. The Government's vision of sustainable development is based on four broad objectives:

- **social progress which recognises the needs of everyone:** for example, tackling social exclusion and reducing harm to health from poverty, poor housing, unemployment and pollution. Budget 99 includes a better deal for families with children and for pensioners;

- **effective protection of the environment:** limiting global threats such as climate change; reducing hazards such as poor air quality and toxic chemicals; and protecting things that people value, such as wildlife and the landscape. Budget 99 introduces measures to tackle climate change and improve local air quality;

- **prudent use of natural resources:** making sure that we use our natural resources efficiently; and that renewable resources such as water, are not used in ways that could endanger those resources. Budget 99 includes measures to limit the impact of land use, promote energy efficiency and to encourage sustainable waste management; and

- **maintenance of high and stable levels of growth and employment,** so that everyone can share in high living standards and greater job opportunities. As well as locking in stability, Budget 99 introduces a further package of measures to promote enterprise and investment, to deliver Welfare to Work, to make work pay and to help improve skills.

In November, the Government published a consultation paper, *Sustainability Counts*, setting out proposals for a set of headline indicators of sustainable development. These will help track progress across the range of areas covered by sustainable development. As well as economic indicators, the proposed headline indicators cover social and environmental aspects, including expected years of healthy life, educational qualifications at age 19, emissions of greenhouse gases, populations of wild birds, days of air pollution and road traffic.

A MODERN MACROECONOMIC FRAMEWORK

The monetary policy framework

Why low inflation is important

2.4 Stability is essential for high levels of growth and employment. Maintaining low and stable inflation is the best contribution monetary policy can make to long-term economic and social prosperity. High and variable inflation damages the real economy. It leads to an inefficient allocation of resources because people find it difficult to distinguish price movements associated with changes in the demand and supply for particular goods and services from general increases in the price level due to excessive demand across the economy. More generally, planning for the future becomes much more difficult. Costs are also incurred as people seek to protect themselves from the effects of inflation rather than concentrating on the creation of new wealth. This damages productivity and growth.

2.5   High and variable inflation also involves social costs that are likely to fall particularly hard on those people on lower incomes. By damaging growth, high inflation leads to lower average incomes than otherwise. High inflation and macroeconomic instability can also affect those on low incomes through their impact on the distribution of income. This can occur, for example, from arbitrary changes in wealth caused by unexpected movements in inflation; through the impact of uncertainty on decisions to invest in human capital (which is an important mechanism by which people can raise their earning potential); and because of the deterioration in the skills of low income workers who tend to be those most affected by boom and bust cycles.

2.6   Low and stable inflation plays a central role in creating the stable macroeconomic environment which individuals and businesses need to make sound investment and saving decisions. By ensuring that monetary policy focuses on maintaining low inflation, both sharp slowdowns and runaway booms can be avoided. It is now widely accepted that tolerating more inflation does not lead to higher growth or lower unemployment in the long term. Indeed, it is increasingly accepted that high inflation adversely affects long-term growth and is unfair (see Box 2.2).

Box 2.2: Monetary policy, opportunity and fairness

Maintaining low inflation is an integral part of the Government's strategy to achieve high levels of growth and employment. There are good reasons to think that low inflation will also help ensure that the benefits of growth are shared fairly.

The relationship between inflation and income (both its level and distribution) has been examined in a recent study.[1] Based on data for 19 OECD economies and a wider group of 66 countries, the authors conclude that:

> *"On average, the poor are much better off in countries where monetary policy has kept inflation low and aggregate demand stable".*

Furthermore, they argue that although expansionary policy can lead to temporarily lower unemployment, thus raising incomes at the lower end of the distribution, the effect is just that – temporary.

[1] *Monetary policy and the well-being of the poor, National Bureau of Economic Research, No 6793, C.D. Romer and D.H. Romer, 1998.*

The new monetary framework

2.7   The Government reformed the monetary framework immediately upon coming to office to ensure that monetary policy makes the best possible contribution to achieving high and stable levels of growth and employment. The primary objective of monetary policy is price stability. But, subject to that, the Bank of England must also support the Government's economic policy objectives, including those for growth and employment. The Government's inflation target – reaffirmed in this Budget – is $2^1/_2$ per cent for the 12-month increase in the Retail Price Index excluding mortgage interest payments (RPIX).

2.8   The new monetary policy framework, set out in the Bank of England Act 1998, has several features that ensure the benefits of low inflation are realised fully:

- transparency and accountability are central to the framework:

    - the roles of those concerned and what they are responsible for are clear. The Government sets, and is answerable for, the inflation target consistent with the goals of its economic policy. The role of the Bank of England's Monetary Policy Committee (MPC) is to set interest rates to meet the inflation target; and

- in discharging its responsibility, the MPC is subject to Parliamentary scrutiny, for example, by the House of Commons Treasury Select Committee and a House of Lords Select Committee. The MPC is also required to publish the minutes of its meetings, which now occurs within two weeks.

- the inflation target is symmetrical. Inflation outcomes below target are viewed just as seriously as outcomes above the target;

- the target for inflation applies at all times and the MPC is accountable for any deviations from it. It is required to justify any such deviation on its merits. For example, following a supply shock, regaining the target immediately might require such a severe policy response as to cause unwarranted damage to the economy. The onus is on the MPC to explain how it proposes to return inflation back to its target level; and

- furthermore, if inflation is more than 1 percentage point higher or lower than the target, the 'open letter' system requires that the Governor of the Bank of England write to the Chancellor, explaining why the divergence has occurred, the policy action being taken to deal with it, the period within which inflation is expected to return to the target and how this approach meets the Government's economic policy objectives, including those for growth and employment. Any such letter must be published so as to facilitate public scrutiny.

> **Box 2.3: The Harmonised Index of Consumer Prices (HICP)**
>
> The Government's inflation target is expressed in terms of the Retail Price Index excluding mortgage interest payments (RPIX). This measure is familiar in Britain – an important factor underpinning the credibility of the new framework. Within the European Monetary Union, the European Central Bank uses the Harmonised Index of Consumer Prices (HICP) for assessing compliance with its price stability objective. A paper outlining the differences between the HICP and the RPIX was published with the Pre-Budget Report in November 1998.
>
> The Government believes it is important to establish a record of sticking to the RPIX target, but it is monitoring the HICP since this index is useful for comparing Britain's inflation performance with other European countries. Starting with the figures for January 1999, the Office for National Statistics (ONS) began publishing the UK's HICP and RPIX together for the first time.

Assessing the new framework 2.9   The new monetary policy framework has been in place for less than two years but there are already signs that it is yielding significant benefits:

- inflation has remained very close to target since last summer, with monthly outturns for RPIX inflation at or around 2.5 per cent;

- financial market inflation expectations have fallen towards the target level. Inflation expectations 10 years ahead, derived from index-linked and conventional gilts yields, have fallen from 4.3 per cent in April 1997 to 2.6 per cent in February 1999;

- base rates peaked at $7^1/_2$ per cent for 4 months in 1998 compared with a peak of 15 per cent for a year in the last economic cycle, and have since fallen to $5^1/_2$ per cent. Long-term interest rates have recently been at their lowest level for over 40 years and the differential between the yields on 10-year government bonds in the UK and Germany has fallen from 1.7 percentage points in April 1997 to 0.5 percentage points in February 1999; and

- debt interest payments by the Government are falling due to lower long-term interest rates and inflation.

2.10 The forward-looking and transparent nature of the new monetary policy framework means interest rates have been changed when necessary in a more timely fashion than in the past. This has helped to keep output closer to trend, preventing a repeat of the large boom seen in the late 1980s. With inflation close to target, the UK is now in a better position to steer a course of stability and respond to the current global economic slowdown.

2.11 Macroeconomic policies aimed at achieving sustained growth, sound public finances and low inflation should also promote exchange rate stability, consistent with the Government's objective of a stable and competitive pound in the medium term. The strength of sterling during 1997 caused difficulties for some firms, especially manufacturers trading within Europe. Most of sterling's appreciation took place before the new monetary framework was introduced. Over recent months, however, sterling has fallen back close to its level at the time of the last General Election.

The fiscal policy framework

2.12 The Government's new fiscal policy framework constitutes the second key element of its strategy to promote economic stability. The framework also serves to support some of the Government's other important goals, notably the more efficient use of resources in the public sector, thus contributing directly to raising productivity in the economy.

Problems with the previous approach

2.13 The new framework has been designed to tackle head-on a number of key deficiencies associated with the previous approach:

- fiscal policy objectives were not precise and were subject to change. Observers found it difficult to tell whether the objectives were being met. Consequently, structural deficits were not identified sufficiently quickly to be tackled without significant costs;

- the framework promoted neither the economic stability nor long-term focus vital to economic success. Output and inflation in Britain were more variable than in most other major industrial countries;

- current spending often took precedence over capital, even if the latter offered better value for money. In particular, capital spending – the benefits of which tend to accrue primarily in the future – was an easy target for cutbacks when the fiscal position deteriorated; and

- fiscal decisions did not accurately reflect the impact of current public spending on future generations.

The new fiscal policy framework

2.14 *The Code for Fiscal Stability* sets out the new fiscal policy framework and gives it a statutory basis. It was approved by the House of Commons on 9 December 1998, in accordance with the requirements of the Finance Act 1998.

2.15 Five principles lie at the heart of the Code – transparency, stability, responsibility, fairness and efficiency. The Government is required to conduct fiscal (and debt management) policy in accordance with these principles. In particular, it must state explicitly its fiscal rules and objectives. These must be consistent with the principles.

2.16 The Government has set two strict fiscal rules to deliver sound public finances:

- *the golden rule* – on average over the economic cycle, the Government will borrow only to invest and not to fund current spending; and

- *the sustainable investment rule* – public sector net debt as a proportion of GDP will be held over the economic cycle at a stable and prudent level.

2.17   The golden rule ensures that the Government does not pass on the costs of services consumed today to the taxpayers of the future – each generation is expected to meet the current costs of the public services from which they benefit. This approach is consistent with achieving fairness between generations.[1] The golden rule, supported by the new regime for planning and controlling spending (discussed further below), also removes any bias against capital spending by providing for separate current and capital budgets. Now both types of spending are treated equally on a value for money basis.

2.18   Although the golden rule means that, over the economic cycle as a whole, the Government should not borrow to meet current spending, borrowing is permitted to finance public investment. This is because capital spending generates assets that confer benefits to both current and future generations. It is fair, therefore, that future generations should help pay for the benefits they receive, including servicing the associated borrowing.

2.19   High levels of public debt, however, can reduce the Government's ability to buffer the economy against major shocks. Debt may also impose other costs, such as higher interest rates and efficiency losses due to the higher tax rates needed to service the debt. The Government has, therefore, set the sustainable investment rule to ensure that public debt (net of financial assets) remains at prudent levels. The current level of net public debt is not high by historical or international standards. Nonetheless, the Government believes that a modest reduction is desirable, other things equal, to below 40 per cent of GDP over the economic cycle.

2.20   Transparency is an integral and pervasive feature of the new framework, so ensuring that Parliament and the public can scrutinise the economic and fiscal plans. This should encourage a longer-term approach to government decision-making. *The Code for Fiscal Stability* provides for a number of reports, of which the EFSR is one, that together set out a comprehensive account of the Government's economic and fiscal strategy and the state of the public finances. In order to ensure that the public is fully informed about Budget decisions, the Government will propose an amendment to the *Code for Fiscal Stability*, requiring that, in future, a leaflet be sent to every household informing them of tax and spending decisions.

2.21   The Budget includes some technical changes to allow the Debt Management Office (DMO) to take over the Government's cash management from the Bank of England as intended in last year's Finance Act. The transfer of cash management will complete the separation of monetary policy and debt management operations announced by the Chancellor in May 1997. These changes improve the transparency and efficiency of the Government's debt management operations.

2.22   It is important that information is of high quality and presented in a form which provides the basis for good policy-making. The Government is in the process of implementing a major new initiative in the public sector – Resource Accounting and Budgeting (RAB). RAB will put the Government's accounts on a similar footing to those found in the private sector (see Box 2.4). In addition, the Office for National Statistics is undertaking a number of improvements to key economic statistics, relating to both economic activity and the public finances (see Box A2 in FSBR Annex A and Box B2 in FSBR Annex B).

---

[1] As discussed in EFSR Annex A, current fiscal policy settings in Britain do not appear to result in significant generational imbalance, in contrast to many industrial countries.

> ### Box 2.4: Resource Accounting and Budgeting
>
> Resource Accounting and Budgeting (RAB) is a further step in the process of fiscal reform. It will enhance the effectiveness of the changes to the fiscal policy framework and to the spending control regime. RAB takes the distinction between current and capital spending one stage further, by planning, controlling and accounting for departmental spending on a full accruals basis. This involves recognising the capital costs (ie depreciation and interest) of public investments and assets as they occur, consistently and alongside other current spending. New capital spending will continue to be budgeted for separately.
>
> Departmental spending measured on a RAB basis will fit more readily within the fiscal policy framework which measures spending on the same basis (ie including capital costs). This means that, under RAB, there will be a closer link between the planning process and the fiscal framework which it is intended to support.
>
> Departments are on course to produce the first set of audited 'dry-run' resource accounts for 1998–99. The first full set of published audited resource accounts will be for 1999–2000. The intention is that the next spending review, in 2000, will be the first full round of resource budgeting, conducted on the basis of resource accounting information. Subject to Parliament's agreement, Estimates for the year 2001–02, the first year of the new plans, will also be presented on a resource basis.

Planning and controlling spending

2.23 The new fiscal policy framework is supported by a new regime for planning and controlling public spending, first announced in the 1998 EFSR. This regime anticipates the planned introduction of RAB, and will play an integral part in allowing the Government to deliver on its wider economic and fiscal strategy.

2.24 The previous control regime – like the fiscal policy framework with which it was associated – encouraged short-term planning and favoured spending on consumption rather than investment. It led to planning on an incremental basis and a failure to coordinate and integrate new spending so as to maximise its effectiveness.

2.25 The new regime addresses these shortcomings. All public sector spending (excluding financial transactions) is contained under the heading Total Managed Expenditure (TME). Within TME, current and capital expenditures are planned and managed separately, consistent with the distinction made in the fiscal rules.

2.26 Around half of TME is managed through Departmental Expenditure Limits (DEL). Spending within DEL is subject to firm multi-year limits covering a three-year period. These limits, set in cash terms, provide departments with a solid basis for planning and a strong incentive to manage their own costs. The Government is now allowing departments the freedom to carry over any part of their spending within DEL from one financial year to the next, a major new flexibility which should greatly improve value for money.

2.27 The other half of TME, expenditure which cannot reasonably be subject to firm multi-year limits, is known as Annually Managed Expenditure (AME). AME – a large part of which is social security spending – is subject to tough annual scrutiny as part of the Budget process. The scrutiny is to ensure that spending within AME is consistent with achievement of the fiscal rules.

2.28 Controlling the quantity of spending is just one aspect of the new regime. It is equally important to control the quality of spending. The Government made clear that the increased public investment announced in last year's Comprehensive Spending Review (CSR) would be linked to modernisation and reform to deliver enhanced efficiency and effectiveness in public spending.

2.29   The Government is delivering on that commitment. It is publishing for the first time measurable targets for the full range of the Government's objectives for public services in the form of ground-breaking Public Service Agreements. Departments' performance against their targets is being scrutinised by a high level Cabinet committee (PSX), chaired by the Chancellor, and supported by a Public Services Productivity Panel of outside experts from business, consultancy and audit. Each department will publish a Departmental Investment Strategy, and this will inform decisions by the Government on the allocation of resources from the Capital Modernisation Fund.

Benefits of the new approach   2.30   The Government is well on track to meet both its fiscal rules. A full assessment of the performance of the new fiscal policy framework is set out in detail later in this chapter.

Stability in the international context

2.31   The UK is an open economy, and therefore events in the world economy and financial markets have a substantial impact. Reform of the domestic macroeconomic policy framework has improved the UK's ability to respond to external events. But the UK has also taken the lead in promoting macroeconomic stability across the world, so as to reduce the likelihood of future global shocks. It has also been at the forefront of proposals to improve the international community's ability to respond to shocks when they occur.

Stability abroad   2.32   Recent world events, especially those in Asia, Russia and Brazil, have served to emphasise the importance of taking steps to improve crisis prevention and resolution. Lessons learned include the need for: an open and transparent international financial system; co-operation and co-ordination between international and national bodies; prevention of moral hazard (where investors take on undue risk in anticipation of being 'bailed out' if a crisis occurs); official financing able to stem contagion; and mechanisms to protect vulnerable groups in crisis countries. Transparency and accountability have just as powerful a role to play in avoiding poor policy making and poor outcomes internationally as they have in the domestic economy.

2.33   Responding to these events, the UK led the G7 in a Declaration on 30 October 1998, which committed G7 countries to:

- introduce codes of good practice on fiscal policy, monetary and financial policy, corporate governance, and accounting, to ensure public and private sector transparency;

- establish a mechanism for co-ordination and co-operation between international financial institutions, international regulatory bodies and key national authorities. This should improve surveillance of financial supervision and regulation, thus fostering stability and reducing systemic risk. The President of the Bundesbank, Hans Tietmeyer, was tasked with consulting on how to bring this about;

- involve the private sector in crisis prevention and resolution, for instance, through collective action clauses in bond issues;

- establish a new, contingent IMF financing facility to prevent contagion, backed up by private sector involvement and bilateral financing as appropriate; and

- ask the World Bank to draw up principles of good practice in social policy, to reduce the impact of economic adjustment on vulnerable groups and ensure that development goals were taken fully into account in programme design, especially during crises.

2.34   Good progress has already been made in implementing this reform agenda. At their 20 February meeting this year, G7 Finance Ministers and Central Bank Governors endorsed Herr Tietmeyer's proposal for a Financial Stability Forum, to co-ordinate the identification of systemic risk, the implementation of codes of good practice, and promotion of international financial stability. They noted the completion by the International Accounting Standards Committee of its core set of internationally-agreed accounting standards, and the agreement of a new format for the IMFs Special Data Dissemination Standard – both to increase transparency. They welcomed the implementation of the agreed increase in the IMF's quotas, including the New Arrangements to Borrow. They also published a detailed timetable for the implementation of all the remaining reforms agreed in the October Declaration.

2.35   As they are progressively implemented, these reforms should help to reduce the volatility of financial markets and increase the prospects for economic stability and prosperity, both in Britain and abroad.

Economic stability in Europe   **2.36**   The UK has a strong interest in economic stability in Europe, irrespective of whether or not it chooses to join the single currency. Around half of the UK's trade and 40 per cent of overseas investment is with the euro area.

2.37   Along with other Member States, the Government submitted its Convergence Programme to the European Community in December 1998, in line with the requirements of the Stability and Growth Pact. The Convergence Programme shows how the new stability-oriented policy framework provides an essential platform for closer convergence of the economic performance of the UK and other Member States.

2.38   The first outline National Changeover Plan for possible entry to the European single currency was published by the Treasury in February 1999. This is a consultative document which sets out the practical steps which would be needed for the UK to join the euro – if that is what Parliament and the British people decide. Government policy on UK entry to the single currency was set out in the Chancellor of the Exchequer's Statement to Parliament on 27 October 1997. This makes it clear that the determining factor as to whether the UK joins should be the national economic interest, and whether the economic case for doing so is clear and unambiguous

2.39   In a statement to Parliament on 23 February 1999, the Prime Minister explained that preparations need to be made now so that, should the economic tests be met, a decision to join a successful single currency could be made early in the next Parliament. The public sector has given a clear signal of its commitment to prepare, involving some spending to give Britain the flexibility it would need to make the changeover as quickly and cost-efficiently as possible.

MACROECONOMIC PROSPECTS: MEETING THE FISCAL RULES

Summary of the economic forecast

2.40   Developments in the economy since the Pre-Budget Report (PBR) have been broadly in line with expectations. Growth slowed a little further in the fourth quarter of 1998 and RPIX inflation has remained very close to its target level of $2^{1}/_{2}$ per cent. Survey measures of confidence have shown signs of improvement following reductions in interest rates. As a result, there is little change to the economic forecast, or in the assumptions underpinning the fiscal projections. A summary of the forecasts for output and inflation is presented in Table 2.1. (A detailed assessment is set out in FSBR Annex A.)

Table 2.1: Summary of the economic forecast

	1998	1999	Forecast 2000	2001
GDP growth (per cent)	$2^{1}/_{4}$	1 to $1^{1}/_{2}$	$2^{1}/_{4}$ to $2^{3}/_{4}$	$2^{3}/_{4}$ to $3^{1}/_{4}$
RPIX inflation (per cent, Q4)	$2^{1}/_{2}$	$2^{1}/_{2}$	$2^{1}/_{2}$	$2^{1}/_{2}$

2.41   The forecasts for GDP growth are presented in the form of opportunity ranges. The upper end illustrates the potential for higher sustainable growth based on improved supply side performance of the UK economy. As in the PBR and previous forecasts, the public finances projections are based on the lower end of the GDP opportunity ranges. They are consistent with a deliberately cautious assumption for trend economic growth of $2\frac{1}{4}$ per cent a year over the medium term.

2.42   GDP grew by $2\frac{1}{4}$ per cent in 1998, a little lower than forecast in the PBR, but in line with the forecast made a year ago in the last Budget. Growth in the fourth quarter of 1998 showed a further slowing, but was in line with the PBR projection. Manufacturing output fell, but this was more than offset by continued robust growth in the service sector. This was accompanied by strong labour market activity during the second half of 1998, with growth in employment showing a marked upturn compared with the first half of the year.

2.43   RPIX inflation averaged $2\frac{1}{2}$ per cent in the fourth quarter, as projected in the PBR. The latest evidence, including a slowing of earnings growth, lower pay settlements and historically low rates of producer output price inflation, supports the view that RPIX inflation may move marginally, and temporarily, below $2\frac{1}{2}$ per cent during 1999, returning to target later in the year. The fall in average earnings growth over the past six months, as revealed in the newly reinstated series, is encouraging. As the Chancellor has said on a number of occasions, including last year's Budget, stability requires wage responsibility across the public and private sectors.

2.44   Growth in the United States remains strong and wider financial market contagion as a result of the Brazilian devaluation has been relatively limited. However, prospects for growth in Europe have deteriorated and, overall, the outlook for UK export markets is weaker than previously expected. This is balanced by the marked easing in domestic monetary policy in recent months and firm domestic consumer confidence.

2.45   Growth is expected to be slower this year than last at 1 to $1\frac{1}{2}$ per cent. The fiscal projections are based on GDP growth of 1 per cent in 1999-2000. However, the factors necessary for stronger growth in 2000 and beyond are expected to build during the course of this year:

- prompt monetary policy action to tackle earlier pressures on inflation – supported by fiscal policy action to restore the public finances to a sound structural position – has allowed interest rates to fall at an early stage. With world financial market turbulance receding, survey measures of business confidence appear to be improving;

- as the impact of past policy tightening wears off, healthy private sector fundamentals should begin to dominate once more. Both companies and households are in better shape than at the beginning of the decade: neither sector appears over-borrowed and balance sheets are relatively strong; and

- the Budget continues to lock in sound public finances, while providing some £6 billion of support for the economy during its below trend phase.

2.46   Overall, there is no reason to alter the assessment that this cycle is likely to be much more moderate than those in recent decades. The independent consensus remains one of moderate growth in 1999, followed by higher growth thereafter. Uncertainties remain, including ongoing risks to the world economic outlook. Nonetheless, around two-thirds of independent growth forecasts lie in a relatively narrow band of $\frac{1}{2}$ percentage point either side of the low end of the forecast opportunity ranges for both 1999 and 2000.

Recent fiscal trends and short-term outlook

2.47   The public finances improved further in 1998-99. The current budget moved into surplus for the first time in eight years, and public sector net debt has fallen to around 40 per cent of GDP.

2.48   Chart 2.1 below shows the improvement in the fiscal position from a longer-term perspective. From the early 1970s, the current budget was continuously in deficit apart from three years during the late 1980s boom. The deficits in the early 1990s were the largest since the Second World War. Although net investment was falling as a share of GDP, net borrowing also reached its highest post-war level in the early 1990s. As a result, public sector net debt doubled over the first half of the 1990s.

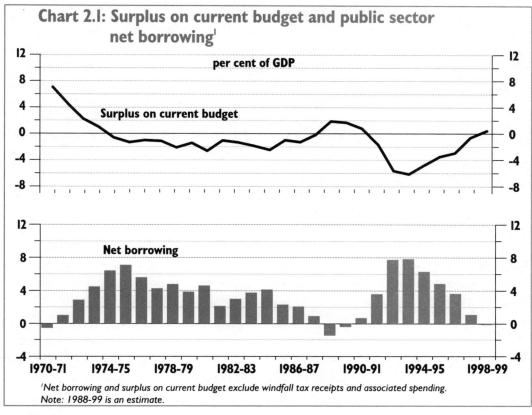

Chart 2.1: Surplus on current budget and public sector net borrowing[1]

per cent of GDP

Surplus on current budget

Net borrowing

[1]Net borrowing and surplus on current budget exclude windfall tax receipts and associated spending.
Note: 1988-99 is an estimate.

2.49   Table 2.2 compares the latest outturns and short-term forecasts with the forecasts in the PBR. The estimate for net borrowing in 1998-99 is a net repayment of £1 billion. This compares with a £1½ billion repayment forecast in the PBR. The current budget surplus in 1998-99 is estimated to be about £1½ billion lower than forecast in the PBR.

Table 2.2: Comparison of updated forecasts with 1998 PBR

	£ billion	
	Estimate	
	1998–99	**1999–00**
Current budget[1]		
1998 PBR	5·5	1
Budget 99	4·1	2
Public sector net borrowing[1]		
1998 PBR	–1·5	4
Budget 99	–1·0	3

[1] Excluding windfall tax receipts and associated spending.

2.50 These differences are small. They largely reflect lower than expected receipts, particularly for corporation tax and VAT. Public sector current receipts in 1998-99 are estimated to be about £1³/₄ billion lower than forecast in November. The Control Total – which under the new spending control regime will cease to exist after the current financial year – is £³/₄ billion lower than forecast in the PBR, mainly reflecting lower expenditure on social security benefits. The Government is set to meet its objective of working within the previous Government's spending plans in its first two years in office.

2.51 Forecasts of receipts for 1999-2000 on a pre-Budget basis have been revised downwards by £3 billion. In part, this reflects some of the estimated shortfall in receipts in 1998-99 (especially of VAT) carrying forward. In addition, the forecast of tobacco receipts has been revised down by over £¹/₂ billion and national insurance contributions are now expected to grow less strongly next year. This partly reflects the effect on receipts of the 1998 Budget reforms. Total Managed Expenditure for 1999–2000 is over £4¹/₂ billion lower than forecast in the CSR, largely reflecting lower than expected spending on debt interest and on social security (even after adjusting for the effects of the economic cycle).

2.52 These changes result in a higher forecast of the surplus on current budget in 1999–2000 of £2 billion, compared with the PBR projection of £1 billion, whilst net borrowing is £3 billion – £1 billion lower than projected in the PBR.

Medium-term fiscal projections

Fiscal policy and economic activity   **2.53** The key requirement of fiscal policy is that it delivers sound public finances, and thus prevents government itself being a source of adverse shocks to the economy.

2.54 Fiscal policy can also play an important role in supporting monetary policy. The substantial tightening of the fiscal stance during 1997–98 supported monetary policy in containing the pressures on inflation that were emerging when the economy was above trend, as well as restoring the public finances to a sound position.

2.55 More recently, the economy has slowed as the world economy has weakened. In these circumstances, the Government judges it appropriate that the Budget measures should continue to lock in the structural improvement in the public finances. At the same time, it is appropriate and sensible to continue to allow fiscal policy to support monetary policy in the below trend phase of the cycle. The Budget measures provide a £6 billion discretionary boost to the economy over the next 3 years, safeguarding stability, while continuing to meet the fiscal rules.

Medium-term fiscal projections   **2.56** The Government's latest medium-term projections for the public finances are summarised in Table 2.3 (£ billion) and Table 2.4 (per cent of GDP) below. A more detailed breakdown can be found in Annex B of the FSBR.

Table 2.3: Summary of public sector finances

				£ billion			
	Outturn	**Estimate**			**Projections**		
	1997–98	**1998–99**	**1999–00**	**2000–01**	**2001–02**	**2002–03**	**2003–04**
Current receipts	315·7	334·2	335	364	385	405	425
Current expenditure	304·3	313·5	329	346	362	379	398
Depreciation	14·0	14·6	15	15	16	16	17
Surplus on current budget[1]	**–5·1**	**4·1**	**2**	**4**	**8**	**9**	**11**
Net investment	4·0	3·4	5	7	10	12	15
Public sector net borrowing[1]	**9·1**	**–1·0**	**3**	**3**	**1**	**3**	**4**

[1] *Excluding windfall tax receipts and associated spending.*

Table 2.4: Summary of public sector finances

	Outturn 1997–98	Estimate 1998–99	Per cent of GDP Projections				
			1999–00	2000–01	2001–02	2002–03	2003–04
Current receipts	38·9	39·4	39·2	39·4	39·5	39·6	39·7
Current expenditure	37·5	37·0	37·4	37·4	37·1	37·1	37·1
Depreciation	1·7	1·7	1·7	1·6	1·6	1·6	1·6
Surplus on current budget[1]	**–0·6**	**0·5**	**0·3**	**0·4**	**0·8**	**0·9**	**1·0**
Net investment	0·5	0·4	0·6	0·8	1·0	1·2	1·4
Public sector net borrowing[1]	**1·1**	**–0·1**	**0·3**	**0·4**	**0·1**	**0·3**	**0·4**
Public sector net debt	**42·5**	**40·6**	**39·4**	**38·2**	**36·8**	**35·6**	**34·6**

[1] Excluding windfall tax receipts and associated spending.
[2] Includes accruals adjustment for the capital uplift on the redemption of the 2½ per cent 2001 and 2003 index linked gilt.

2.57   Over the three-year planning period from 1999–2000, Departmental Expenditure Limits are essentially unchanged from those set out in the CSR in July 1998[2]. However, the components of AME have been reviewed since the CSR, leading to downward revisions to the forecasts of spending on debt interest and on social security benefits (even after adjusting for the effects of the economic cycle).[3] The AME margin has been set at the same level as in the CSR.

2.58   Public sector net investment is set to double to 1 per cent of GDP by 2001–02. For later years, it is assumed that current spending continues to grow at 2¼ per cent per year in real terms while net investment rises to 1½ per cent of GDP.

2.59   It is assumed that there are no further tax changes other than those announced in the Budget, which include the annual real increases in fuel and tobacco duties and the indexation of rates and allowances.

2.60   Actual public borrowing is expected to become positive again during the below trend phase of the economic cycle. But the underlying position remains strong. Net debt continues to fall as a percentage of GDP and the current budget remains in surplus.

2.61   Chart 2.2 shows public sector net debt is projected to fall below 35 per cent of GDP in 2003–04. The improvement in the debt ratio reflects sustained strength in the structural position of the public finances. The chart also shows that net wealth is projected to stabilise broadly as a proportion of GDP, in marked contrast to the experience during most of the 1990s.

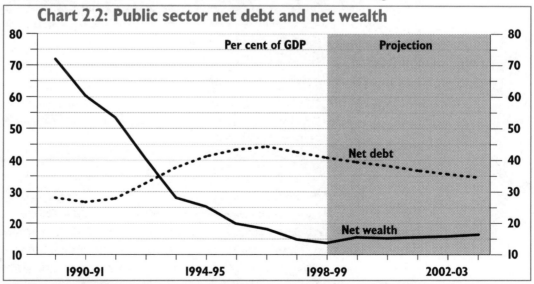

Chart 2.2: Public sector net debt and net wealth

[2] £250 million of the Capital Modernisation Fund has been brought forward from 2001–02 to 1999–2000.
[3] The reduction in forecast AME spending on social security occurs despite the adoption of a new, more cautious planning assumption underpinning the public finances. It has been decided to base the projections of social security expenditure in this Budget on the average of outside forecasts of unemployment compiled in *Forecasts of the UK Economy* (latest edition, HM Treasury, February 1999). This approach does not reflect the Government's views on the prospects for unemployment. When unemployment is projected to fall by outside forecasters, the flat assumption will again by be used. This approach has been endorsed by the National Audit Office (see their report, HC 294).

2.62 Table 2.5 reconciles the revised medium-term projections of the surplus on current budget and public sector net borrowing with those published in the PBR, with the difference split between those accounted for by Budget initiatives and those due to forecasting and other changes. Before Budget measures are taken into account, tax revenues are slightly lower than projected previously over the period, but spending – notably on debt interest and social security – has fallen faster still.

Table 2.5: Changes in surplus on current budget and public sector net borrowing since the PBR

	£ billion					
	1998–99	1999–00	2000–01	2001–02	2002–03	2003–04
Surplus on current budget[1,2]						
1998 PBR	5·5	1	3	8	10	11
Effect of Budget measures		–1	–1	–4	–4	–4
Effect of revisions/forecasting changes	–1·4	2	2	3	3	4
Budget 99	4·1	2	4	8	9	11
Net borrowing[1,2]						
1998 PBR	–1·5	4	5	2	2	1
Effect of Budget measures		1	1	4	4	4
Effect of revisions/forecasting changes	0·5	–3	–3	–5	–2	–1
Budget 99	–1·0	3	3	1	3	4

[1] Excluding windfall tax and associated spending.
[2] Figures may not sum due to rounding.

Taking account of the cycle　**2.63** For the purposes of assessing the underlying strength and therefore sustainability of the public finances, it is necessary to take account of the impact of the economic cycle. The method used to produce estimates of the impact of the economic cycle on the public finances is discussed in Box 2.6.

Box 2.5: The public finances and the economic cycle

The economic cycle has an important short-term impact on the public finances. These effects need to be taken into account when assessing the underlying (structural) position of the public finances. Failure to do so could lead to inappropriate policy decisions. This is why the *Code for Fiscal Stability* requires the Government to publish estimates of the cyclically-adjusted fiscal position.

Recent Treasury estimates[1] suggest that, after two years, a 1 per cent increase in output relative to trend leads to:

- a decrease in the ratios of net borrowing and net cash requirement to GDP by just under $^3/_4$ percentage point; and

- an increase in the ratio of the surplus on current budget to GDP by just under $^3/_4$ percentage point (since public investment does not vary systematically with the economic cycle).

About two thirds of the effect derives from the change in the ratio of expenditure to GDP reflecting the fact that a large part of expenditure is fixed in cash terms. The remaining third reflects the fact that tax receipts tend to move more than proportionately with GDP. These estimates are necessarily uncertain since measuring the economic cycle and its impact on the public finances is is a difficult task. However, it is worth noting that studies by the OECD, IMF, the European Commission and other independent commentators have produced similar results.

[1]See *Fiscal policy: public finances and the cycle*, HM Treasury.

2.64 Based on the judgement that the economy was on trend, on average, in the first half of 1997, Table 2.6 below presents cyclically-adjusted estimates of the key budget balances. With the economy projected to undergo a fairly modest cycle by historical standards, the difference in the paths of actual and cyclically-adjusted measures of borrowing is less than it has been in the past.

Table 2.6: Cyclically-adjusted budget balances[1]

					Per cent of GDP		
	Outturn	Estimate			Projections		
	1997–98	1998–99	1999–00	2000–01	2001–02	2002–03	2003–04
Surplus on current budget	–0·7	0·2	0·6	1·0	1·1	0·9	1·0
Net borrowing	1·1	0·1	0·0	–0·2	–0·1	0·3	0·4

[1] Excluding windfall tax receipts and associated spending.

2.65   The Budget continues to lock in the sound structural position of the public finances, while allowing fiscal policy to play its role in supporting the economy during its below trend phase of the cycle. As Chart 2.3 shows, cyclically-adjusted public sector net borrowing remains close to balance over the period covered by the projections and is very similar to that set out in the PBR. This conclusion is reinforced in Table 2.7 which shows the cumulative fiscal tightening since 1996–97.

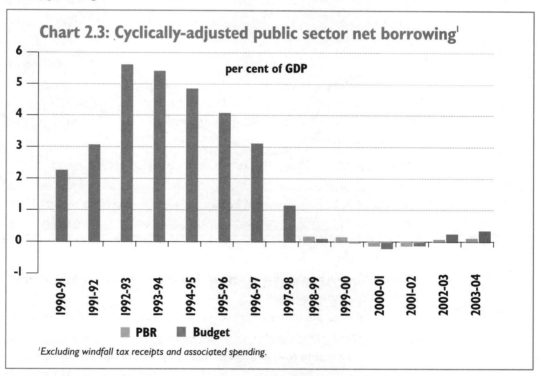

Chart 2.3: Cyclically-adjusted public sector net borrowing[1]

per cent of GDP

■ PBR   ■ Budget

[1] Excluding windfall tax receipts and associated spending.

Table 2.7: The fiscal tightening – cumulative change since 1996–97

	per cent of GDP			
	1997–98	1998–99	1999–2000	2000–01
Public sector net borrowing (cyclically-adjusted)[1]				
1998 EFSR (ESA95 basis)	–2	–2³⁄₄	–3	–3¹⁄₄
1998 Pre-Budget Report	–2	–2³⁄₄	–3	–3¹⁄₄
March 1999 Budget	–2	–3	–3¹⁄₄	–3¹⁄₄

[1] Excluding windfall tax receipts and associated spending.

Fiscal policy in an uncertain world

2.66 Projections of the public finances necessarily involve a significant element of uncertainty. This is because public revenue and spending projections depend heavily on economic growth and, in particular, on assumptions made about the position of the economy in relation to its sustainable long-term trend. The demand for public spending can also vary unpredictably in response to evolving needs and opportunities.

2.67 The medium-term projections discussed above are based on deliberately cautious assumptions audited by the National Audit Office. In addition, they imply a small surplus on the current budget over the economic cycle, providing a safety margin over what would strictly be necessary to meet the golden rule.

2.68 Chart 2.4 illustrates a still more cautious case in which trend output is assumed to be 1 per cent lower than in the central projection (the same degree of caution as in the PBR). This scenario would imply that a greater proportion of the projected surplus on current budget was due to cyclical strength in the economy. Nonetheless, even under this scenario, the Government would still remain on track to meet the golden rule, while the sustainable investment rule would be met comfortably.

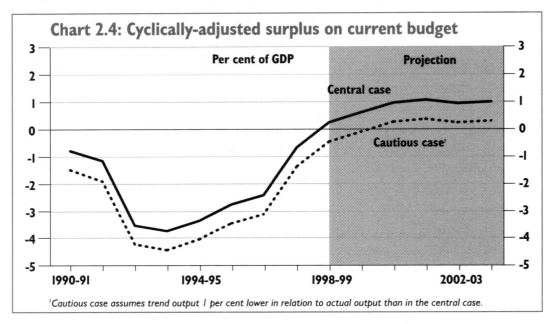

Chart 2.4: Cyclically-adjusted surplus on current budget

¹Cautious case assumes trend output 1 per cent lower in relation to actual output than in the central case.

Assessment against the fiscal rules and European commitments

2.69 Table 2.8 illustrates the Government's progress in meeting its fiscal rules and against the criteria set out in the Maastricht Treaty. As the table shows:

- the surplus on current budget is expected to average 0.4 per cent of GDP over the economic cycle, thus meeting the golden rule;

- public sector net debt is projected to decline to well below 40 per cent of GDP by 2003–04, an outcome consistent with the sustainable investment rule; and

- the Maastricht Treaty and Stability and Growth Pact requirements – reference values for general government net borrowing below 3 per cent and general government gross debt less than 60 per cent of GDP – are met comfortably.

Table 2.8: Progress against the fiscal rules and Maastricht Treaty criteria[1]

	Outturn 1997–98	Estimate 1998–99	Projections 1999–00	2000–01	2001–02	2002–03	2003–04
			Per cent of GDP				
Surplus on current budget	−0·6	0·5	0·3	0·4	0·8	0·9	1·0
Average surplus since 1997–98	−0·6	−0·1	0·0	0·1	0·3	0·4	0·5
Public sector net debt	42·5	40·6	39·4	38·2	36·8	35·6	34·6
Average debt since 1997–98	42·5	41·6	40·8	40·2	39·5	38·9	38·2
Maastricht deficit[2]	0·6	−0·6	0·3	0·2	0·2	0·1	0·3
Maastricht debt ratio[3]	49·6	47·6	46·6	45·3	43·5	42·2	41·0

[1] Excluding windfall tax receipts and associated spending.

[2] General government net borrowing on a ESA79 basis. The Maastricht definition does not exclude the windfall tax and associated spending.

[3] General government gross debt.

Box 2.6: Fiscal policy and the Stability and Growth Pact

The Stability and Growth Pact was agreed in Amsterdam in 1997. It strengthened and clarified the excessive deficits procedure outlined in Article 104c of the Maastricht Treaty. This procedure was designed to ensure fiscal stability in the Eurozone. The Maastricht Treaty prohibits Member States participating in the single currency from running excessive government deficits – defined as over 3 per cent of GDP, on a general government basis.

The Stability and Growth Pact outlined the procedure for sanctions for EMU entrants, and introduced a medium term budgetary objective for Member States of close to balance or in surplus. This objective is designed to allow the automatic fiscal stabilisers of Member States to operate over the economic cycle without breaching the 3 per cent reference value.

Long-term fiscal projections

2.70   Illustrative long-term projections of the public finances are presented in EFSR Annex A, as required by the *Code for Fiscal Stability*. These projections show a sound fiscal position, broadly in line with the results of a recent study by the National Institute of Economic and Social Research which constructed a first set of generational accounts for the UK. They show that, unlike in many countries, Britain does not have long-term fiscal problems in store. In addition, even a small rise in trend productivity growth could strengthen the long-term sustainability of the public finances considerably.

Conclusion

2.71   The modern macroeconomic policy framework described above is set to deliver the economic stability that Britain needs to achieve its goal of high and stable levels of growth and employment. But while economic stability is a necessary condition for prosperity, it is not sufficient – policies aimed at encouraging work, raising productivity, and promoting fairness and opportunity are also needed. The next three chapters consider the Government's strategy on each of these fronts.

3 RAISING PRODUCTIVITY

This chapter sets out the Government's strategy for raising productivity in the British economy. Raising productivity is the key to high rates of growth in people's incomes. The Government's strategy to raise productivity focuses on:

- raising investment;

- encouraging enterprise and innovation;

- improving skills;

- promoting competition and better regulation; and

- raising public sector productivity.

This Budget builds on that strategy and the steps already taken to deliver a better deal for enterprise and business. Key measures include:

- a new 10p corporation tax rate and extension of 40 per cent capital allowances for small and medium sized enterprises (SMEs) to encourage investment and growth;

- a new research and development tax credit to encourage small and medium sized companies to invest in R&D;

- a new Small Business Service to coordinate the delivery of services for SMEs and to take on a new role helping businesses comply with regulations;

- a new Automatic Payroll Service, offered by the SBS, for new small employers;

- new enterprise management incentives for SMEs, to help small growing firms recruit talented managers and new proposals for an all-employer share ownership scheme;

- further reform to the Enterprise Investment Scheme to promote serial entrepreneurship;

- new measures to boost venture capital, with a £20 million Venture Capital Challenge to finance early stage high-technology businesses across the UK, and a commitment to a new tax incentive for corporate venturing in 2000; and

- new Individual Learning Accounts to enable the low-skilled to obtain the qualifications that they need.

INTRODUCTION

3.1   The Government's central economic objective is to achieve high and stable levels of growth and employment. Raising productivity is vital to achieving this aim. Some UK companies and sectors produce world class performance. The challenge is to drive this top quality performance to all parts of the economy, making the UK as productive as other leading economies.

3.2   The UK's productivity lags behind other major economies and has done so for decades. This Government is determined to tackle this gap. The Government's strategy to achieve this recognises that:

- economic stability is fundamental to establishing the conditions for effective microeconomic reform. In the past, boom and bust cycles have undermined efforts to improve long-term performance. The macroeconomic and public expenditure reforms outlined in Chapter 2 will provide a stable environment for people and businesses to plan, innovate and invest;

- the package of reforms to raise productivity has to be coherent and comprehensive. Policy effectiveness is increased if linkages between elements are recognised. For example, policies to raise skills create a better environment for investment and innovation;

- an open and consultative approach is necessary to deliver the strategy. Real change will only be achieved if there is a shared commitment to making it happen on the ground. That is why the Government held a series of Productivity Roadshows after the publication of the Pre-Budget Report and Competitiveness White Paper, allowing people across the nation to contribute to the productivity debate.

3.3   This chapter examines the productivity challenge and explains the Government's strategy for tackling it. It outlines some of the initiatives that are already contributing to improving UK performance and sets out how this Budget builds on them to deliver a better deal for enterprise and business. Further details will be announced by the DTI.

THE PRODUCTIVITY CHALLENGE

3.4   The Government's approach to the productivity challenge starts from a clear understanding of the nature of the problem.

Understanding the productivity gap

3.5   Productivity in the UK is lower than other major economies Chart 3.1, reproduced from the PBR, shows the UK has a gap in whole economy output per worker of approaching 40 per cent with the US and around 20 per cent with France and Germany. If the alternative measure of output per hour is used a substantial gap still remains. The gap with France increases to around 30 per cent and, that with the US falls to around 25 per cent. Measures vary over the cycle, but they are substantial and provide a clear rationale for action, a position endorsed by business leaders attending last summer's Productivity Seminars and the Regional Roadshows.

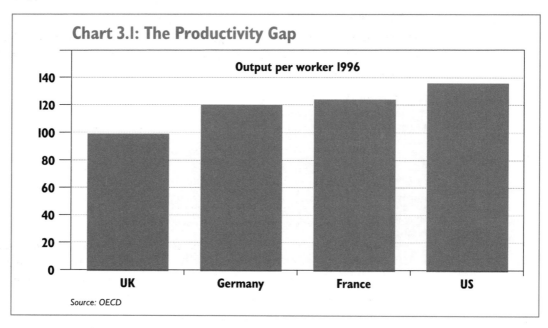

Chart 3.1: The Productivity Gap

Output per worker 1996

Source: OECD

3.6   A productivity gap also remains when Total Factor Productivity (TFP) levels are compared. The recent figures from the National Institute of Economic and Social Research confirm this. TFP is designed to measure 'technical progress'– that part of growth that is not explained by an increase in inputs of either capital or labour. Because TFP calculations compare countries after controlling for differences in capital stock the gap is generally smaller than that measured by output per worker, or per hour, but this is unsurprising given the UK's historically poor investment performance.

The Government's strategy: rising to the challenges of the modern economy

3.7   The Government has identified five key drivers of productivity performance. They help diagnose past failings, and set out a framework for improving performance. They tackle weaknesses in inputs, in the use of existing technology, and in the creation and exploitation of new technology. The five drivers are:

- investment in physical capital;
- enterprise and innovation;
- education and skills;
- competition and regulation; and
- public sector productivity.

Box 3.2: Growth accounting – growth, productivity and total factor productivity

A 'growth accounting' framework breaks down the sources of output growth into growth due to a greater quantity of inputs (labour and capital) and that due to better use of those inputs through technological progress or other efficiency gains, often called total factor productivity.

Using this framework, traditional analysis of growth argued that the only way permanently to increase the growth rate was to increase the rate of technical progress or total factor productivity growth. An increase in the proportion of people in employment, or in physical capital or human capital, would lead to a higher level of output, and per capita incomes as a result, but would not permanently raise the growth rate. The economy would grow faster for a period, until it reached its new higher level, but thereafter it would return to its original growth rate.

However, more recent studies suggest that investment in physical and human capital can increase both the level of output and permanently raise the growth rate. There are three key mechanisms:

- increasing the speed of diffusion and adoption of new production methods. New investment embodies new inventions and new techniques so that newer capital is more productive than older capital. And a higher level of skills in the economy is important in getting best use from new investment.

- spillover effects whereby one firm's investment creates new growth opportunities for other firms. This is perhaps best seen in the development of 'clusters' of firms whereby the opportunity of a particular firm to make profits depends crucially on the presence and prior investment of other firms; and

- increasing the rate at which knowledge and innovations are generated. As the OECD have argued, an increase in investment in R&D can increase the rate at which new knowledge is created. There can be pervasive spillover effects since unlike the consumption of goods, the fact that one person is using a new idea or insight, does not prevent others from exploiting the idea too.

So policies to increase skills and investment, and which recognise the links between the two, become vital to an economy's long run growth performance, and hence are central to improving UK productivity and growth.

3.8   The box above sets out how a growth framework underpins this strategy, and emphasises the potential gains, in terms of permanently higher growth, that can be unlocked by increasing investment in physical and human capital.

INVESTMENT

3.9   Investment is central to productivity improvement. A high quantity and quality of investment has two key influences. The first is that it increases the level of inputs into the economy – increasing the productivity and hence the earnings of workers in a very direct way. But it is also a vital channel for the introduction of new technology and processes. New investment does not just replace existing machinery, but moves forward production possibilities by embodying technical change.

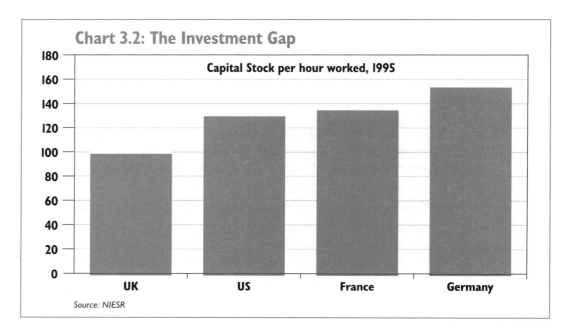

Chart 3.2: The Investment Gap

Capital Stock per hour worked, 1995

Source: NIESR

3.10   The UK's investment record has been poor. In each year since at least 1960, the UK has invested a lower share of GDP than the OECD average. In addition, over the last full international economic cycle between 1982 and 1993, the UK invested a lower share of GDP than any other G7 country.

3.11   The UK has a lower level of capital stock per worker or per hour worked than the United States, France or Germany. The differences in capital stock are not being made up by higher investment in recent years: for example, in the last international business cycle for every £100 per worker invested in the UK, the US and Germany invested £140 and France almost £150.

3.12   Some have argued that the UK does not have an investment gap to reverse because in recent years business investment as a share of GDP has been comparable to other major countries. This is not the case. Britain needs a period of higher investment than other leading economies if it is to begin addressing the under-investment of the past. If the UK carries on investing the same share of a smaller national income it will fall further behind.

3.13   The picture of under-investment is confirmed by figures comparing individual companies. The top 500 UK companies have around two thirds the level of capital expenditure per employee and capital stock per employee of the top 300 international companies.

3.14   The Government's strategy to address under-investment has been taken forward on four main fronts:

- macroeconomic reforms to provide a stable environment;
- greater public investment to reverse a legacy of public sector under-investment;
- a tax framework that encourages investment; and
- promoting efficient national and international capital markets.

3.15   The macroeconomic reforms – set out in Chapter 2 – will help provide a stable environment to encourage long-term investment in physical capital. Greater economic stability can also benefit investment in human capital, for example encouraging employers and employees to invest in training and education.

3.16   The doubling of net public investment announced in the Comprehensive Spending Review will begin to reverse historic public sector under-investment. The new fiscal policy and control regime ensures capital spending will not be cut to meet short term targets.

3.17   The Government's approach to encouraging investment through the tax system and to promoting efficiency in capital markets is set out in more detail below.

A tax framework that encourages businesses to invest

3.18   The Government has put in place a number of tax measures that build on the stable foundations of the new macroeconomic framework and are designed to encourage investment for the long term. The first two Budgets:

- reduced the main rate of corporation tax to 30 per cent, the lowest rate among major industrialised countries, and reduced the small companies' rate to 20 per cent. UK corporation tax rates are now at their lowest level since the tax was introduced;
- reformed Capital Gains Tax (CGT) to encourage long-term investment by introducing a taper to reduce the gain the longer the assets are held. Higher rate payers holding business assets for 10 years will now face a CGT rate equivalent to 10 per cent;
- withdrew payable tax credits to remove the distortion that encouraged companies to pay dividends rather than reinvest, and reduced the compliance burden on small and medium-sized firms that pay dividends by abolishing advance corporation tax (ACT); and
- introduced enhanced first-year capital allowances to encourage investment in plant and machinery by small and medium-sized businesses.

3.19   Budget 99 builds on this to provide further support for business investment through:

Corporation tax
- **the introduction of a 10 per cent rate of corporation tax for the smallest companies.** The 10 per cent rate will encourage investment and enterprise by halving the corporation tax rate for the smallest companies with profits up to £10,000 and it will benefit those with profits of up to £50,000 (some 270,000 companies). These companies will be left with more of their profits for retention, reinvestment and growth; and

Capital allowances
- **the extension of 40 per cent first year capital allowances for SMEs for a further year.** These will include spending by small and medium-sized businesses on machinery and plant in the year ending 1 July 2000.

Efficient national and international capital markets

3.20   The efficiency of national and international capital markets has a direct impact on both the level and quality of investment and is an important factor in understanding the availability of finance for business expansion.

3.21   The Government is working in a number of areas to improve the efficiency of UK and EU financial markets, these include:

- establishing the Financial Services Authority (FSA) to ensure that capital markets regulation complements competition policy and that the regulatory system is strong, effective and fair and does not impose excessive burdens;

- consulting on a proposal to enable any kind of pension vehicle (including stakeholder pensions) to invest in pooled investment funds. This will be a more transparent holding for investments – it should make it easier and cheaper for people to transfer their pension savings from one kind of pension to another and allow savers to monitor more actively their investments; and

- launching a Banking Review, under the chairmanship of Don Cruickshank, which is looking at current levels of innovation, competition, and efficiency in the banking industry and reviewing the services provided.

3.22   The Government is committed to continuing to stimulate competition in the financial services sector to promote efficiency and to ensure that consumers get the best deal.

3.23   To help firms raise capital both at national level and across the EU, the Government:

Prospectuses

- **will bring forward amendments to UK legislation on prospectuses and offers of securities to remove unnecessary restrictions.** The Government is working with the European Commission and other Member States to remove barriers to cross-border offers of securities in the EU.

3.24   Budget 99 also proposes further measures to enhance competition in the financial services sector:

Financial services

- **the Financial Services Authority will consult on league tables for savings and investment products.** These will provide authoritative and reliable information on private pensions, endowments, unit trusts and ISAs; and

Mortgage quotations

- **the DTI will set out proposals to improve information on mortgages and other credit including clarifying how interest rates are quoted to allow borrowers to more easily compare the costs of competing loans.** Further details will be announced tomorrow.

ENTERPRISE

3.25   A dynamic and innovative business sector is vital to long run growth. SMEs have an important role to play as drivers of productivity and innovation in the wider economy.

3.26   Small firms can help increase competitive intensity by introducing new products and through the pressures they put on existing firms to improve efficiency, and compete on price. Markets work best when incumbent firms face competition, or the threat of competition if their performance is lacklustre. Recent work by the OECD highlights the impact on productivity growth that the entry of new, often innovative, firms can have[1]. Competitiveness abroad depends on competition at home.

---

[1] "Decomposition of Industry-level Productivity Growth: A micro-macro Link" OECD 1997.

3.27   The UK has a relatively good record in generating new businesses but has a weaker record at getting such firms to grow. This is a concern because evidence from the US suggests that increasingly it is new, often high-technology businesses that generate growth in high quality employment and output. A smaller, less dynamic UK SME sector means less competitive pressure on the rest of the economy, and a weaker presence in the UK of those firms that have driven significant improvements in productivity performance.

3.28   The Government has a role to play in helping SMEs reach their potential. For example, there can be particular problems for SMEs in raising finance because they may have little track record for the financial community to use in assessing whether to lend money. Their small size means monitoring and transactions costs are high[2].

3.29   High-technology SMEs can face particular problems – such as higher technical risks and difficulties in assessing the value of technology on the part of lenders. As set out in last year's FSBR, to grow these companies need:

- entrepreneurs who have the energy and drive to create a company and the ambition to keep it growing;

- access to finance to allow good ideas and innovations to be developed into saleable products. Such businesses often require significant start up capital to develop products. Providing finance for such businesses is often perceived to be high-risk and in many cases investment may be needed over the long-term to realise significant returns. Bank or standard equity finance is often not available for such ventures; and

- key employees who are willing to join and stay with a small company to develop an idea, obtain finance, and see a product through to the market, even though initial salaries may be low and job security is less than working for a large company.

3.30   But it is important to acknowledge that enterprise is not just about encouraging entrepreneurial behaviour in the SME sector. Firms of all sizes can be innovative and enterprising. The key features of high-productivity, high-wage firms is that they combine innovative approaches to production and continuous improvements in the skills of their staff. And they place emphasis on encouraging all workers to contribute ideas, often backed up by innovative pay systems[3].

3.31   Productivity differences may also reflect different historical attitudes to enterprise and business. A more enterprising culture can be developed – for example by highlighting positive role models amongst business people and entrepreneurs and by encouraging businesses and schools and the wider community to interact.

3.32   The Government's approach to promoting enterprise is focused on:

- encouraging entrepreneurial investment;

- encouraging employees to take a stake in their company; and

- providing small businesses with the advice and support they need to succeed.

---

[2] "Technology, Productivity and Job Creation: Best Policy Practices" OECD 1998.
[3] Newton K. "The Human Factor in Firms' Performance: Management Strategies for Productivity and Competitiveness in the Knowledge-based Economy" (1996).

Encouraging entrepreneurial investment

3.33 Innovative and high-technology small businesses have the potential to make a major contribution to the United Kingdom's economic performance.

3.34 The last Budget began the focus on encouraging risk-taking and entrepreneurial investment through:

- reforming Venture Capital Trusts (VCTs) and the Enterprise Investment Scheme (EIS) to target the provision of equity capital on smaller higher risk trading companies; and

- reforming Capital Gains Tax (CGT) as described in the investment section above.

3.35 Budget 99 builds on this package by:

Enterprise management incentives

- taking forward a new enterprise management incentive scheme which would provide tax relief for certain forms of equity-based remuneration. It will be clearly targeted on small higher-risk trading companies, with the aim of improving their ability to recruit and retain high-calibre management. Further details will be contained in an Inland Revenue technical note, to be issued on 10 March, and the scheme will be announced next year.

Venture Capital Challenge

- creating a Venture Capital Challenge Competition of £20 million from the Capital Modernisation Fund to be invested in new funds for early stage, high-technology businesses, in partnership with private investors. Funds will operate in every part of the UK and will have a significant regional dimension. In England public funding will be administered by the new Small Business Service, in consultation with the Regional Development Agencies;

Corporate venturing

- setting out plans for a new tax incentive to promote corporate venturing. This will be introduced in Budget 2000 and will aim to promote inter-firm collaboration and to improve the flow of investment to early-stage companies; and

Serial EIS investment

- encouraging serial investment through the EIS, by giving CGT taper relief cumulatively on a gain deferred from one EIS investment to another.

3.36 The Government will continue to look at how best to create an environment that supports investment and growth by small and medium sized enterprises.

Encouraging employees to take a stake in their companies

3.37 The Government believes that employee share ownership has an important part to play in raising productivity by harnessing the ambition of employees to see the company they work for succeed. Research evidence suggests that share ownership has a positive effect on employee productivity, particularly when combined with other means of active employee participation.

3.38 Share schemes help recruitment and retention of staff, by encouraging a long-term commitment to the company. However, the current tax advantaged employee share schemes do not effectively promote the long-term holding of shares by employees. Shares are often seen as part of remuneration and there is evidence that a majority of employees dispose of their shares as soon as they can.

3.39   The Government believes that an effective employee share ownership scheme should:

- promote long-term shareholding by all employees to build a stronger sense of partnership in industry and increase productivity;

- promote widespread employee share ownership – in small firms as well as large;

- improve long-term company performance.

Employee share ownership   3.40   **To achieve these objectives Budget 2000 will introduce a new all-employee share scheme.**

3.41   This scheme will encourage companies to give free shares to their employees, and for the first time employees will be able to buy shares from their pre-tax salary, which can be matched with shares given by the company. There will be tax incentives to encourage longer-term shareholding. This new scheme will represent an important step towards the Government's target of doubling the number of companies offering all-employee share schemes.

3.42   An advisory group is being set up, which will assist the Inland Revenue in the development of the new scheme and the further work on the existing employee share schemes. This advisory group will also consider the specific needs of smaller and unquoted companies and how these might be met.

Helping businesses to succeed

3.43   The Government places great emphasis on improving the economic climate for small firms. Small firms are the bedrock of an innovative, adaptable economy and a key provider of employment. Over 45 per cent of the workforce work for companies employing 50 or less people.

3.44   The enterprise and innovation measures set out in this chapter are important steps in ensuring that SMEs and hi-tech businesses are able to invest and grow.

3.45   However the Government believes it also has a role to play in supporting small businesses through the provision of advice and in particular by helping them to minimise the cost of complying with regulations.

3.46   The current framework for providing support and advice to SMEs needs to be given a stronger focus, with much more emphasis on helping SMEs comply with regulations.

Small Business Service   3.47   **The Government will therefore create a new Small Business Service (SBS) to act as a focal point within Government for providing both regulatory, tax and payroll advice and business support to small firms.** The SBS will work to:

- improve help to SMEs in complying with regulations, taking on responsibilities from – and working closely with – the Better Regulation Unit;

- improve the quality and coherence of delivery of government support for small firms including the Business Link programme and the new DTI Enterprise Fund;

- **establish a new automated payroll service for new small employers to reduce the burden of complying with the tax system.**

3.48   The Government will be looking to recruit for the SBS a high-profile and experienced chief executive, who will be accountable directly to Ministers. The Secretary of State for Trade and Industry will consult on further details of the Government's plans.

Compliance **3.49**   Budget 99 also sets out further measures to reduce the costs to business of complying
costs with the tax regulations:

- working closely with the **Small Business Service new Inland Revenue Business Support Teams will provide support and advice to new businesses, who want it, including the provision of one-to-one advice for half a day, by experienced Revenue staff;**

- **an increase in the PAYE quarterly payments limit to £1,000 per month, giving an additional 130,000 small employers the opportunity to reduce costs by paying PAYE quarterly rather than monthly;**

- **businesses will be able to file fax returns over the Internet.** The Government intends to offer a discount on returns filed via the Internet.

- **new business advice service for exporters and importers provided by Customs and Excise;** and

- **a new Government supported standard for payroll software so that small employers can be confident that the software they buy will meet the requirements for effective communications with all parts of the Government this will be available from January 2000.**

INNOVATION

3.50   Innovation and research and development (R&D) are central to technical progress which is a key driver of long-run growth. The process of innovation encompasses all aspects of firm performance, from R&D, through to new processes and products, to a culture of continuous training and improvement. Failure to understand this process was a key weakness in traditional analyses of growth.

3.51   The OECD recently examined the link between R&D and productivity and found:

"There is conclusive evidence at the firm level that R&D-performing firms experience both higher productivity levels and higher productivity growth than other firms."[4]

3.52   So R&D is crucial to productivity, and as chart 3.3 shows, the UK investment in R&D has been weak, as seen also in the fact that the UK has the lowest R&D to sales ratio in the G5.

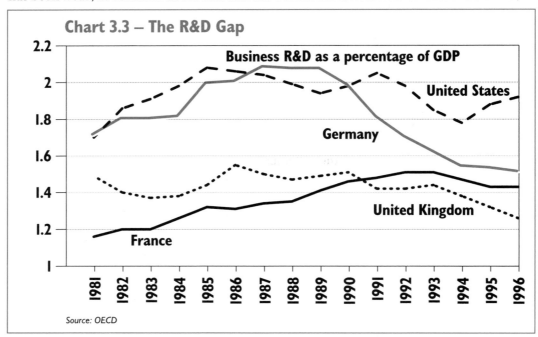

Chart 3.3 – The R&D Gap

---

[4] "Technology, productivity and Job Creation: Best Policy Practices" OECD 1998.

3.53　Both public and private sector research is important. Recent research from the OECD shows that, in the short term, the return to R&D spending in terms of patents is higher for privately funded R&D, but that, in the long run, Government funded R&D has a higher return.

3.54　The Government has a central role in promoting and funding R&D because of the spillover benefits that result from private R&D effort – the firm undertaking the R&D appropriates some of the gains, but other benefits flow to customers, other researchers, and other firms. So the returns to society can be greater than the private return. This means that it is in the interests of the whole economy for the Government to encourage private sector R&D.

3.55　Increasing the linkages between centres of research, such as universities, and business is vital. The experience of MIT in Massachusetts and Stanford in Silicon Valley demonstrate the scale of the economic return that can be generated by partnership between business and academia.

3.56　So the Government's strategy addresses the three key approaches to getting the most out of R&D. The first is to provide adequate funding to basic research. The second is to improve the commercialisation of the research that is undertaken. And the third is to improve the incentive for business to conduct research.

A better deal for basic science

3.57　The Government has acted to improve improve basic science infrastructure through the creation of the £600 million Joint Infrastructure Fund, endowed equally by the Government and the Wellcome Trust, for new university equipment and buildings. This fund was announced in July 1998 as part of a wider increase in funding for science totalling £1.4 billion.

Joint Infrastructure Fund　**3.58**　**To further enhance the Government's efforts to modernise the essential underpinning infrastructure of scientific research carried out in universities, the Higher Education Funding Council for England will add £100 million to the Joint Infrastructure Fund making a total Fund of £700 million.**

Encouraging exploitation of research

3.59　Over the past year the Government has taken a number of steps to begin to generate a step change in attitudes towards the commercialisation of university research. Initiatives include:

- the £50 million University Challenge scheme, launched in last year's Budget, to provide early-stage seed funding to help exploit the commercial potential of university research. Over 40 bids for support from this fund were received and it was over-subscribed by three times;

- the £25 million Science Enterprise Challenge to endow up to eight centres of enterprise to act as beacons of excellence in technology transfer and the teaching of entrepreneurship to scientists and engineers. These will help universities commercialise research and to foster a stronger culture of scientific enterprise; and

- a review of commercialisation of knowledge in public sector research establishments led by John Baker, chairman of Medeva plc.

3.60   The Government has now taken further measures to help improve the exploitation of scientific research:

- the new Venture Capital Challenge with £20 million of funding from the Capital Modernisation Fund will be specifically aimed at financing innovative, high-technology companies needing early stage financing; and

University Challenge

- the Government has allocated further funding of £15 million to University Challenge; there will now be a second round of the competition.

Encouraging business research and development

3.61   The Government has an important role in ensuring that the right incentives are in place for business and finance sectors to exploit science research. In particular the Government wants to ensure that the SME sector is investing in the growth potential of R&D.

3.62   The Pre-Budget Report set out some of the Government's initial proposals on providing a tax credit for SME Research and Development.

R & D tax credit   **3.63**   **The Government intends to introduce for a volume-based R&D tax credit for SMEs, with the aim of introducing the credit in Budget 2000.** The proposed credit will:

- be open to small and medium sized companies spending more than £50,000 a year on R&D;

- increase the existing 100 per cent relief for R&D to 150 per cent. So, a company that is paying tax at the 20 per cent smaller companies rate would receive a total saving of 30 per cent on the cost of R&D; and

- also extend to companies undertaking R&D but not yet in taxable profit. In return for this tax credit payment, companies would surrender the right to carry forward their R&D costs to offset against future profits.

3.64   The details of this proposal will be set out in an Inland Revenue technical note.

3.65   The Government is also concerned to ensure that the tax treatment of intellectual property is simple and fair. The Inland Revenue will issue a technical note, on 10 March, which will discuss ways in which the system could be simplified and reformed so that all expenditure is relieved according to a common regime and clarify the rules on when basic rate income tax should be deducted from royalty payments.

EDUCATION AND SKILLS

3.66   Education and skills are important for growth both in terms of directly increasing labour productivity, and through influencing the impact of new technology and innovations. Improving skills at all levels is vital. For example, weaknesses in basic skills will inhibit the diffusion of new technology and mean the UK will gain less from its research and development effort.

3.67   Skills deficiencies can also impact on other productivity drivers. For example, investment in physical capital – such as machinery – has often been seen as a substitute for investing in workers. But it is increasingly clear that investment in human and physical capital can be complements rather than substitutes – a shortage of skilled labour is a key constraint on investment in physical capital.

3.68   The UK's historic weaknesses in skills have been well-documented and apply throughout the system. Too many people leave school with no qualifications at all; and there is an under-developed culture of lifelong learning. For example, over a quarter of young people still fail to achieve the equivalent of a good GCSE by the time they leave school.

3.69   Tackling this skills gap involves coordinated action across every part of the education sector:

- in pre-nursery, nursery and primary education to provide a sound base for later learning;

- in secondary schools, to ensure that all pupils have the skills necessary to succeed when they enter the workplace;

- in further education to provide accessible opportunities to improve basic and intermediate skills, including for those already in the workforce; and

- in higher education to ensure that courses are relevant to the needs of a modern economy and a modern society.

3.70   The Government has acted to tackle this national priority. The Comprehensive Spending Review allocated an additional £19 billion for the next three years for education, an increase in real terms of 5.1 per cent a year between 1998-99 and 2001-02. The Government has:

- established the Sure Start scheme and is expanding nursery education;

- begun to provide more modern facilities and equipment through an additional £2.2 billion in schools capital funding over the next three years;

- helped make lifelong learning possible for everyone with the establishment of the University for Industry (UfI) which will use the latest technology to bring education and training into the home, the workplace and the community; and

- continued the expansion in higher and further education with a commitment to add over 700,000 extra students a year in further and higher education by 2002.

3.71   Budget 99 builds on the important steps already taken with a major announcement setting out how Individual Learning Accounts will improve skills training in the existing workforce.

3.72   Some 13 million adults have yet to achieve "level 2" – the equivalent of five good GCSEs. The 1998 Labour Force Survey shows that, compared to those with no qualifications, adults with five good GCSEs are:

- up to four times more likely to get further training from their employers;

- likely to earn more than those with no qualifications. Men with five good GCSEs earned on average £110 a week more than those with no qualifications; women earned £80 more; and

- one third as likely to be unemployed.

3.73   The Government's proposals for Individual Learning Accounts (ILAs) are designed to provide lifelong learning opportunities for everyone in the workforce, ensuring people can receive the training that they need to succeed in today's dynamic labour market.

3.74 ILAs should help correct market failures that can lead to under provision of training even when it is clearly in the employer's and the employee's interest. For example:

- some employers do not provide training that would benefit their company because they are afraid that the trained worker will be poached by another firm;

- employees may under-invest in training because they have difficulty in financing it: investment in training does not create a tangible asset which a bank can use as collateral.

Individual Learning Accounts

3.75 Individual Learning Accounts will bridge both sides of this problem. **An initial one million accounts will be opened with the first starter accounts opening in 1999.** The first million accounts will match £25 from the ILA holder with an additional £150 for spending on education and training.

3.76 **Every adult in Britain will be entitled to open an Individual Learning Account in 2000.** These ILAs will comprise:

- a discount of 20 per cent for all ILA holders, on spending on eligible courses of up to £500 a year;

- generous discounts of 80 per cent on the cost of certain key courses, including computer literacy; and

- tax reliefs for employers and employees on employers' contributions to ILAs.

COMPETITION AND REGULATION

3.77 Competition is a key driver of productivity both in individual companies and across whole sectors. The need to compete in terms of price, product and service drives companies to innovate, to improve efficiency and to pass savings on to consumers and the wider economy. Work by Stephen Nickell, for example, has demonstrated the link between higher competitive pressures and higher productivity[6]. And this link was often cited by business participants at the Productivity Roadshows and seminars.

3.78 Entrepreneurs need to know that the competition authorities will be vigilant in preventing incumbent firms from seeking to restrict market access. Otherwise potential entrepreneurs will be unable to grow new firms successfully, and may be dissuaded from even trying.

3.79 The existing competition framework does not set the right environment for competition giving insufficient powers for the authorities to tackle anti-competitive practices and abuses of dominant positions. This is perhaps exemplified by the persistence of price differentials across a broad range of sectors with the US, though there are clearly a number of other factors involved.

3.80 The Government has acted to improve the intensity of competition in the UK through the new Competition Act (which comes into force in March 2000). This will provide the competition authorities in the UK with the powers to fine firms by up to 10 per cent of turnover, and make it a criminal offence to obstruct an inquiry.

3.81 Tough competition regulation is only possible if it is underpinned by sufficient resources. The Pre-Budget Report announced a 20 per cent increase in funds for the Office of Fair Trading to enable it to take a more pro-active approach.

---

[6] "Competition and Corporate Performance." (1996) S Nickell, Journal of Political Economy 104(4).

3.82   The full benefits of competition require markets to be open to trade and investment by overseas firms. This increases competition and facilitates the spread of leading edge technology, thereby stimulating UK firms to deliver productivity improvements, operate at maximum efficiency and continuously innovate.

3.83   **The Government has concluded however that more needs to be done to take forward the competition agenda.** The Secretary of State for Trade and Industry will therefore be making announcements on the framework under which mergers are controlled. The Deputy Prime Minister will review competition in airports in following up proposals in the Government's Integrated Transport White Paper. In addition, starting with industrial and commercial consumers, the Deputy Prime Minister will review competition in the water industry.

Regulation

3.84   The Government believes that sensible regulation can help to balance economic, social and environmental needs. But over-regulation, or regulation that is confusing or contradictory, risks preventing innovative ideas from reaching the market. Many participants at last year's Productivity Seminars suggested that it was important that the impact of regulations on productivity was properly considered.

3.85   The Government has asked the Better Regulation Task Force under Lord Haskins to launch a detailed investigation into the impact of regulation on growth and productivity. The Task Force has already produced its interim report, which emphasised, among other things the need for Government to target the needs of SMEs right through from initial consultation on the need for regulations to final implementation and enforcement. This Budget has begun to address these concerns with measures to help businesses comply with tax and regulation.

3.86   The Deputy Prime Minister has been undertaking a comprehensive examination of the planning system to ensure that it is attuned to the needs of enterprise and business, while still meeting the Government's wider environmental objectives. He will shortly publish a report on progress. The Government attaches particular importance to the development of clusters of business enterprises. A review is currently underway to identify whether the planning system creates any barriers to the development of clusters. Planning guidance issued last month highlighted the need to make "provision for the location, expansion and promotion of clusters or networks of knowledge driven industry."

PUBLIC SECTOR PRODUCTIVITY

3.87   The Government also has a part to play by working to improve productivity in the public sector. In the past the public sector has focused on reducing costs rather than improving the quality of the service provided and has not had the management systems to implement a productivity enhancing strategy.

3.88   The Government has taken forward its commitment to improve public sector productivity with the publication of the Public Service Agreements which set out key targets for improving efficiency and productivity in service delivery. Progress against the PSAs is being overseen by a Cabinet Committee (PSX) chaired by the Chancellor of the Exchequer. This Committee is advised by the Government's Public Service Productivity Panel, a body of private sector management experts.

3.89 Public private partnerships (PPPs), bringing the public and private sectors together in partnership for their mutual benefit, are another element in the Government's strategy. By bringing in private sector management, finance and ownership, PPPs help improve the efficiency and quality of public services and deliver the best return for the economy as a whole from assets and enterprises currently in the public sector.

3.90 The Government is taking forward public private partnerships for many of the remaining commercial organisations in the public sector – for example London Underground, air traffic control, British Waterways and the Commonwealth Development Corporation. The Government believes that such businesses should be structured so they invest and operate effectively, so improving their services to customers and their own chances of long-term commercial success, while delivering value for money for the taxpayer.

4 INCREASING EMPLOYMENT OPPORTUNITY

High levels of labour market participation are central to achieving high and sustainable growth and greater prosperity. The Government has begun an ambitious series of reforms to help people move from welfare to work and to make work pay. Over 350,000 people have benefited from the New Deal. Budget 99 builds on and extends these reforms, increasing employment opportunity for all with a better deal for working people.

The challenge of a changing labour market

The labour market has changed significantly over the last twenty years:

- sharply rising female employment with a corresponding rise in part-time work;

- rises in structural unemployment, alongside wide swings in employment;

- declining rates of labour market participation, particularly among the over 50s, lone parents, people with disabilities and the partners of unemployed people; and

- people on low wages failing to keep pace with the general rise in earnings.

New strategies are needed to tackle these new challenges.

Delivering Welfare to Work

- extra help for young people to ensure everyone takes advantage of the New Deal options available, with no option of simply remaining on benefit;

- a New Deal for the over 50s; and

- an Income Support run-on to ease the transition into work for lone parents.

Making work pay

- a minimum income guarantee of £200 per week for full-time working families, from October 1999;

- from October 1999, families will pay no net income tax until their earnings exceed £235 per week, over £12,000 a year;

- an increase of over 25 per cent in the starting point for employee national insurance contributions over 2 years, to align it with the starting point for income tax;

- cuts in NICs liabilities for low earning self-employed people, continuing the package of work incentive measures recommended by Martin Taylor;

- a £60 per week in-work payment to people over 50 moving back to work;

- a new 10p rate of income tax which halves the tax bill for the low paid; and

- a cut in the basic rate to 22p to reward work and ensure working families are better off.

INTRODUCTION

4.1   Budget 99 builds on the Government's strategy for achieving high and stable levels of employment, through the promotion of employment opportunities for all – the modern definition of full employment for the 21st century. Creating employment opportunities will not only promote economic growth but will ensure that the benefits of growth are shared throughout society.

4.2   The Labour Force Survey (LFS) shows that, since the last election, employment has risen by over 400,000. Unemployment has fallen by over 300,000 on the ILO definition, and by over 360,000 on the claimant definition. Long-term youth unemployment has fallen by over 50 per cent. However, there remain substantial challenges to be faced: over the last 20 years structural unemployment has risen, participation rates among certain groups have fallen dramatically, and the rewards for work for those on low incomes have not kept pace with the general increase in living standards. More is also known about the way the labour market works. In particular, the tax and benefit system can trap people into unemployment and poverty. In May 1997, for example, around three quarters of a million people faced a poverty trap whereby over 70 pence of every extra £1 they earned was lost in tax and benefit clawback.

4.3   Chapter 2 set out the need for a stable macroeconomic environment, an essential precondition for an extension of employment opportunities. However, a better macroeconomic framework alone is not enough. This Government's first two Budgets, together with the Comprehensive Spending Review, have made major steps towards extending employment opportunities. Measures in Budget 99, set out later in this Chapter, build on the Government's strategy to promote employment opportunities for all.

THE CHALLENGE OF A CHANGING LABOUR MARKET

4.4   Since the objective of full employment was first set out in 1944 there have been major demographic and social changes, new developments in the labour market and the global economy and a rise in female and part-time employment. The traditional approach to full employment relied heavily on the levers of macroeconomic demand management to secure full-time male employment. Active Welfare to Work policies were not so important when a high proportion of those looking for work could find it relatively quickly. Skills mattered less when there were plentiful job opportunities for people without qualifications. Distortions in the tax and benefit system had a much lesser impact when work took people substantially above the level of benefits. Family-friendly work practices were less relevant when fewer women were in work and fewer people needed to balance work and family responsibilities. And it was more valid to focus only on the claimant unemployed when those outside the work force altogether were not denied the chance of employment opportunity. The new challenge facing the Government is to promote employment opportunity for all in the very different labour market of today.

Changing patterns of employment   4.5   In the UK today over 27 million people – over 70 per cent of the working age population – are in work. This is a relatively high rate of employment compared with many other European countries, although below the levels of Japan and the US. Female employment rates have increased sharply over the last few decades. In 1975, 59 per cent of working age women were in employment compared to 69 per cent today. Two-thirds of working mothers now return to work within one year of the birth of their child, compared to 38 per cent in 1979, and those who return within a year do not appear to suffer the loss in subsequent earnings faced by other mothers. The UK is also notable for providing a wide range of opportunities to fit work around personal and family circumstances, and has been relatively successful at supporting the increased participation of women in the labour market.

Structural unemployment   4.6   High structural unemployment is the most obvious sign of a failure in the labour market. Although unemployment today is lower than in many other European countries, it remains well above the levels seen in the 1950s and 1960s. Chart 4.1 shows how registered unemployment has varied since the 1950s. Unemployment in the UK fluctuated between 1 per cent and 3 per cent of the workforce from the 1950s until the middle of the 1970s, before rising to around $4^{1}/_{2}$ per cent by the end of that decade. But since 1980, it has averaged around

8½ per cent. Alongside high levels of structural unemployment, the employment rate has also been very variable over the economic cycle – reflecting the swings in output there have been over the last 20 years.

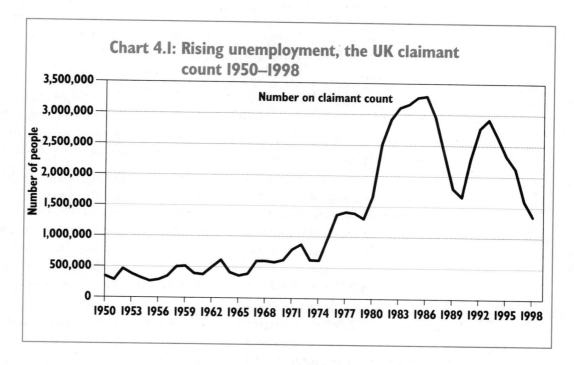

Chart 4.1: Rising unemployment, the UK claimant count 1950–1998

4.7 The headline picture on unemployment hides a more complex, dynamic picture. The unemployment rate is the product of substantial labour market flows into and out of employment. Every quarter, around 2 million people move into a new job, of whom around 40 per cent were previously out of work. This means that, despite lower growth this year, millions of new job opportunities will continue to emerge. The Government's employment strategy will mean that individuals are better placed to take advantage of those opportunities.

4.8 Most people who become unemployed, at whatever stage of the economic cycle, return to work within the first few months. But a significant proportion of the labour force are at risk of repeated or prolonged periods of unemployment, amounting to a significant detachment from work. The increase in unemployment over the last 25 years is largely explained by increases in the duration of unemployment, rather than the number of people who become unemployed.

4.9 The build up of long-term unemployment associated with previous recessions was immensely damaging for individuals – destroying their connections with the labour market, their skills and employability. Typically, the long-term unemployed find it much harder to find work and those who do leave unemployment are much more likely than the short-term unemployed to move onto other benefits. The Government's strategy – through the New Deal – aims to reattach the long-term unemployed to the labour force, and give them a fair chance of competing for the available vacancies. In this way, employers are also given a wider choice of potential employees for their vacancies, and the risks which they perceive in hiring a long-term unemployed worker are reduced. The economy can then grow more rapidly without running into skill shortages and unsustainable wage inflation. The Welfare to Work programme raises the effective supply of labour, and hence can help raise the sustainable level of employment.

Rising inactivity 4.10   Many other groups of people are excluded from the labour force altogether – neither employed nor unemployed. Lone parents, people with disabilities, and the partners of unemployed people all have low employment rates. Whilst 69 per cent of mothers in couples work, only 45 per cent of lone mothers are in work. Where the youngest child is under 5, the differences are even more marked: more than twice as many mothers in couples, with a child under 5, are working, compared with lone mothers. The UK also has one of the lowest employment rates among lone parents in the developed world.

4.11   Worklessness is increasingly concentrated – about 3 million households with at least one adult member of working age have no one in work – or 17·6 per cent, compared to 9 per cent 20 years ago. People whose partners are unemployed are themselves only half as likely to move into work as people whose partner is in work. Increased worklessness is particularly acute among families with children, a major factor behind child poverty (see Chapter 5).

4.12   There has also been a particularly sharp fall in labour market participation among men over 50 which has partly offset increases in female labour market participation – see Chart 4.2. The proportion of men aged 50-64 who are outside the labour market has risen from 12·6 per cent in 1979 to 27·4 per cent today. And older women have seen much smaller increases in participation than those which have been so prominent among younger women. If the participation rate of people over 50 had followed the same pattern over the last 20 years as for those aged 25-50, there would be 700,000 more people in employment today.

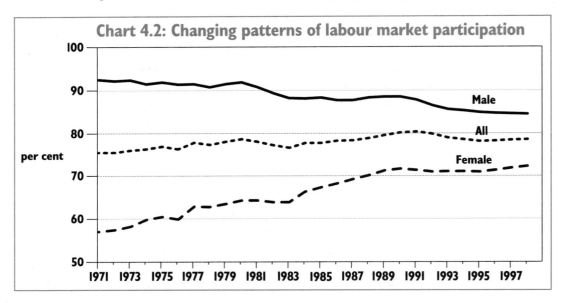

Chart 4.2: Changing patterns of labour market participation

Persistent low 4.13   Income inequality has increased sharply over the last 20 years. This is not
income   representative of a world-wide trend: only New Zealand has seen similarly widening inequality. Alongside this has been a substantial increase in the number of people living on relatively low incomes. 12 million people, nearly a quarter of the population, live on a household income below half the national average. This is almost three times the number 20 years ago. For a couple with no children it means living on less than £129 a week after housing costs. There has been no improvement in absolute incomes for people at the bottom of the income scale either. As many people in the mid 1990s were living on the equivalent of less than £92 a week after housing costs – half average income 20 years ago – as at the end of the 1970s.

4.14   For most people low income is transitory, lasting for no more than a year. But for some people it is a long-term experience, indicative of a persistent lack of opportunity and constrained life chances. Between 1991 and 1996, one quarter of those who started in the poorest 20 per cent of the income distribution remained there for all six years, and one in ten of the whole population never got above the poorest 30 per cent during these six years.

4.15   Lack of work and low pay are the main risk factors for short-term and persistent low income. Employment and earnings changes are the most important events associated with entry and escape from low income. Changes in family structure – divorce, bereavement and childbirth – also feature heavily in relation to entries into low income. But work is clearly the most important route out of low income:

- two-thirds of working age households on persistently low incomes are workless and 8 out of 10 are not fully employed;

- around two-thirds of movements out of low income occur through people gaining work or increasing their earnings; and

- between 1991 and 1995, 8 out of 10 people on low incomes who moved from worklessness into work also moved from out of the bottom fifth of the income distribution.

4.16   Getting a job is the most effective route out of low income, but one in five low-income households remains stuck on low income even though all the working-age adults in their household have jobs. Many of these people will become caught in a low-pay, no-pay cycle. This occurs where people move between unemployment and low-paid jobs, and are not able to move up the earnings ladder.

4.17   Women are more likely to be low paid than men. Around 11 per cent of women, compared to four per cent of men, currently earn less than the National Minimum Wage. Women are also less likely to move out of low pay, up the earnings ladder. Over two-thirds of women earning below half median hourly earnings in one year will remain below this threshold in the following year, compared to around 44 per cent of men. But, the number of men who were either continuously low paid, or caught in a low-pay, no pay cycle, doubled, from seven per cent in the period 1979–83 to 14 per cent in the period 1990–94.

THE GOVERNMENT'S STRATEGY FOR INCREASING EMPLOYMENT OPPORTUNITY

4.18   The Government has already implemented policies to reduce structural unemployment, increase labour market participation and make work pay. In addition to the New Deal programmes for 18-24 year olds and the long-term unemployed, the New Deal is offering help to lone parents, people with disabilities and partners of unemployed people to move back into work. Reforms to make work pay – including new measures in Budget 99 building on previous reforms – will make it worthwhile for those currently outside the labour force to move into employment. And extra help for the over 50s moving back into work will begin to tackle the sharp decline in participation among this group, and help to prevent them becoming the next generation of poorer pensioners.

4.19   The Government will also introduce a Single Work-Focused Gateway in 12 pilot areas, providing a personal adviser to help all benefit claimants of working age to become more independent. There will be a fundamental shift away from a system that asks simply "what money can we pay you?" to one that also says "how can we help you become more independent?". The Government is not forcing lone parents or disabled people into work, but many people who want to work are being written off as unemployable when they may have a good chance of finding a job. The Single Gateway will ensure that everyone is given the opportunity to discuss their prospects of finding work.

4.20   To build a stronger economic future, the Government will build on these reforms to provide a better deal for working people. So Budget 99 extends the New Deal, contains new measures to make work pay, and, because the Government is determined to reform the tax and benefit system to put work first, it introduces a 10p rate of income tax.

WELFARE TO WORK

4.21 The Government is delivering its Welfare to Work programme: already, over 350,000 people have participated in the New Deal, and more than 70,000 have got jobs. The Government is committed to continuous improvement of all aspects of the New Deal. Budget 99 builds on the New Deal by:

- **intensifying the gateway** for 18-24s, providing extra help for those young people who need it most, and ensuring that there is no option of a life on benefit;

- **a New Deal for the over 50s**, providing tailored advice and support to help people over 50 return to work; and

- **supporting lone parents** moving into work, by continuing their Income Support payments for two weeks, to guarantee their income in the critical transition to the Working Families Tax Credit.

Box 4.1: Experiences of the New Deal

The New Deal for 18-24s has already secured 58,000 jobs for young people. Among them are:

Andy, 18, from Perthshire, had been made redundant from his previous employer before joining the New Deal. He found a subsidised job with a local tree surgeon, and after just six months has now been promoted and gained qualifications as a chainsaw operator, climber and first aider, overcoming the problems of dyslexia to do so.

Emma, 23, from Cheltenham, wanted to work as a nursery assistant but had no relevant experience to offer an employer. She had been unemployed for a year prior to joining the New Deal. Her personal adviser was able to find a place for Emma with a local nursery, through the voluntary sector option. This gave Emma valuable experience and enabled her to work towards her Montessori Teaching Diploma. Emma was taken on as an employee by another nursery in February.

Lee, aged 23, had been unemployed for four years before starting on the New Deal. He got a job as a security guard at the local multi-storey car park, under the employment option, and has now been taken on as an unsubsidised employee. What a difference the last year has made for Lee: "This time last year I had no money, nothing to do and was moving around a lot as I had nowhere to live. I had never had a job. Since joining New Deal I have found a flat of my own."

Already, over 6,000 people have been helped into work by the New Deal for 25+:

Graham, 34, from South Shields, had been unemployed for nearly 2½ years before joining the New Deal. He attended a series of intensive interviews with his New Deal personal adviser and subsequently applied for a vacancy in the car industry. The company remarked on Graham's enthusiasm and keenness to work and have taken him on as a trainee press setter preparing precision components.

> **The New Deal for lone parents has already helped over 6,000 lone parents into work, including:**
>
> **Diane, 38, with a nine-year old son, had been out of work for six years and desperately wanted to work in catering. Her New Deal adviser helped her to write a CV and arranged an interview for her as a part-time cook. Diane got the job. She is now £33 per week better off and is able to work around her son's school hours.**

New Deal for 18-24 year olds

4.22   Men who are unemployed for more than a year by the time they are 23 spend nearly six times longer in unemployment over the following ten years than those who were unemployed for less than six months by age 23, and over 14 times longer than those who were not unemployed at all before 23. For women, the pattern is less acute for unemployment, but stronger for non-employment. The New Deal for 18-24 year olds, running nationwide since April 1998, helps young unemployed people to secure jobs as the most effective way of enhancing their earnings, increasing their skills and securing their future economic independence.

4.23   Over 230,000 young people have joined the New Deal, initially entering a gateway where they receive intensive support from a personal adviser. And already over 58,000 jobs have been secured for young people – over 43,000, or 74 per cent, unsubsidised. In addition, nearly 50,000 young people are gaining valuable training and work experience in New Deal options.

4.24   The Government has made considerable progress in developing its continuous improvement strategy for the New Deal for 18-24s, to ensure progressively better performance in helping young unemployed people find and retain jobs. Performance by each area delivering the New Deal will be measured against a set of nine indicators including the number of people moving into jobs, how long participants remain in employment, and how well people from ethnic minorities do. League tables showing performance by each area against the first objective of getting participants into jobs have already been made available. The Government intends to publish data on the performance measures in May. It is also developing a strategy to ensure that effective and timely action is taken to tackle poor performance and to drive forward performance across the board.

4.25   As part of the continuous improvement strategy, an Innovation Fund will enable enhancements to the New Deal to be tested. In particular, some young people might gain from a more intensive initial gateway at the beginning of the New Deal, to inject greater pace and purpose into their job-seeking activities. The Government hope to announce pilots later in 1999. And for those still in the gateway after three months, their final month will be made more intensive to reinforce the message that there is no option of continuing on benefits, and to make sure every young person has the help they need.

4.26   An effective balance between rights and responsibilities is an important element of the New Deal for 18-24 year olds. The vast majority of young people have engaged enthusiastically with the New Deal and are taking full advantage of the new opportunities it offers. Given the substantial public investment involved, and the wide ranging opportunities provided by employers and by the voluntary and environmental sectors, it is right that all young people should be required to meet their side of the bargain.

New Deal for the long-term unemployed

4.27   Since June 1998, those aged 25 and over and unemployed for over two years have been eligible for a £75 per week subsidy to help them into work. So far, around 95,000 long-term unemployed people have started on the New Deal. Most participants are still in the advisory interview process. But already over 6,000 have found jobs.

4.28   The last Budget announced the extension of the New Deal through a series of innovative pilots, based on the intensive approach pioneered for 18-24 year olds. The pilots were launched at the end of November 1998. Those unemployed for over 18 months, or for over 12 months in some areas, start an intensive gateway of job search activities. Those who do not find work enter a period of full-time activity for three months. The choice of options depends on individual need, but can include work trials with employers, training, work experience, and support for self-employment. On-going support is available to those most at risk of remaining unemployed.

4.29   60,000 people are expected to enter the pilots in Great Britain. In Northern Ireland, as part of the Chancellor's Economic Initiative which he announced in May 1998, these opportunities will be open to all those who have been unemployed for over 18 months – up to 30,000 people.

4.30   The pilots will be extensively evaluated, including the use of random assignment in two areas, to yield evidence about what works and what does not. The evidence will inform the future development of the Welfare to Work programme.

A New Deal for the over 50s

4.31   The employment rate of men over 50 has fallen sharply in the last 20 years, whilst women over 50 have not seen the large increases in participation that are so marked among younger women. **A New Deal for the over 50s will provide personalised advice for people over 50, where they or their partner have been on benefits for more than six months, to help them return to work.** The programme will be voluntary, and available to people who are economically inactive as well as unemployed. The programme will complement the new Employment Credit for over 50s (see paragraph 4.68). Pathfinders will start in October 1999, prior to national roll-out of the programme in 2000.

4.32   Many workers over 50 have skills that may have been superseded, or become rusty from a period out of the labour force. In addition to an Employment Credit, the over 50s will be eligible to up to £750 in-work training grants to help them acquire accredited training to take up and keep a new job.

New Deal for lone parents

4.33   The New Deal for lone parents was launched nationwide on 26 October 1998. It offers a personalised service combining job search help, advice and training to all lone parents on Income Support. It is the first serious national attempt to help lone parents improve their prospects and living standards by taking up and increasing paid work.

4.34   At the end of January 1999, over 39,000 lone parents had attended an initial interview with a trained personal adviser, with 32,000 of those attending a first interview deciding to participate in the New Deal. Over 6,000 lone parents participating in the New Deal have already moved into employment.

4.35   Lone parents have much lower employment rates than mothers in couples. Removing the financial uncertainty which lone parents often experience when moving into employment for the first time will encourage work and provide financial security for lone parents and their children. **To help lone parents to make the transition from welfare to work, their out of work Income Support (IS) will be extended for two weeks, from October 1999, when they move into employment.** Extending IS payments will help to bridge the gap between benefits and work, ensuring financial security in the transition to the Working Families Tax Credit (WFTC). The extended payments will be available to all lone parents who have been claiming IS for at least 26 weeks prior to finding work and claiming WFTC. The Government will consider whether there is a case for extending this run-on to other groups on the basis of evidence from lone parents.

New Deal for partners of unemployed people

4.36   The New Deal for partners of unemployed people was launched in three pathfinder areas in February 1999 and it will be rolled out nationally in April 1999. It will ensure that partners of people unemployed for six months or more can receive specialist advice to help them back to work. Childless partners aged 18-24 will be brought into the New Deal for 18-24s from 2000, subject to legislation, and will be able to volunteer to join it from April 1999.

New Deal for disabled people

4.37   In the past, the benefit system defined people with disabilities by what they could not do, condemning them to a life of benefit dependency and low expectations. The New Deal for disabled people offers people with disabilities the opportunity to work and achieve their full potential. In six pilot areas, a personal adviser service offers individually tailored support. A further six, run by private, voluntary and public sector agencies, will start soon. Already over 1,000 people with disabilities have benefited. Because the needs of people with disabilities have been ignored too often in the past, new strategies need to be developed and tested. Further pilot services will be launched during 1999.

New Deal for Communities

4.38   Unemployment and deprivation are often concentrated in small areas. The New Deal for Communities provides funding for the intensive regeneration of some of our poorest neighbourhoods. £800 million over three years was allocated in the Comprehensive Spending Review to help local people improve their areas, particularly by tackling worklessness, reducing crime, raising educational attainment and improving health. Already, 17 pathfinder areas are developing ideas on how to narrow the gap between their neighbourhood and the rest of the country. Further announcements, extending the programme to more areas, will be made later in 1999.

Employment Zones

4.39   Employment Zones tackle the problems faced by areas where long-term unemployment is particularly high and persistent, complementing the New Deal for Communities. The Government aims to have at least 14 Employment Zones up and running for two years from April 2000, helping about 48,000 long-term unemployed people aged 25 and over to find and keep work. A key innovation in Employment Zones will be the personal job account. It will allow the pooling of funds that would be available to individuals through, for example, entitlement to training programmes and European support and the equivalent of benefit spending. The individual and a personal adviser will agree how this can be spent most effectively and flexibly to help the individual back to work.

Rapid Response Units

4.40   The New Deal is primarily focused on those who are the most detached from the labour market. The Government is also developing new approaches to improve the service available to people when they lose their jobs. Rapid Response Units have been established to help people who lose their jobs through major redundancies. Co-ordinated by the Employment Service and bringing together a variety of local agencies, the Rapid Response Units provide assistance and guide people to the help they need to move quickly into new jobs.

Windfall Tax

4.41   The Welfare to Work programme is funded from the receipts from the one-off Windfall Tax on the excess profits of the privatised utilities. The second and final instalment of the Windfall Tax was due in December 1998 and £2·6 billion was collected. In total, the Windfall Tax raised £5·2 billion. Table 4.1 sets out the latest estimates of the allocation of the Windfall Tax receipts between programmes.

Table 4.1 Allocation of the Windfall Tax

£million	1997–98	1998–99	1999–00	2000–01	2001–02	1997–02
Spending by programme[1]						
New Deal for 18-24 year olds[2]	50	300	820	690	690	**2550**
New Deal for over 25s[3]	0	30	260	110	120	**520**
New Deal for over 50s	0	0	10	20	20	**50**
New Deal for lone parents	0	40	60	50	40	**190**
New Deal for disabled people[4]	0	10	40	80	80	**210**
New Deal for partners of unemployed people	0	10	20	15	15	**60**
New Deal for schools[5]	90	300	280	360	270	**1300**
Childcare[6]	0	40	0	0	0	**40**
University for Industry[7]	0	5	0	0	0	**5**
Total Expenditure	**140**	**730**	**1490**	**1320**	**1230**	**4910**
Unallocated						**290**
Windfall Tax receipts	**2600**	**2600**				**5200**

[1] *Rounded to the nearest £10 million. Constituent elements may not sum to totals because of rounding. Outturns for 1997–98, estimates for 1998–99 onwards.*

[2] *Includes £10 million for 18-24 year old childless partners of unemployed people, subject to legislation.*

[3] *Includes £10 million for the Small Business Service.*

[4] *Includes £10 million in 1999–00, an element of the November 1998 announcements on Welfare Reform.*

[5] *Capital spending on renewal of school infrastructure, to help raise standards – announced in the 1997 Budget.*

[6] *Includes £30 million for out-of-school childcare. The costs of the 1997 Budget improvements in childcare support through Family Credit are included from April 1998 until October 1999, when the measure will be incorporated within the Working Families Tax Credit.*

[7] *Start-up and development costs. Other costs of the UfI are funded from within departmental expenditure limits.*

MAKING WORK PAY

4.42   People are reluctant to take work that does not pay. Too often, the gap between in-work and out-of-work income is too small to encourage people to move off benefits – the unemployment trap. Once in work, too many people cannot improve their in-work income even if they earn more, because they simultaneously pay more tax and receive less benefit – the poverty trap. These distortions have frustrated the ambitions of people on low incomes, and contributed to family poverty. They have also contributed to high levels of structural unemployment and low levels of labour market participation. The Government is determined to make work pay by tackling the unemployment and poverty traps.

Working Families Tax Credit   4.43   Different groups of people face different obstacles to work. Those with families, in particular, can find it harder to move from welfare into work, because of the way the tax and benefit system works. That is why the 1998 Budget announced a number of reforms aimed at making work pay for families with children. In particular, the introduction of the Working Families Tax Credit, from October 1999, with its generous childcare tax credit. The WFTC will boost the incomes of low and middle income working families with children. As a tax credit, payable through the wage packet from April 2000, it will demonstrate more clearly the rewards of work over welfare. By 2001, about 1·4 million working families will be receiving the WFTC, around 500,000 more families than would have received Family Credit.

4.44   The WFTC's childcare tax credit will provide help with 70 per cent of eligible childcare costs, up to a limit of £100 per week of costs for families with one child and £150 per week for families with two or more children. In addition, there will be a full disregard of child maintenance payments for the calculation of income for WFTC, making a significant contribution to work incentives for poorer families as working families will be able to benefit from the full value of their maintenance payments.

The low paid   **4.45**   All low paid workers will benefit from the reform of national insurance contributions (NICs) announced in the last Budget. The old structure meant that NICs penalised the low paid and discouraged job creation at the lower end of the earnings distribution. Changes to both employer and employee NICs, in April 1999, will remove the "entry fees" and "steps" in the system, removing labour market distortions and reducing the burden on the low paid.

4.46.   From April 1999 the point at which employers start paying NICs will be increased from £66 per week and aligned with the personal tax allowance at £83 per week. The complicated system of four separate rates of employer NICs will be replaced with a single employer rate of 12·2 per cent. This will remove distortions from the system and make it easier for employers to understand and administer their NICs. The NICs burdens on employers in respect of the vast majority of workers earning up to £460 per week will decline, encouraging job creation at these earnings levels. This reform was originally estimated to be revenue neutral, but on the basis of the latest economic assumptions, the Government Actuary's Department now estimate that employers will pay over £600 million less NICs in 1999–2000 as a result of the reform. And for employees, the NICs entry fee of two per cent for people earning £66 per week or more, on all earnings below that level, will be abolished. This is worth £1·32 per week in 1999–2000 for all employees. The abolition removes a major cause of marginal rates of deduction of over 100 per cent on the low paid and is a significant step towards making work pay.

The National   **4.47**   The National Minimum Wage will help underpin the Government's welfare reforms.
Minimum Wage   Together with tax and benefit reforms, the minimum wage will help to promote work incentives. It will ensure greater fairness at work and remove the worst exploitation. The National Minimum Wage will boost the hourly wage of almost 2 million low paid workers – two thirds of them women – by an average of 30 per cent. From April 1999 the following rates will apply:

- £3·60 for adult workers aged 22 and over;

- £3·20 for trainees – workers aged 22 and over and in the first six months of employment and receiving training leading to a recognised qualification; and

- £3·00 for workers aged 18-21 inclusive, rising to £3·20 in June 2000.

BUDGET 99: A BETTER DEAL FOR WORKING PEOPLE

4.48   Budget 99 takes these reforms a step further. It will extend employment opportunity, and reduce the tax burden on **all** the low-paid, to ensure greater fairness and to make work pay. Budget 99:

- increases the **minimum income guarantee** from October 1999 under the WFTC to every family with children and with full-time earnings to **£200 per week** or £10,400 per year;

- ensures that no family earning less than **£235 per week** (over £12,000 per year) will pay any net income tax from October 1999;

- introduces a **new 10p rate of tax** from April 1999;

- cuts the **basic rate to 22p**, from April 2000, to reward work and ensure working families are better off;

- introduces a further reform of **employee NICs** so that the low paid take home more of their earnings;

- reforms **self-employed NICs** to improve work incentives for low earners; and

- further reforms **employer NICs** so that the cost of employing low and middle income workers falls.

10p rate of tax

4.49 **To put work first in the tax and benefit system, the Government will introduce a 10p rate of income tax.** From 6 April this year, taxpayers will pay only 10 pence in the pound on their first £1,500 of taxable income. This is the lowest starting rate of tax since 1962–1963, and will reduce the marginal rate of tax from 20p to 10p for 1·8 million people.

4.50 When the 10p rate is introduced, there will be three main rates of income tax – 10, 23 and 40 per cent. Basic and top rate taxpayers will gain £1·15 a week from the change. But those on the lowest incomes (below £8,835) will gain more, because the three rate structure helps to target the gains from the 10p rate on the lowest paid: 1·8 million people, of whom 1·5 million are low paid, will see their tax bill halved, and a further 300,000 people will be taken out of income tax altogether.

4.51 The new 10p band will help to ease the poverty trap whereby people on low pay are discouraged from climbing the earnings ladder. At present, around 700,000 people lose more than 70 pence for every extra pound they earn. After the implementation of Budget 99, this figure will fall by around two-thirds (see Table 4.2).

4.52 Taken with other measures announced since the Government took office, the new 10p band will help to make work pay and ease the unemployment trap. From April 2000 a number of further measures will also help to reward work.

Basic rate cut to 22p

4.53 **The cut in the basic rate to 22p will take effect in 2000–2001.** This is the lowest basic rate level for 70 years. Someone on average earnings of £20,000 will gain £2·72 a week from this measure alone.

4.54 By 2001–2002, the effective tax rate on a family on average earnings with two children will have fallen below 20 per cent for the first time since 1979, and be at its lowest level since 1972. These changes, alongside other reforms in Budget 99, create a modern income tax system to meet the challenges of today's labour market, and ensure fairness for all working people. They will mean the main income tax rates will be 10, 22 and 40 per cent. Further details of the impact on families are given in Chapter 5.

National insurance contributions

4.55 **Employees on low earnings will find their position improved still further by the alignment of the threshold above which employees pay NICs with the single person's tax allowance.** This means the threshold for paying NICs will increase from £64 per week as it is now to £76 per week in April 2000 and then to £87 per week[1] in April 2001 – an increase of over 25 per cent. All employees will gain from this, but it will be particularly valuable to the low paid, many of whom currently earn too little to pay income tax, but still have to pay national insurance contributions. This move will take around 900,000 people out of NICs altogether, of whom 560,000 will be women, and will significantly improve work incentives.

4.56 The Government has undertaken to protect the benefit entitlements of those taken out of NICs by this change. So a zero-rate band of NICs will apply on earnings between the lower earnings limit and the new threshold for NICs. This will ensure that employees build up the same entitlement to benefits that they have now. However, for the longer-term, the Government believes that employers too must benefit from the alignment of income tax and NICs. The Government has already decided to bring together the organisations that administer tax and NICs: the Contributions Agency merges with Inland Revenue on 1 April 1999. The Government will look at ways to reduce the administrative burden on employers, and report back with proposals for the way forward in the Pre-Budget Report.

---

[1] 2001–2002 income tax personal allowance derived by applying indexation and statutory rounding rules.

4.57   Historically, the upper earnings limit (UEL) for national insurance contributions has been between 6½ and 7½ times the earnings point at which NICs first become payable. **With the latter being raised by over 25 per cent in two years, it is right to raise the UEL as well: to £535 per week from April 2000 and to £575 per week from April 2001.**

4.58   **From April 2000 the position of self-employed workers with lower profits will be improved.** Following the recommendations of Martin Taylor's report on work incentives, the flat-rate Class 2 NICs charge that is currently payable once profits reach £69 a week will be reduced from £6·35 per week as it is now to £2 per week. This will continue to yield benefit entitlements for this group and remove an excessive marginal deduction rate on low earners, improving their work incentives. Self-employed people with profits of under £4,420 in 2000–2001 will pay around £240 less in NICs a year.

4.59   **In addition, self-employed women will become entitled to the full rate of Maternity Allowance, which at present is restricted.** Both these moves should make work a more attractive prospect for self-employed people on low earnings. **The revenue lost through reducing the NICs burden on low earners will be recouped by aligning the starting point at which Class 4 contributions become payable with the income tax personal tax allowance (the equivalent of £83 per week at 1999–2000 prices) and by increasing the contribution rate to seven per cent, and by raising the upper profits limit to £535 in April 2000 and £575 from 2001.** Overall these changes will align more closely the benefits the self-employed are entitled to with the amount of NICs they pay, whilst improving work incentives for low earners. Self-employed NICs will still be lower than NICs for employees.

4.60   Changes to employees and self-employed NICs continue implementation of the package of reforms recommended by Martin Taylor, which the Government began in the 1998 Budget. Chart 4.3 shows the combined effects of the Government's reforms on employee NICs for the low paid.

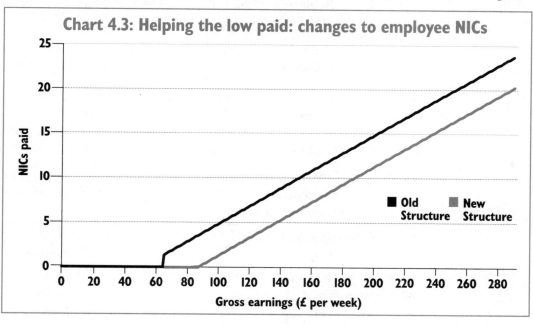

Chart 4.3: Helping the low paid: changes to employee NICs

Gross earnings (£ per week)

NICs paid

■ Old Structure   ■ New Structure

Benefits in kind   4.61   **As part of further alignment of the tax and NICs systems recommended by Martin Taylor, employer NICs on benefits in kind will be extended from April 2000 to cover not just cars and car fuel, as at present, but other benefits in kind which are already subject to income tax.** Making this change places no additional administrative burden on employers since they already need to record and report benefits in kind for tax purposes.

4.62   Taken together with the reform described in paragraph 4.46, employers will be paying no more NICs in aggregate in 2000–2001.

Lower rates for employers 4.63   From April 2001, the rate of employer NICs will be reduced by 0·5 per cent. This will bring the headline rate down from 12·2 per cent to 11·7 per cent. Combined with reforms in the last Budget, this will cut employer NICs in respect of most workers on earnings of around £30,000 per year or less. This measure will come into force at the same time as the climate change levy, described in Chapter 5, and will ensure that the introduction of the levy entails no increase in the burden of tax on business as a whole. This shift of the tax burden from employment to environment should promote employment opportunities and the efficient use of energy.

BETTER OFF IN WORK

4.64   This package increases the rewards to work, while targeting the benefits on the low paid. It radically improves work incentives, following the recommendations of Martin Taylor's report. The 10p rate halves the income tax bill for 1·8 million taxpayers, 1·5 million of whom are in low paid work. Reforms in Budget 99 and Budget 98 eliminate the unfair national insurance bill for around a further 900,000 people who earn too little even to pay income tax. The cut in the basic rate will reward work and ensure working families are better off. As a result of Budget 99 and Budget 98, the income of working households will rise by an average of £450 a year. For working families with children the gain is even greater – an average of £740 a year.

4.65   For a one earner couple with two young children on earnings of £200 per week, the average entry wage for men with families, the gain from work will have gone up since before Budget 98 by around £25 per week, an increase of around 25 per cent. Chart 4.4 shows the effect of the Government's reforms on the weekly net income for families on low incomes. As some examples of the combined effects of these reforms:

- a one earner couple, with two children aged under 11, working 35 hours at the National Minimum Wage of £3·60, will have an effective hourly wage rate of £6·69; and

- a lone parent, with one child under 11, working 35 hours at the National Minimum Wage, will have an effective hourly wage rate of £5·81.

4.66   In 1997 nearly three-quarters of a million people faced effective "tax" rates of over 70 per cent. The combined effect of Budget 99 and the Government's reforms since the election means that this will fall by two-thirds, significantly alleviating the poverty trap. Table 4.2 shows the effects of the Government's reforms on marginal deduction rates.

Table 4.2: Keeping more of what you earn: combined effect of the Government's reforms on high marginal tax and benefit withdrawal rates

Marginal deduction rate[1]	Before	After
100 per cent or more	5,000	0
90 per cent or more	115,000	15,000
80 per cent or more	255,000	175,000
70 per cent or more	715,000	230,000
60 per cent or more	730,000	950,000

[1] Figures are for families where at least one partner works 16 hours or more, and are based on estimated 1998–99 caseload and take-up rates.

An Employment Tax Credit 4.67   The Working Families Tax Credit will provide guaranteed minimum levels of in-work income for families with children. The Government sees a case for extending this principle to all those in work, as part of a better deal for all working people. This would be reform for the longer-term which needs to be carefully considered. The Government will explore the options and bring forward further proposals in due course.

An Employment Credit for the over 50s

4.68   In the meantime, the priority is to tackle low levels of in-work income for those over 50 moving off welfare back into work. Those over 50 face a very steep penalty if they lose their job. Their wages when re-entering work from unemployment are, on average, 25 per cent below their previous job – a much larger fall than for younger workers. Many may stand to earn so much less that they do not return at all.

4.69   **As a first step towards longer-term reform, the Government will introduce an Employment Credit as part of the New Deal for the over 50s.** People over 50 who return to full-time work after six months or more on benefits will be eligible for £60 per week for the first year back in work. This guarantees a minimum income of £175 per week for the over 50s moving back into full-time work. Those taking up part-time work, of 16 hours a week or more, will be eligible for £40 per week. The Employment Credit will be available not just to unemployed people on Jobseeker's Allowance, but also to the over 50s not participating in the labour force: those on Income Support and disability benefits, and to partners of unemployed or economically inactive benefit claimants in workless households. The Employment Credit will be available in New Deal for the over 50s pathfinder areas from October 1999 prior to national roll-out of the programme in 2000.

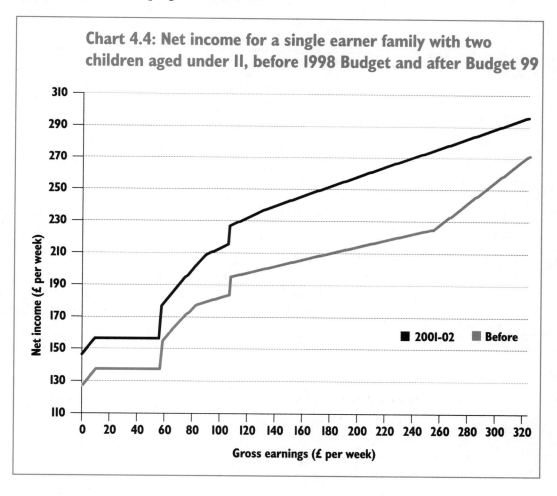

Chart 4.4: Net income for a single earner family with two children aged under II, before 1998 Budget and after Budget 99

Net income (£ per week) vs Gross earnings (£ per week)

Legend: ■ 2001-02   ■ Before

The Disabled Person's Tax Credit

4.70   The 1998 Budget announced that from October 1999 a new Disabled Person's Tax Credit (DPTC) would replace the Disability Working Allowance. The new Credit would be more generous than the benefit it replaces, with higher earnings thresholds (£70 for singles, £90 for couples) and reductions in the taper (from 70 per cent to 55 per cent). As a result the DPTC will provide a guaranteed minimum income of at least £155 a week for a single disabled person who moves from benefit to full-time work earning the National Minimum Wage, and £230 for a couple with one earner moving from benefit to full-time work and one child under 11.

4.71   In the November 1998 Pre-Budget Report, the Chancellor announced he would be consulting on a new Fast-Track to the Disabled Person's Tax Credit (DPTC) targeted at helping with the retention of employees who become sick and disabled while working. The proposal received a very positive and constructive response. **In the light of this response, the new Fast-Track will be available from October 2000.** People will be able to claim after 20 weeks on Statutory Sick Pay or related benefits, provided they meet the current Disability Working Allowance test, their condition is likely to last at least another six months, and their continued employment depends on a reduction in earnings of 20 per cent, as a result of reduced hours or taking a lower paid job.

5   BUILDING A FAIRER SOCIETY

> The Government is committed to building a fairer society in which everyone has the opportunity to fulfil their potential and enjoy the benefits of high and stable levels of economic growth and employment while protecting the environment. This Chapter highlights measures designed to ensure that all have the chance to share in rising prosperity, including:
>
> - **modernisation and reform of public services**, such as health and education, through the CSR;
>
> - **investment in innovative projects to enhance key services** through the Capital Modernisation Fund;
>
> - the Government's commitment to a **better deal for families with children**, including:
>
>   - the replacement of the married couple's allowance with a new Children's Tax Credit, worth £8 a week (£416 a year);
>   - a package of measures to provide targeted financial help for poorer families;
>
> - a package of measures for **pensioners worth £1 billion** every year;
>
> - proposals to encourage more **donations to charity** as part of the Review of Charity Taxation;
>
> - the Government's commitment to **tackling tax abuse** to ensure individuals and businesses pay their fair share of taxes; and
>
> - further proposals designed to **protect the environment**, including measures aimed at:
>
>   - encouraging energy efficiency and tackling climate change;
>   - improving local air quality and supporting the integrated transport strategy;
>   - encouraging sustainable waste management;
>   - limiting the impact of land use and water pollution.

INTRODUCTION

5.1   To achieve the Government's goal of high and stable levels of growth and employment **everyone** of working age in Britain must have the chance to share in rising economic prosperity. Economic growth, opportunity and fairness go hand in hand: an economy in which a significant proportion of the population is unable to fulfil its potential will be poorer and less productive. The Government is therefore committed to:

- ensuring that everyone has access to **high quality public services,** including decent schools and a modern health service;

- supporting **families with children;**

- targeting support on:

  - **work as the best way out of poverty** (as set out in Chapter 4);

- **help for those not in work,** including giving a better deal to **pensioners;**

- ensuring that **economic growth takes place in a sustainable** way which respects the environment and is fair to both current and future generations.

5.2   The CSR focused on how public services could be modernised to meet these goals, and put in place Public Service Agreements that set explicit aims, objectives and targets to be achieved by the public sector with the funding provided. Budget 99 focuses on tax and other measures that will make Britain a fairer society and help protect the environment.

High Quality Public Services

5.3   High quality public services are the bedrock of a fair society and affect the quality of all of our lives. The outcome of the CSR announced last July set out how the Government will invest in and reform key public services over the next three years. These reforms mean public services will be able to meet the changing demands of a modern world and promote wider opportunities for the many people using them.

5.4   Key elements of these plans include:

- additional investment of £19 billion in education, doubling the capital budget for schools, expanding further and higher education, and providing resources to meet manifesto commitments on reducing class sizes;

- £21 billion for health, modernising the NHS and supporting the largest hospital building programme in the history of the NHS;

- a new integrated transport strategy, supported by £1.7 billion of additional spending on public transport and the road and rail network; and

- £4.4 billion to regenerate cities and housing, tackling the council house repairs backlog, and providing a New Deal for Communities – expanding economic opportunity, improving neighbourhood management, and bringing housing and regeneration together in some of the most deprived neighbourhoods in the country.

5.5   The CSR also provided for the Invest in Britain Fund which will double public sector net investment over the next three years. Departmental Investment Strategies have been prepared to ensure efficient use of this investment, and will be published shortly.

5.6   Within the Invest in Britain Fund (and the overall CSR spending plans), a £2.5 billion Capital Modernisation Fund (CMF) was set aside to fund additional innovative investment projects. The CMF is being allocated competitively across the Government's priorities to provide specific step changes in the quality of designated public services and infrastructure. This will complement the improvements across the public sector as a whole set out in the Public Service Agreements.

Box 5.1: Capital Modernisation Fund

The Government has announced a major boost to investment in access to computers, a modern NHS and the fight against crime, financed from the Capital Modernisation Fund totalling £1.1 billion over the next three years. The £2.5 billion Fund was set up in the CSR to support capital investment to improve public services. It initially provided £1 billion for spending in 2000-01 and £1.5 billion in 2001-02. The Government now believes, consistent with the fiscal rules, that there is scope for a more rapid start in these three key areas and has brought forward £250 million of the Fund from 2001-02 to 1999-2000.

The national IT Strategy

- As part of the £1.7 billion national IT strategy, £470 million has been allocated from the CMF to provide extensive access to technology in the community, in schools and in homes:

    - for communities, it will fund a network of learning centres for adults across the country, allowing maximum scope for partnerships with local authorities, companies and others, supporting the University for Industry network and alongside additional investment from the New Opportunities Fund (NOF);

    - for schools, to raise standards further, it will offer super-specialist facilities, building on the National Grid for Learning, and subsidised loans to teachers to buy computers, so that they can make the most of their NOF-financed training; and

    - in homes, it will support a scheme for renting computers for family use, which will complement a tax relief for employees who are loaned computer equipment by their employers.

Modernising the Health Service for the 21st Century

- £430 million will be invested in the NHS over the next three years to modernise hospitals and primary care. This will complement existing programmes modernising Accident and Emergency departments, further improving primary care facilities and ensuring that patients get faster and more convenient access.

Safer Communities

- £170 million will provide a substantial boost to the Government's fight against crime, building on the Crime Reduction Programme.

Further allocations from the CMF will be announced in due course.

Support for all families with children

5.7   To build a strong economic future, the Government recognises the need to invest in children. The share of tax paid by households with children has increased since the 1970s. Since 1972 the tax burden for a one earner couple with two young children on male mean earnings has increased from around 18 per cent of earnings to 21 per cent in 1997-98. This Budget and the last reverse the decline in the provision society makes for families with children through the tax and benefits system.

5.8   The Government has made clear that support for children will in the future be built on universal Child Benefit paid to the main carer and, as a recognition of its importance, Child Benefit for the eldest child will be raised from April 1999 by £2.95 a week. From April 2000, Child Benefit, as a result of Budget 99, will be increased by a further 3 per cent in real terms to £15 for the first child and £10 for subsequent children.

5.9   Budget 99 goes further in ensuring that financial support provided through the tax and benefits system is fairer, and that the tax burden on families with children is further reduced to its lowest level since 1972.

5.10   The married couple's allowance and related allowances are not simply restricted to married couples, being available at the same flat rate to single parents and unmarried parents living together. The MCA does not serve its purpose in recognising marriage because it is possible for twice the normal level of allowances to be paid in the year a married couple with children separate.

Children's Tax   **5.11**   The married couple's allowance and its related allowances will be removed from April
Credit   2000. **It will be replaced with a new Children's Tax Credit from April 2001.** The Children's Tax Credit will be available to families with one or more children. It will be worth £416 a year compared to a married couple's allowance worth £197. It will go to around 5 million families.

5.12   The Chancellor made clear in his last Budget that the Government was determined to increase substantially support for families with children and to do so in the fairest way. The new Children's Tax Credit will therefore be tapered away for families where there is a higher rate taxpayer. Chapter 1 of the FSBR contains further details. In the light of this reform, the Chancellor has decided not to tax Child Benefit in this Budget.

5.13   The Government sees a case for improving the transparency and administration of income-related payments for children through the tax and benefit system. **It is examining, for the longer term, the case for integrating the new Children's Tax Credit with the child premia in Income Support and the Working Families Tax Credit – an integrated child credit.** This could allow families' entitlement to income-related child payments to be assessed and paid on a common basis. A single seamless system, without disruptions in financial support, would provide a secure income for children in the family's transition from welfare to work. Such an integrated child credit, for those in and out of work, could be paid to the main carer, complemented by an employment tax credit paid through the wage packet to working households, with or without children (see paragraph 4.67 above).

Targeted support   **5.14**   The Government also recognises the challenges and difficulties faced by low income families, especially at particular times in their children's lives. The evidence shows that:

- one in three children is growing up in poverty – this is the highest rate in Europe;

- most children are poor because their parents do not have work or have insufficient work. The number of children growing up in workless households is higher than in any other EU country;

- disadvantaged children fall behind from a very early age – by 22 months there are significant differences in educational development;

- once they have fallen behind they are very unlikely to catch up through school, but early intervention programmes are effective; and

- the incomes of families with children have fallen relative to other families and 10–15 per cent of families fall into poverty when they have a child.

5.16   Reducing the number of workless households with children is crucial to relieving childhood disadvantage. Chapter 4 sets out the strategy and measures for encouraging and equipping people to move into work.

Working Families Tax Credit

5.16   A key element of this strategy is to make work pay. The tax burden on poorer families has increased sharply over the past 30 years. In 1972, a one earner couple with two young children on half male average earnings paid 2.1 per cent of their earnings in tax. By 1997-98 this figure had risen to 8.8 per cent. The introduction of the Working Families Tax Credit in October 1999 will provide extra help to 1.4 million families on lower incomes. Budget 99 increases the level of support available through the Working Families Tax Credit – ensuring all low-paid working families will see the benefit of increased support for children.

5.17   From October 1999, the basic credit in the Working Families Tax Credit will also be increased by £2.50 and the under-11 child credit will be increased by £4.70 with a further increase of £1.10 over and above indexation from April 2000. These measures, along with the new 10p rate of income tax, will mean that from October 1999 the minimum income guarantee for families with someone in full-time work will be £200 a week or £10,400 a year.

5.18   Families are most likely to be under pressure when their children are young. The Government is targeting extra support for children under 11. It announced increases of an extra £2.50 a week for each child under 11 to families on income-related benefits in the last Budget.

5.19   Budget 99 increases the under 11 child credit in WFTC and, from October 1999, gives an extra £4.70 per week for children under 11 in families on income-related benefits, with a further £1.05 in April 2000 over and above indexation. There will be additional increases to ensure that families on income-related benefits enjoy the full value of the planned increases in Child Benefit.

Sure Start Maternity Grant

5.20   The period before and immediately after birth is also crucial to a child's development. The Social Fund Maternity Payments paid to mothers in low-income households to help with the initial costs of having a new child have been frozen at £100 since 1990. This is an increasingly inadequate contribution towards providing new babies with early essentials. In this Budget a new Sure Start Maternity Grant will replace the Maternity Payment with the payments doubled to £200. The increased payments will be linked to contact with a healthcare professional to ensure expert advice on child development and services.

5.21   A strategy to help families and children must also recognise that parents need support in balancing family life with work. At the moment women in low-paid part-time work do not qualify for paid maternity leave. Entitlement to Maternity Allowance will be extended to women earning less than the lower earnings limit (£66 pw) but at least £30 a week. This will mean that, for the first time, all pregnant working women can feel able to take adequate time off around childbirth. Research shows that improvements in UK maternity provisions have been crucial in reducing the financial penalties of motherhood. Similarly, the new parental leave provisions will mean that from next December working fathers and mothers can each take up to 3 months off work, with job protection, to be with a young child. This should also help families achieve a better balance between work and family life, whilst retaining their jobs. Many of these families will already be entitled to claim WFTC or Income Support during such leave.

> **Box 5.2: Public Services to help the youngest children**
>
> To prepare children to be ready to thrive at school the Government allocated a total of £540 million to Sure Start as part of the CSR. This is a new programme to pioneer a coordinated approach to services for families with children aged under 4, covering childcare, early education and play, health services and family support. The Sure Start Public Service Agreement set a target of 250 local programmes by 2001-02.
>
> The Government has also provided nursery places for all eligible 4 year olds whose parents want one since September 1998. The CSR included provision to increase the number of nursery places for 3 year olds, targeted on areas of greatest social need, from 34 per cent to 66 per cent by 2001-02.

Effect of Budget 99 for families with children

5.22   The last Budget gave an increase in support for children to the seven and half million households with children. Budget 99 will build on that, cutting the tax burden for working families. The combination of both budgets will mean that households with children gain on average £740 a year compared to all households who gain on average £380 a year.

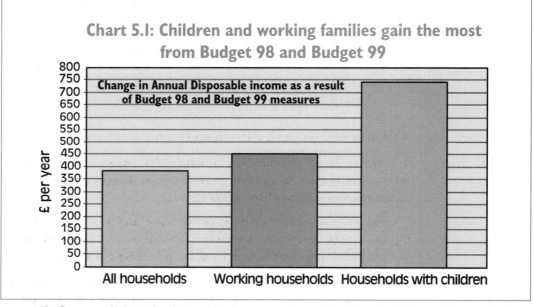

Chart 5.1: Children and working families gain the most from Budget 98 and Budget 99

Change in Annual Disposable income as a result of Budget 98 and Budget 99 measures

¹ The figures underlying the chart are for the average change in net household income from all the direct tax and benefit measures announced in Budget 99 and Budget 98 which take effect in 1999-00 to 2001-02. The changes are relative to indexation.

5.23   Taken together Budget 99 and the last Budget will mean that a one earner couple with two children on £20,000 (average male earnings) will be £460 a year better off. For the same couple the effective tax rate will fall from 21 per cent in 1997-98 to 19 per cent in April 2001, the lowest since 1972. Chart 5.2 shows how the tax burden on a family on average earnings with two children will change as a result of the Budget measures.

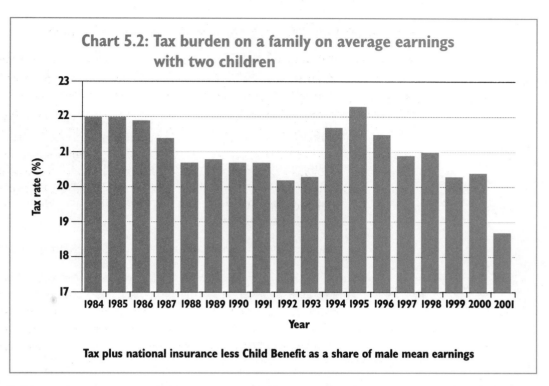

Chart 5.2: Tax burden on a family on average earnings with two children

Tax rate (%)

Year

Tax plus national insurance less Child Benefit as a share of male mean earnings

5.24   Support for low income families has also been increased. As a result no family with children will pay net income tax on earnings of less than £235 a week.

5.25   On average, WFTC will give families an extra £24 a week compared to Family Credit.

5.26   The measures announced in this Budget and the last will take around 700,000 children out of poverty.

Box 5.3: Women and the Budget

The Government is committed to deliver for women. The average increase in weekly income for women as a result of measures in Budget 99 and Budget 98 will be £5.40, compared to £4.20 for all individuals.

Women make up a disproportionate number of the poorest groups in society. Budget 99, together with previously announced measures, will particularly benefit low-earning women and women who work part-time, increasing the average take home pay of women.

The new measures in Budget 99 demonstrate the Government's commitment to ensuring that women get a fair deal out of the tax and benefits system. Women will gain from the introduction of the 10p rate of income tax, from the further National Insurance reforms, as well as from the extension of maternity pay to low-earners and from the new Sure Start Maternity Grant.

This is on top of measures announced in previous Budgets which will benefit women: the Working Families Tax Credit with its childcare tax credit, the National Minimum Wage, the National Childcare Strategy and the forthcoming legislation on parental leave and part-time workers.

Fairness to Pensioners

5.27   Pensioners also need fair and decent support. The Government has continued to honour its commitment to providing more help for pensioners. The first step came with the package of measures for pensioners in the CSR, including:

- an allocation of £500 million over three years from April 1999 to make winter fuel payments of £20 to all pensioner households;

- a minimum income guarantee through Income Support. For single pensioners aged between 60 and 74 this will be set at £75 per week from April 1999 – over three times the increase pensioners would have received under normal uprating; and

- the introduction of free eye tests for pensioners from April 1999.

5.28   Building on this foundation, Budget 99 introduces a new package of measures for pensioners worth a further £1 billion every year. This package includes:

- a fivefold increase in the winter allowance from £20 to £100. This increase helps every pensioner household;

- a commitment to uprate the minimum income guarantee by earnings rather than prices in April 2000. The minimum income guarantee, which will be introduced from April 1999, itself represents an increase several times above indexation compared to previous Income Support rates for pensioners. The commitment to uprate by earnings in April 2000 ensures that poorer pensioners will continue to benefit; and

- the introduction of the Minimum Tax Guarantee. Age-related income tax personal allowances will be increased by up to £200 over indexation. This will mean that no pensioner aged between 65 and 74 with income of £110 per week or less will pay income tax. For those aged 75 or more, no pensioner with income of £115 per week or less will pay income tax. And pensioner couples who already receive the married couple's allowance will be able to keep this entitlement.

5.29   Combined with the new 10p and 22p tax rates, 200,000 pensioners will be taken out of income tax altogether as a result of measures in Budget 99. Moreover, the average pensioner household will be £240 per year better off. Together with the CSR package, the additional £1 billion of spending each year on pensioners ensures that the Government is meeting its manifesto pledge to help pensioners "share fairly in the increasing prosperity of the nation".

5.30   Pensioners with savings will also be offered more choice. The Government will introduce new pensioner bonds offering fixed monthly income as existing Pensioner Bonds do, but at terms of less than five years. This will give pensioners the security of a guaranteed income, without having to lock away their savings for as long as five years.

5.31   Finally, the Government has undertaken to ensure adequate pension incomes for future pensioners. The Pensions Green Paper sets out proposals to improve provision by dramatically improving state second pension rates for people on low earnings compared to SERPS. The aim is to ensure that people who have spent a lifetime in work get more out of their pension and do not have to rely on means-tested benefits in retirement.

5.32   The Green Paper also sets out details of the stakeholder pension, a central element to the Government's savings strategy.

Fairness in saving

5.33   The Government wants to encourage people to save, both to underpin long-term investment and to secure their own financial welfare for the future. This underpins the Government's policy of work for those who can and security for those who cannot.

5.34   Encouraging people to save does not mean compulsion. It means encouraging more of those who are able to take responsibility for their own security through saving. It means promoting awareness of saving opportunities and improving investor confidence through reforming the regulatory framework. And it means challenging the industry to produce better, low-cost, simple savings products.

5.35   Government is introducing or has introduced:

- **Stakeholder pensions.** This new type of pension will combine the low overheads and high security of occupational pensions with the flexibility of personal pensions, and will be available to all. They are particularly designed to help those on middle incomes between £9,000 and £20,000. Tax relief will be available on contributions to stakeholder pensions in a similar way to occupational and personal pensions, but will have simpler limits;

- **Individual Savings Accounts (ISAs),** which will start on 6 April 1999. The aim of ISAs is to extend the savings habit to the half of the population that has little or no savings at the moment. Savers will be able to put their money into bank or building society accounts, including National Savings, life insurance products and stocks and shares. Interest, dividends and capital gains on assets held within the account will not be liable to income or capital gains tax and a 10 per cent tax credit will be payable on dividends from UK equities during the first 5 years. And savers can get access to their savings in an ISA whenever they want to.

5.36   But the Government also wants people to consider where to put their savings to see if they fit the level of risk and reward they find acceptable. It is important that those wishing to invest and get tax relief are all able to do so confidently. To this end:

- there will be a wide variety of ISAs on offer and CAT standards will help savers recognise fair Charges, easy Access and decent Terms for each of these;

- we are consulting on a Pooled Pension Investment (PPI) to enable any kind of pension vehicle (including stakeholder pensions, when available) to invest in pooled investment funds. The PPI should make it easier and cheaper for people to transfer their pension savings from one kind of pension to another. And because the PPI is transparent it should help demystify pensions and make it harder for mis-selling to occur.

Fairness in Housing

5.37   A modern housing policy is essential if we are to ensure that everyone has the opportunity of a decent home. But Britain's current housing system is failing those in need.

Mortgage Interest Relief   5.38   Successive Governments have reduced both the rate and level of tax relief on mortgage interest payments. Both short-term and long-term interest rates have fallen considerably over the last year. The Government has therefore decided to abolish Mortgage Interest Relief from April 2000, to improve the functioning of the housing market and to contribute to the long-term stability of the economy.

Reforming Rented Housing Policy

5.39   Alongside reforms for owner-occupiers, the Government is planning reforms for renters. In the social rented sector, there are few incentives for efficient use of the housing stock; and rents bear little relationship to the size, location and condition of properties. Under-occupation of council housing exists side by side with homelessness and overcrowding.

5.40   Housing Benefit can exacerbate these problems. Many other European countries have a flat rate element in personal housing support. In Britain, tenants on Housing Benefit are often given little interest in the rent – provided it falls within local limits, it can be reimbursed in full. This means that there are few checks on the rents that landlords can charge at the bottom end of the private rented sector. This pushes up the welfare bill and hits those on low and middle incomes but not on Housing Benefit.

5.41   The current housing system is bad for the labour market as well as the housing sector. For many families, Housing Benefit is a disincentive to work, contributing to the poverty trap and the unemployment trap. Evidence suggests that the low visibility of Housing Benefit as an in-work benefit is a major disincentive to taking a job. A number of independent studies have proposed the integration of personal housing support with the tax credit system for those in work.

5.42   Housing Benefit is extremely complex. This makes it difficult for local authorities to administer; difficult for claimants to understand; and extremely prone to fraud. It is estimated that as much as £600 million a year is lost through Housing Benefit fraud.

5.43   The Government's ambition is to tackle these problems by modernising housing policy. In the social rented sector, the Government is investing heavily to improve the stock and to modernise service delivery. It is drawing up a national strategy for neighbourhood renewal, to tackle problems on our most deprived estates, to bring vacant properties back onto the market and to reduce rough sleeping. Moreover, the Government has been working in partnership with local authorities to develop proposals for simplification and improvement of the existing system of Housing Benefit.

5.44   For the future, the Government is looking at options for strengthening the link between social rents and the size, location and condition of properties. Other options for study include the possibility of wider reforms to the system of personal housing support.

5.45   Further details will be announced in a Housing Policy Green Paper later in the year, which will complement the Urban White Paper and the Rural White Paper already announced. Thereafter, there will be extensive consultation with all stakeholders. It is important that any reforms help make the housing market and labour market fairer for all concerned.

Recognising the contribution of charities

5.46   The Government recognises the excellent work that charities do delivering services and supporting individuals and communities, complementing but not replacing the role of Government.

5.47   It is reviewing charity taxation in order to move towards a tax system which encourages more people and businesses to give to charity and is as simple as possible for donors and charities to operate.

5.48   As part of this ongoing review, the Government is publishing today a consultation document setting out options for change. It includes options to:

- reduce the minimum limit for Gift Aid payments from £250 to £100 from 2001 and allow donations to be made by instalments;

- encourage take-up of the Payroll Giving scheme by removing the current upper limit on the size of donations, and providing a "kick-start" top up on donations;

- simplify and improve the tax system for charities, including the alignment of direct and indirect tax rules for fund-raising events, and a single helpline that charities can ring for advice on all aspects of tax; and

- modernise and simplify the existing VAT reliefs, including the relief for advertising.

5.49   The Government also wants to encourage businesses to give to charity. In Budget 99 the Government is therefore extending to all charitable causes the tax relief for gifts of trading stock and equipment by business.

Tackling tax abuse

5.50   Budget 99 shows the Government's commitment to promoting opportunity and fairness for all. When individuals and businesses abuse the system to avoid paying tax or reduce their liability, it undermines the fairness of the system, leading to higher burdens falling on the majority of taxpayers.

5.51   The Government is committed to countering abuses and contrived avoidance schemes, whilst recognising the right of businesses and individuals to manage their tax affairs efficiently.

5.52   Budget 99 contains a package of measures to ensure that individuals and businesses pay their fair share of tax. Further details are listed in the FSBR. Among the key measures are:

- rules to prevent individuals avoiding income tax by providing personal services through intermediaries, such as service companies;

- rules to prevent companies avoiding tax by channelling UK dividends through controlled foreign companies;

- a package of measures to combat avoidance of VAT; and

- an independent evaluation of the strategy to counter excise duty fraud and evasion, and in particular the growing threat of tobacco smuggling.

PROTECTING THE ENVIRONMENT

5.53   The Government is committed to ensuring that economic growth takes place in a sustainable way which respects the environment and is fair to future generations.

5.54   Environmental objectives must be achieved in the most efficient way available, taking into account the advantages and disadvantages of different policy options for securing those objectives.

5.55   This agenda has been taken forward in an open and consultative way, and the Government has sought to build consensus where possible on the best way forward. Examples of this approach include:

- the Task Force led by Lord Marshall on the role of economic instruments and the business use of energy;

- a consultation document on a graduated Vehicle Excise Duty (VED) system for cars to encourage cleaner vehicles; and

- the publication of the results of reviews (e.g. on landfill tax) and research (e.g. on the environmental costs and benefits of aggregates extraction).

5.56   Budget 99 presents the biggest ever package of environmental tax reforms in this country. This includes measures aimed at:

- tackling climate change;

- improving local air quality and supporting the Government's integrated transport strategy;

- encouraging sustainable waste management; and

- limiting the impact of land use and water pollution.

Chapter 1 of the FSBR contains full details of these measures.

5.57   Box 5.4 explains how the Government is also reviewing its policies aimed at improving the quality of life in urban areas.

Box 5.4: Urban renaissance and the Urban White Paper

The Government's objective is to offer everyone the opportunity of a decent home. Population and household projections indicate that over the next two decades the number of households in England will substantially increase, as the population lives longer and forms more one-person households.

A White Paper will be published later this year setting out the Government's approach to improving the quality of urban areas. This will complement the work of the Urban Task Force, led by Lord Rogers of Riverside, which is due to report in the early summer on how urban areas may be rejuvenated.

The Government will also consider what measures might be appropriate to encourage the repair and better use of the existing housing stock, a significant proportion of which is empty or under-used.

Climate change

5.58   Climate change is recognised as one of the greatest environmental threats facing the world. Latest forecasts from the Meteorological Office's Hadley Centre estimate that average temperatures will rise by up to 3.5°C by the end of the next century.

5.59   A consultation document was published on 26 October 1998 which set out a range of possible options for meeting the UK's legally binding target of a 12.5 per cent reduction in greenhouse gas emissions on 1990 levels by 2008-2012, and for moving towards the Government's domestic goal of a 20 per cent reduction in carbon dioxide emissions on 1990 levels by 2010. The consultation period closed on 12 February. Over 700 responses were received. The Government has been assessing these responses, with a view to producing a draft programme later this year.

5.60   All sectors of the economy will need to play their part in tackling the problem of climate change. A mix of policy instruments will also be needed. As part of this, the Government is taking forward Lord Marshall's recommendation on a dry run emissions trading pilot, and is discussing with industry the details of setting up such a scheme. This could give industry and Government valuable experience of trading, and help to give the UK a lead in this area.

5.61   In March 1998, the Chancellor asked Lord Marshall to consider whether, and if so, how best, economic instruments could be used to improve energy efficiency in business and reduce greenhouse gas emissions from this sector. In developing its strategy on climate change, the Government has considered carefully the recommendations made by Lord Marshall, published in November 1998.

5.62   The Government agrees with Lord Marshall that there is a role for a tax, as part of a package of measures, alongside negotiated agreements and emissions trading, if businesses of all sizes and from all sectors are to contribute to improved energy efficiency and help meet the UK's emissions targets. But the Government is also mindful of the need to protect the competitiveness of UK industry.

Climate change 5.63   The Government therefore intends to bring forward legislation in the Finance Bill 2000 levy   to introduce a climate change levy from April 2001 raising around £1.75 billion in its first full year.

5.64   The Government also agrees with Lord Marshall's recommendation that the levy must be designed in a way that protects the competitiveness of UK firms. The Government therefore intends to recycle the revenues to business through a cut of 0.5 percentage points in the main rate of employer NICs. Businesses will also benefit from schemes aimed at promoting energy efficiency directly and stimulating the take-up of renewable sources of energy, like solar and wind power. The introduction of the climate change levy will therefore entail no increase in the burden of taxation on business.

5.65   The Government also recognises the need for special consideration to be given to the position of energy intensive industries given their energy usage, the separate Integrated Pollution Prevention and Control regulation and their exposure to international competition. In line with the recommendations made by the CBI, there will not be taking a blanket 'across the board' approach to setting the appropriate level of the new levy. Subject to any legal and practical constraints, the Government intends to set significantly lower rates for those energy intensive sectors that agree targets for improving energy efficiency which meet the Government's criteria.

Supporting integrated transport

5.66   The White Paper *A New Deal for Transport: Better for Everyone*, published in July 1998, set out the Government's integrated transport strategy. This aims to extend choice in transport and secure mobility in a way that supports sustainable development.

5.67   A mix of policy instruments is being used to address the environmental problems associated with road transport. The White Paper proposed a number of new measures affecting road traffic, such as powers for local authorities to introduce road user charges and workplace parking charges to reduce congestion and to generate revenue to fund complementary local transport projects. Box 5.5 shows how measures in Budget 98 complemented measures in the White Paper aimed at meeting the accessibility needs of rural areas.

5.68   Economic instruments have an important role to play in influencing travel choice. They can ensure that the price of transport reflects all costs, including environmental costs. The previous 2 Budgets have reinforced the integrated transport strategy by:

- increasing the commitment to raise road fuel duties from 5 per cent in real terms a year to at least 6 per cent. This remains the key policy instrument for reducing emissions of carbon dioxide from this sector;

- moving towards a fairer tax treatment of petrol and diesel, when calculated on an energy or carbon basis. This means that the duty on diesel should be higher than that for unleaded petrol;

- increasing the duty differential between ultra low sulphur diesel (ULSD) and standard diesel to encourage the use of this cleaner fuel. This will reduce emissions of particulates and nitrogen oxides from existing vehicles and, over time, encourage the use of cleaner diesel technology. Box 5.6 describes the dramatic impact this policy has had already on the take-up of ULSD;

- encouraging the use of road fuel gases, which produce much lower emissions, especially of particulates, than conventional fuels; and

- increasing the fuel scale charges for company cars.

Box 5.5: Rural transport

As evidence of the Government's commitment to improve public transport services in rural areas, and as part of its developing integrated transport strategy, the Budget 98 allocated an additional £50 million a year to assist public transport in rural areas. The majority of these funds (£32.5 million) are being used to provide new and additional bus services in England, and funds are also being used to support services in Wales, Scotland and Northern Ireland. Many new services are now running.

In addition, forty six bids have been approved for grant under the Rural Bus Challenge competition to promote innovative local authority bus schemes in England. The Challenge competition attracted a wide variety of bids and was heavily over-subscribed. In England, £4.2 million of the new money has also been made available each year for a Rural Transport Partnership scheme. The purpose of the scheme is to reduce rural isolation and social exclusion by supporting community based projects which enhance access to jobs and services.

The rural transport fund will benefit by a further £20 million, with £10 million from the Capital Modernisation Fund, over the next two years. This extra funding will provide further support for the Government's integrated transport strategy, securing accessibility and mobility in a way which supports sustainable development.

Box 5.6: The National Air Quality Strategy and the increasing use of ultra low sulphur diesel

The Government is committed to reducing air pollution and its impact on health and the environment. A consultation document on the Government's review of the National Air Quality Strategy was published on 13 January 1999.

Road traffic makes a significant contribution to levels of particulates and nitrogen dioxide, especially in congested urban areas. Tax incentives to encourage cleaner fuels and vehicles can make an important contribution to the delivery of air quality objectives, complementing improved fuel quality and vehicle emission standards of the European Auto Oils programme. Budget 98 announced that the difference in duty between ultra low sulphur diesel and standard diesel would increase from 1 pence a litre to 3 pence a litre over 2 years.

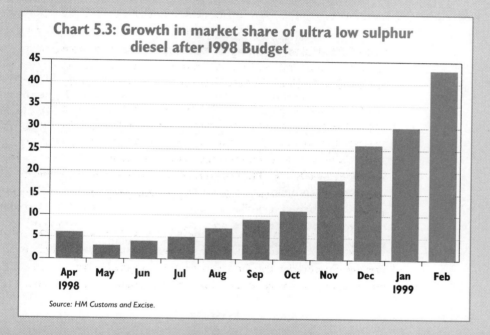

Chart 5.3: Growth in market share of ultra low sulphur diesel after 1998 Budget

Source: HM Customs and Excise.

Chart 5.3 shows the dramatic effect this policy has had on the use of ultra low sulphur diesel. The proportion of diesel sold which meets this specification had increased to 43 per cent by February 1999. The further increase in the duty differential in Budget 99 will turn almost the whole diesel market to ULSD by the end of this year, leading to significant reductions in emissions from diesel fuelled vehicles, and contributing to improved air quality for everyone, especially in congested urban areas.

5.69 Budget 99 includes a series of major reforms which will help meet the Government's environmental objectives, and help underpin its integrated transport strategy. These include:

- a fundamental reform of the company car tax regime to be implemented on a revenue neutral basis in April 2002. This will replace incentives to drive extra miles with an incentive to use more fuel efficient cars. Reductions in business mileage discounts and older car discounts in April 1999 are a first step towards this longer term reform. Box 5.7 contains additional details;

- a new £100 reduced rate of Vehicle Excise Duty for cars with engines up to 1,100cc to be introduced from 1 June 1999. From Autumn 2000, Vehicle Excise

Duty rates for new cars will be based primarily on their carbon dioxide emission rates. In Budget 2000, Vehicle Excise Duty rates will be set to secure a revenue neutral system;

- a package of seven measures to encourage employers to establish "green transport plans" and promote environmentally sensitive commuting by their employees;

- honouring the commitment to increase fuel duties, and altering duty differentials to further encourage ultra low sulphur diesel and road fuel gases; and

- a package of Vehicle Excise Duty measures for heavy goods vehicles to discourage the use of heavy lorries and encourage cleaner ones.

Box 5.7: Major reform of company car taxation

Company car drivers are currently taxed on 35 per cent of the list price of the car. There are discounts on this percentage for those drivers doing higher business miles, and also for older cars. The current system of discounts therefore provides incentives to company car drivers to drive extra business miles to reduce their tax bills. This increases the total number of miles driven, and the amount of carbon dioxide and pollution emitted.

Company cars tend to have larger engines than private cars. As Chart 5.4 shows, three-quarters of company cars have engines greater than 1,600cc, but less than a third of private cars are of a similar size. Although the relationship between engine size and fuel consumption is a complex one, company cars therefore tend to produce more carbon dioxide than private cars for every mile travelled.

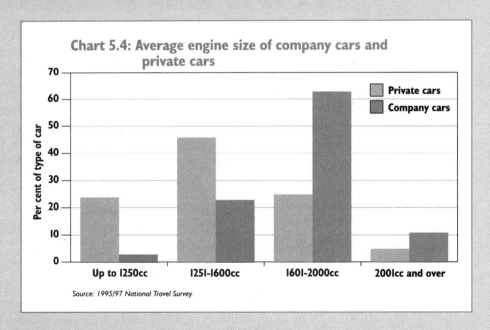

Chart 5.4: Average engine size of company cars and private cars

Source: 1995/97 National Travel Survey.

From April 2002, the existing tax regime will be replaced by a charge on a percentage of list price that varies with the car's carbon dioxide emissions. This revenue-neutral reform will remove tax incentives to drive extra business miles and encourage company car drivers to choose more fuel efficient models.

Land use and water pollution

Landfill tax 5.70 The Government announced its intention to review the existing National Waste Strategy in January 1998. A consultation paper for England and Wales, *Less Waste: More Value*, was launched on 9 June 1998. A draft strategy will be published later in the Spring, with a view to adopting a final strategy by the end of this year. Parallel strategies are being developed for Scotland and Northern Ireland. The new strategy will set out the Government's vision of sustainable waste management over the next twenty years.

5.71 In March 1998, the review of the operation and level of the landfill tax was published. To ensure that the tax continues to help minimise the environmental damage of landfill, Budget 98 announced:

- an increase in the standard rate of landfill tax from £7 a tonne to £10 a tonne from April 1999; and

- an exemption for inert waste used in restoring landfill sites and filling mineral workings.

5.72 The Government intends to reinforce the signals to move towards a more sustainable waste management system. **As part of that, Budget 99 announces an escalator in the standard rate of landfill tax of £1 a tonne each year, from April 2000 until at least 2004, when the National Waste Strategy will be subject to further revision.** The rate increases will mean that more money will be available to be claimed as tax credits for contributions to environmental bodies. A number of changes will also be made to the environmental bodies scheme to clarify and simplify the rules. This will make it easier for landfill operators to support environmental projects, including research and education on recycling and other forms of sustainable waste management.

Extraction of aggregates 5.73 Budget 98 announced that the Government was pursuing further work into the environmental costs of the extraction of aggregates, such as noise, dust, visual intrusion, loss of amenity and damage to biodiversity, and considering a tax alongside other options as a means of addressing these costs.

5.74 Results from the second round of research into the environmental costs of aggregates extraction shows that there are significant environmental costs associated with the extraction of aggregates. The Government believes there is a case, in principle, for an aggregates tax. As a result of the consultation on how a possible aggregates tax might work, draft legislation for a tax on the extraction of sand, gravel and hard rock used as aggregates will be published shortly for consultation.

5.75 However, before coming to a final decision on whether to proceed with a tax, the Government would like to pursue further the possibility of a package of voluntary environmental improvements by the quarrying industry. Should the industry not be able to commit to an acceptable improved offer, or fail to deliver an acceptable package of voluntary measures, the Government would then introduce a tax.

Water pollution and pesticide use 5.76 The quality of rivers has improved significantly in recent years. In the UK about 95 per cent of river length is now classified as "very good", "good" or "fair". However, the Government wishes to see further improvements in water quality. Much of the investment necessary to deliver these quality improvements will be agreed as part of the Periodic Review of water company price limits.

5.77   Against this background of further targeted improvements, the Department of the Environment, Transport and the Regions commissioned research into the practicalities of a national tax or charge on water pollution discharges. The emerging results of the research suggest that a national tax or charge may not be the most effective way to secure further improvements in water quality. The Government is therefore not inclined to introduce a national tax or charge on pollution discharges. Improvements in water quality will continue to be sought, however, through focused use of the regulatory system.

5.78   The Government has also been considering the case for introducing a pesticide tax, as part of its policy for pesticide minimisation. A research report commissioned by the Department of Environment, Transport and the Regions on the possible impact and design of a tax or charge on pesticides will be published shortly. **The Government will seek views on a number of issues the report raises before reaching a conclusion on this issue.**

Environmental appraisal of the Budget measures

5.79   The Government is committed to ensuring that environmental impacts are taken into account in assessing different policy options. Central government guidance makes clear that appraisal systems should try to take account of all environmental costs and benefits, even when they are not easily quantifiable. There is detailed guidance on how to do this, including issues of proportionality and the extent of quantification and valuation.

5.80   The establishment of the Environmental Audit Committee of the House of Commons, with its remit to scrutinise the contribution that government departments make to environmental protection, has helped reinforce the Government's commitment to environmental appraisal.

5.81   The requirement to appraise properly the environmental consequences of policy applies to all Budget measures, irrespective of whether a primary aim of those measures is environmental improvement. All potential Budget measures from the Chancellor's departments must therefore undergo an environmental appraisal.

5.82   Budget 98 contained, for the first time, a table showing the environmental appraisal of Budget measures. That approach is developed in Budget 99 in Table 5.1, which includes those measures which have a significant impact on the environment or whose aim is primarily environmental.

5.83   Wherever possible, the Government attempts to quantify these environmental effects. For example, estimates are quoted of the savings of carbon dioxide emissions from the road fuel duty escalator. There are significant margins of error surrounding these estimates and undue weight should not be placed upon the figures shown. In other cases, it is extremely difficult to quantify the environmental effects, or the precise details of the reform are not yet well defined.

5.84   Table 5.1 also refers to the draft "headline" indicators of sustainable development which were set out in the consultation document *Sustainability Counts*, published on 26

November 1998. One of the aims behind these indicators is to convey complex environmental issues in a more readily understandable format. Table 5.1 integrates the indicators as a way of improving the accessibility of the table and emphasising the role of environmental taxation in underpinning the Government's commitment to sustainable development.

Table 5.1: The environmental impact of Budget measures

A – Budget measures	Environmental impact[1]	Policy objective
Climate change levy	Estimated to produce savings of around 1.5 million tonnes of carbon (MtC) a year by 2010[2], a reduction of 2% in estimated CO_2 emissions from business in 2010	Kyoto target of 12.5% reduction in UK greenhouse gas emissions on 1990 levels by 2010 Domestic goal of 20% reduction in CO_2 emissions by 2010
Company car tax reform	Estimated to produce savings of around 0.5 to 1 MtC[3]	Kyoto target of 12.5% reduction in greenhouse gas emissions
Tax measures to encourage green transport plans	Small reductions in congestion and emissions of carbon dioxide and local air pollutants	Encourage more environmentally sensitive commuting and business travel
Fuel duty increases[4,5]	Escalator over the period 1996 to 2002 estimated to produce carbon savings of 2 to 5MtC[6] by 2010, some 5 to 12% of CO_2 emissions from transport in 2010; and a reduction of 1% in NO_x emissions and 1.2% in particulate emissions[7]	Kyoto target of 12.5% reduction in greenhouse gas emissions National Air Quality Strategy (NAQS) targets
Increase duty on standard diesel[4] relative to unleaded petrol	Reduction of 1-3% of particulates and NO_x.[5,7] Very small increase in emissions of CO_2	NAQS targets
Increase duty differential for ULSD[4]	Reduction of 21% of particulates and up to 2% of NO_x[5,7]	NAQS targets
Reduction in duty on road fuel gases	Reduction in emissions of particulates and NO_x	NAQS targets
Minor oils duties	Small reduction in emissions of CO_2 and other local air pollutants	Kyoto target NAQS targets
Graduated Vehicle Excise Duty for cars	Reduction of emissions of CO_2, NO_x and particulates[3]	Kyoto target NAQS targets
New rates of Vehicle Excise Duty for lorries	Reduce road wear	Internalise costs of lorry use
Increase Vehicle Excise Duty reduction for clean lorries and buses up to £1,000	Reduction in emissions of particulates and NO_x	NAQS targets
Increase standard rate of landfill tax by £3 this year, and £1 for the following five years	Reduction in proportion of waste going to landfill	Reduce landfill and encourage recycling
B – Measures under consideration		
Package of voluntary measures as a possible alternative to an aggregates tax	Possible reductions in noise, dust, visual intrusion, damage to wildlife habitats and other environmental impacts	Internalise environmental costs of aggregates extraction Encourage use of recycled aggregate
Pesticides tax	Improve water quality, biodiversity and reduce impact on wildlife	Reduce use of pesticides

[1] *These estimates are subject to significant margins of error.*
[2] *See Lord Marshall's report on the Use of Economic Instruments for the Business Use of Energy. Estimates calculated using the DTI energy model.*
[3] *Exact size of effects will depend upon design of the measures.*
[4] *Based on assumption that the fuel duty escalator continues at its present level, increases of at least 6 per cent a year on average in real terms, until the end of this Parliament.*
[5] *The reductions in particulates and NO_x emissions are calculated as a percentage of 2010 emissions from urban road transport. The reductions in CO_2 emissions are the estimated annual reduction by 2010.*
[6] *Estimated carbon savings based on DETR's 1997 Road Traffic Forecast and the methodology set out in Energy Paper 65, DTI 1995.*
[7] *Estimates of effect on emissions of local air quality pollutants based on DETR's 1997 National Road Traffic Forecast.*
[8] *The "prudent use of natural resources" is one of the four aspects of sustainable development, not a draft headline indicator of sustainable development.*

Other relevant policy initiatives	Draft sustainability indicator affected
See climate change consultation document *UK Climate Change Programme*, DETR October 1998	Emissions of greenhouse gases
Measures in *A New Deal for Transport: Better for Everyone*, DETR July 1998; and *Breaking the Logjam*, DETR December 1998	Emissions of greenhouse gases Road traffic
Measures in *A New Deal for Transport: Better for Everyone*, DETR July 1998	Road traffic Days of air pollution
Consultation document *UK Climate Change Programme* Measures in *A New Deal for Transport: Better for Everyone* and *Breaking the Logjam* Consultation document *Report on the Review of the National Air Quality Strategy*, DETR January 1999	Emissions of greenhouse gases Road traffic Days of air pollution
Consultation document *Report on the Review of the National Air Quality Strategy*, DETR January 1999	Days of air pollution
Consultation document *Report on the Review of the National Air Quality Strategy*, DETR January 1999	Days of air pollution
Consultation document *Report on the Review of the National Air Quality Strategy*, DETR January 1999	Days of air pollution
Consultation document *Report on the Review of the National Air Quality Strategy*, DETR January 1999	Emissions of greenhouse gases Days of air pollution
Consultation document *Report on the Review of the National Air* DETR October 1999	Emissions of greenhouse gases Days of air pollution
See *Sustainable Distribution*, DETR March 1999	Road traffic
Consultation document *Report on the Review of the National Air Quality Strategy*, DETR January 1999	Days of air pollution
Consultation document *Less Waste: More Value*, DETR June 1998	Waste and waste disposal
See *Minerals Planning Guidance: Guidelines for Aggregates Provision in England*, DoE 1994	Prudent use of natural resources[8]
Consultation document *Economic Instruments for Water Pollution*, DETR November 1997	Rivers of good or fair quality Populations of wild birds

ILLUSTRATIVE LONG-TERM FISCAL PROJECTIONS

This annex presents the first set of long-term fiscal projections as required by the Code for Fiscal Stability. It also examines the effects of alternative economic and fiscal assumptions on long-term sustainability. The key points are:

- long-term projections of the public finances assist in assessing sustainability and intergenerational equity;

- given the projected profile for transfers and the assumption of a constant tax share, public current consumption can increase as a share of GDP in the long term and still remain consistent with the golden rule;

- increases in productivity and labour force participation would strengthen the long-term sustainability of the public finances, creating the potential for improvements in the quality and quantity of public services or reductions in taxation. This reinforces the Government's focus on encouraging work and raising productivity; and

- the Government must balance current spending and investment objectives to maintain intergenerational equity, meet its spending objectives and support economic growth.

A1 It is important to examine and plan for the effects of demographic and other influences on long-term spending and taxation. Over the next 30 years, the structure of Britain's population and the nature of the services they will require is likely to undergo substantial change. In particular, as shown in Chart A1, around one in five people in the UK will be aged over 65 by 2026, compared to around one in seven in 1998.

Chart A1: The UK population is ageing

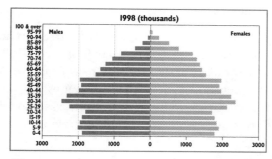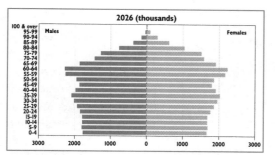

A2 To capture these trends, a key requirement of the *Code for Fiscal Stability* is to publish illustrative long-term projections for a period of no less than 10 years into the future. The presentation of this first set of long-term projections meets this requirement and reflects the Government's commitment to long-term planning.

A3 This Annex represents a first step in developing long-term projections. The Government will continue to analyse long-term spending trends to ensure that the public finances remain sustainable and provide fair outcomes for present and future generations.

KEY ASSUMPTIONS AND APPROACH

A4 The approach taken in this report is to examine the resources available to fund current spending while meeting the Government's fiscal rules over the long term. This is done by projecting forward taxation and transfer payments (mainly social security payments, current grants and debt interest payments) with the difference between them representing the available resources for current consumption spending, for example spending on health and education. Investment is projected forward at a constant share of GDP, consistent with the sustainable investment rule. To show the trends more clearly, the projections extend for a period of 30 years, 20 years longer than the minimum period required by the *Code for Fiscal Stability*.

Economic assumptions **A5** The key economic assumptions underlying the projections are set out in Table A1. The range of plausible assumptions is large, producing outcomes that differ significantly. The baseline case used is at the pessimistic end of this range and, therefore, represents a cautious scenario. The upper end of the range represents a stronger, but plausible, growth scenario which may result from the Government's productivity and labour market reforms. The benefits of stronger productivity and labour force growth are shown later in this Annex. In all cases, the projections presented in Annex B of the FSBR are used for the period from 1998–99 to 2003–04.

Table A1: Long-term economic assumptions

	Annual real growth	
	Per cent	
	2004–05 to 2009–10	2010–11 to 2028–29
Productivity	$1^3/_4$–$2^1/_4$	$1^3/_4$–$2^1/_2$
Labour force	$^1/_4$	0–$^1/_4$
GDP	2–$2^1/_2$	$1^3/_4$–$2^3/_4$
Inflation	$2^1/_2$	$2^1/_2$

A6 Tax revenues are subject to a number of effects in both the short and long term. For example, patterns of income and spending are changing frequently, giving rise to considerable uncertainty about taxation bases. For this reason, the approach used is to project total current receipts as a constant share of GDP without making assumptions about the source of that revenue. This provides a simple, but workable, assumption about the long-term resources available to meet the Government's spending programmes.

Spending assumptions **A7** The assumptions about spending relate to the growth in transfer payments. The largest transfer is social security spending where projections of spending have been developed in consultation with the Department of Social Security and the Government Actuary's Department. The projections represent a plausible outcome based on the interaction of the current social security system with demographic, economic and other factors. They do not pre-empt policy decisions beyond this Budget and so cannot be interpreted as reflecting the direction of future policy.

A8 Debt interest payments are calculated based on an assumed average interest rate and the path for the debt stock. In the baseline projections, net investment is assumed to continue at its 2003–04 share of GDP. The effect of higher investment is shown as an alternative scenario. For simplicity, other transfers are projected forward at a constant share of GDP.

THE BASELINE PROJECTIONS

A9   The baseline long-term fiscal projections are set out in Chart A2. These illustrative projections show that, given the assumptions for transfer payments, public current consumption can grow at an average real rate of around 2½ per cent for the next 30 years and still remain consistent with the fiscal rules. On average, this equates to rises of around £5 billion each year, or £126 billion in total (in 1998–99 terms) from 2004–05.

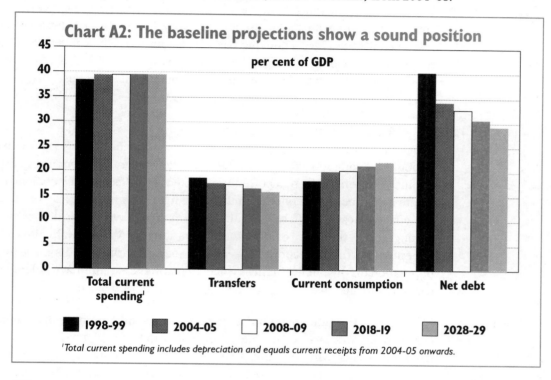

Chart A2: The baseline projections show a sound position

per cent of GDP

Legend: 1998-99, 2004-05, 2008-09, 2018-19, 2028-29

Categories: Total current spending[1], Transfers, Current consumption, Net debt

[1] Total current spending includes depreciation and equals current receipts from 2004-05 onwards.

A10   The main reason for the declining trend for transfers is the projected path for social security benefits. As the majority of benefits are indexed by prices, they remain constant in terms of purchasing power and fall as a share of GDP over time. Falling debt interest payments as a share of GDP also contribute to the decline in transfers.

Demographic changes and the public finances **A11**   Long-term demographic trends, however, are expected to place pressure on some types of spending, and particularly health and education, independent of any policy changes. These effects are set out in Table A2. In total, they do not become significant until after 2018–19. Demographic pressures require an additional £4 billion of spending by 2028–29.

Table A2: Additional spending required for demographic reasons[1]

	£ billion (1998–99 terms)				
	1998–99	**2004–05**	**2010–11**	**2018–19**	**2028–29**
Health[2]	0·0	0·2	1·0	2·8	5·7
Education[3]	0·0	–0·1	–1·1	–2·1	–2·1
Total Health and Education	**0·0**	**0·2**	**–0·1**	**0·8**	**3·7**

[1] England only and abstracting from any other long-term effects and efficiency gains.

[2] Hospital and community health services.

[3] Spending on primary, secondary and tertiary education for those aged 18 and over.

Health   **A12**   The cost of providing hospital and community health services is expected to rise along with the number of people aged over 65. This reflects the fact that, at present, the average annual cost of providing health care to each person aged over 65 is over $3\frac{1}{2}$ times the average for the remainder of the population. Satisfying this demographically-driven demand for services would require real health spending to grow by $\frac{2}{3}$ per cent each year, independent of current policies to improve the speed and quality of treatment.

Education   **A13**   At the same time, demographic trends will also reduce the pressure in some spending areas. For example, the falling proportion of children in the population is expected to reduce primary and secondary school pupil levels over time and thus be reflected in lower education spending than would otherwise be the case. While this would partly offset the increase in health spending, it takes no account of current initiatives to raise standards in schools that can be expected to lead to increased participation in tertiary and higher education.

Uncertainties   **A14**   These data, therefore, need to be interpreted with caution as the impact of current policies and future demographic trends on the public finances is uncertain over such a long period. Changing mortality, morbidity, fertility or migration trends may produce a different population profile from that currently expected with effects on the demand for social security, health and education services. Similarly, the figures do not take account of improvements in the effectiveness or efficiency with which public services are delivered. In addition, the demographic trends provide no information on 'expected healthy life', which adds uncertainty to the projections of health and social security spending. The impact of an ageing population on the public finances will depend on the extent to which longer life shifts health care costs to later ages, rather than extending the period of care.

A15   Aside from demographic uncertainty, there are a number of expenditures which the Government will face in the future for which the cost is uncertain, for example, nuclear decommissioning. In addition, there are uncertainties about the demand for, and cost of providing, public services over time. For example, changes in the structural level of unemployment and deviations in public sector pay, particularly relative to productivity, may affect spending pressures. Similarly, efficiency gains in all spending areas should reduce the cost of providing services.

Policies for the   **A16**   These future uncertainties require the Government to develop policies that take the
long term   ageing of the population into account and minimise the risk of the public finances becoming unsustainable. The future increase in the retirement age for women from 60 to 65 will play a key role in reducing long-term spending pressures. In addition, the Government has announced:

- programmes to raise productivity and labour market participation, and hence increase trend economic growth;

- policies to deliver welfare reform and service modernisation;

- assistance for people to provide for retirement incomes for themselves through the State Second Pension and stakeholder pensions; and

- reforms, such as Public Service Agreements and the Public Service Productivity Panel, aimed at raising productivity throughout the public services and ensuring resources are used to their best effect.

A17   These developments will all play an important role in ensuring sustainable public finances in the long term.

ALTERNATIVE SCENARIOS

A18 This section examines the sensitivity of these projections to economic growth and the rate of public investment.

Stronger economic growth **A19** The Government's central economic objective is to maintain high and stable levels of growth and employment. The productivity and labour market reforms designed to achieve this objective are set out elsewhere in this report. However, one of the benefits of this objective becomes evident in looking at the long-term projections – even a small increase in productivity or labour market participation can be demonstrated to have a substantial effect on the public finances over time.

A20 Table A3 shows the effect of higher economic growth on the public finances. The first scenario shows the effect of achieving long-term growth of $2^1/_4$ per cent. The second scenario represents the top of the growth range shown in Table A1 ($2^3/_4$ per cent in the long-term). These scenarios clearly show that higher economic growth substantially improves the public finances, primarily because higher growth not only benefits individuals through greater wealth and employment opportunities but also results in higher receipts for the Government. This outcome occurs even though the overall tax burden is unchanged as a proportion of income.

Table A3: Alternative growth scenarios[1]

	£ billion (1998–99 terms)				
	1998–99	**2004–05**	**2010–11**	**2018–19**	**2028–29**
Current receipts					
$2^3/_4$ per cent growth scenario	334	385	447	556	729
$2^1/_4$ per cent growth scenario	334	384	439	524	655
Baseline	334	383	430	494	588
Current consumption					
$2^3/_4$ per cent growth scenario	154	191	235	311	431
$2^1/_4$ per cent growth scenario	154	190	228	285	371
Baseline	154	190	221	260	316
Potential spending increase/taxation cuts from higher growth					
$2^3/_4$ per cent growth scenario	–	2	14	51	115
$2^1/_4$ per cent growth scenario	–	1	7	25	55

[1] All scenarios use projections in Annex B of the FSBR for the period 1998–99 to 2003–04.

A21 The gains from higher growth are many times greater than the additional costs projected to arise from demographic trends in the UK. For example, achieving long-term economic growth of $2^3/_4$ per cent would allow public current consumption to rise, on average, by almost an additional £5 billion (in 1998–99 terms) each year. This would nearly double the sustainable rate of real growth in current consumption in the baseline projection.

A22 In each of these scenarios, the benefits of higher growth show up as higher current consumption. However, this does not mean that this is the only choice available to the Government. Indeed, the Government would be able either to fund greater expenditure (either as consumption or transfers) or cut taxes or do a combination of both. For example, in the high growth case above, the Government could maintain the existing level of public services but reduce the effective tax rate by around 16 per cent from what it would be otherwise.

Higher public investment

A23   In determining its spending plans, the Government considers options for both current and capital spending. Both types of spending have roles to play in providing public services and achieving higher economic growth. However, current spending generally provides immediate benefits while capital spending typically provides benefits over time. In recognition of this difference, the fiscal rules and the new spending regime make a clear distinction between current and capital spending.

A24   Decisions about current and capital spending, however, cannot be taken independently. This is reflected in the fact that the surplus on current balance includes the cost of not only current spending but also the costs of financing and consuming capital. The mix of current and capital spending, therefore, has implications for intergenerational equity, as well as for the fiscal rules and economic growth.

A25   The level of net investment from 2003–04 (1·4 per cent of GDP) is consistent with the net debt to GDP ratio stabilising at around 33 per cent of GDP (given the baseline economic assumptions). This is compared in Chart A3 with a scenario in which net investment is increased by a further ½ per cent of GDP. This higher level of investment would stabilise net debt at around 44 per cent of GDP.

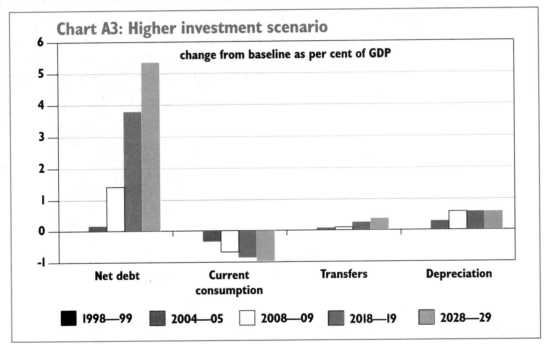

Chart A3: Higher investment scenario

change from baseline as per cent of GDP

Net debt · Current consumption · Transfers · Depreciation

1998—99 · 2004—05 · 2008—09 · 2018—19 · 2028—29

A26   Ultimately, the levels of current consumption and investment are linked to the rate of economic growth. However, in this scenario and in the absence of additional economic growth, the higher investment, and increased consumption of capital and interest payments, would require a reduction in current consumption, from the increases shown in Chart A2, of around £1 billion on average each year (in 1998–99 terms) to meet the golden rule.

A27   In the short-term, lower consumption spending to fund higher investment may be sensible however. This is because investment produces returns (both financial and social) to both the current and future generations, which in the case of well-targeted investment will be at least equal to the costs. In addition, public investment can play a key role in promoting economic growth and employment. The benefits of higher growth shown in the earlier scenario, particularly in terms of allowing greater consumption and investment spending, therefore highlight the importance of an appropriate level of well-targeted investment. A detailed assessment of spending proposals to achieve the optimal mix of current and capital spending is essential to ensure both intergenerational equity and sustainable public finances.

FUTURE DEVELOPMENTS

A28   To ensure that the fiscal position remains sustainable in the long term, it is important that the Government continues its analysis of long-term spending pressures.

Generational accounts

A29   The Treasury has also been supporting a wider examination of the sustainability of the public finances. Along with the Bank of England and the Economic and Social Research Council, the Treasury funded the development of generational accounts for the UK by the National Institute of Social and Economic Research (NIESR). NIESR's results were published in December last year (see Box A1).

Box A1: Generational accounts

Generational accounting measures the burden that current fiscal policies are likely to impose on future generations. The accounts aim to estimate the relative net financial position, in terms of taxes paid and benefits received from public spending, for each generation over its remaining lifetime, for given policy assumptions. The key statistic is the relative burden on those still to be born compared with those born today.

Compared with other leading industrial countries such as the US, Japan and Germany, NIESR finds that "the imbalance in UK generational policy is ... quite modest; i.e. there is not a major intergenerational problem". This imbalance would disappear if the Government's measures to improve productivity and encourage wage restraint prove successful.

A30   The Government is considering how to make further use of both the long-term projections and the generational accounts framework to ensure its fiscal policies are sustainable.

FINANCIAL STATEMENT AND BUDGET REPORT

BUDGET MEASURES

INTRODUCTION

This chapter sets out the measures announced in Budget 99[1]. The financial implications are displayed in Table 1.11 and explained in Appendix 1A. Tax changes announced before the Budget are set out in Appendix 1B. Appendix 1C provides estimates of the revenue costs of some of the main tax allowances and reliefs.

PERSONAL TAXES AND BENEFITS

Income tax 1999-2000

Bands, rates and personal allowances

A new rate of tax at 10 per cent will be introduced on the first £1,500 of income from 6 April 1999. The existing 20 per cent band on non-savings income will disappear. (8)

Income tax on savings eligible for the lower rate up to the basic rate limit will continue at 20 per cent up to that limit and 40 per cent above it, except for dividends which from 6 April 1999 will be taxed at 10 per cent up to the basic rate limit and 32.5 per cent above it.

The personal allowance will increase to £4,335 as already announced. The blind person's allowance and the basic rate limit will rise in line with statutory indexation.

The married couple's allowance and related allowances will rise in line with indexation to £1,970 at 10 per cent in 1999–2000. The age-related married couple's allowance will also rise in line with indexation. (These allowances had already been increased for 1999–2000 on account of the change in the rate of relief to 10 per cent.) (7)

Personal allowances for older people will be increased by up to £200 more than statutory indexation – to £5,720 and £5,980 respectively for people aged 65–74 years and 75 years and over. The income limit for the age-related allowances will be increased in line with statutory indexation to £16,800. (24)

Working Families Tax Credit

The basic tax credit in the Working Families Tax Credit (WFTC) will be increased by £2.50 and the tax credit for children under 11 years will be increased by £4.70 from October 1999. (20)

Other measures

The maximum earnings for which pension provision may be made with income tax relief (the "earnings cap") will be increased in line with statutory indexation to £90,600. (*)

The Government will confirm that annuities paid by free standing voluntary contributions schemes are taxable in full on receipt. (–)

Investors in court common investment funds will be treated in the same way as investors in shares, authorised unit trusts or open-ended investment companies. (*)

There will be no tax charge where an employer provides an employee with a mobile telephone which is used for private calls. (57)

To make the repayment arrangements for the new income-contingent student loans fairer to borrowers, interest on amounts they have overpaid will be tax-free. (*)

---

[1] The effect of the Budget measures on Government revenues is set out in Table 1.11. The number in brackets after each measure refers to the line in Table 1.11 where its yield or cost is shown. The symbol "-" means that the proposal has no effect on revenue. "*" means that it has negligible effect on revenue, amounting to less than £3 million a year.

Table 1.1: Bands of taxable income 1999–2000[1]

1998-99	£ a year	1999–00	£ a year
Lower rate 20 per cent	0 – 4,300	Starting rate 10 per cent	0 – 1,500
Basic rate 23 per cent	4,301 – 27,100	Basic rate 23 per cent	1,501 – 28,000
Higher rate 40 per cent	over 27,100	Higher rate 40 per cent	over 28,000

[1] *The rates of tax applicable to savings income in Section 1A ICTA 1998 remain at 20 per cent for income below the basic rate limit and at 40 per cent above that, apart from the rates applicable to dividends, which for 1999-00 becomes 10 per cent for income below the basic rate limit and 32.5 per cent above that.*

Table 1.2: Income tax allowances 1999–2000

	£ a year		
	1998–99	1999–00	Increase
Personal allowance	4,195	4,335	140
Married couple's allowance[1], additional personal allowance[1] and widow's bereavement allowance[1]	1,900	1,970	70
For people aged 65-74			
– personal allowance	5,410	5,720	310
– married couple's allowance[1]	4,965	5,125	160
For people aged 75 and over			
– personal allowance	5,600	5,980	380
– married couple's allowance[1]	5,025	5,195	170
Income limit for age-related allowances	16,200	16,800	600
Blind person's allowance	1,330	1,380	50

[1] *Tax relief for these allowances is restricted to 15 per cent for 1998-99 and 10 per cent for 1999-00. The amounts for age-related MCA in 1999-00 were increased so that the value of this allowance for people aged 65 and over would be protected. For consistency, the figures shown in 1998-99 for these allowances reflect these increases. Only the further increase (in line with indexation) is reflected in the table.*

Income tax 2000-2001

Bands, rates and personal allowances

From 6 April 2000, the basic rate of income tax will be reduced from 23p to 22p. (9)

The married couple's allowance, for a husband and wife aged under 65, and related allowances, will be removed from 6 April 2000. Couples in which at least one of the spouses was born before 6 April 1935 will remain entitled to claim the married couple's allowance. Tax relief for maintenance payments will cease for payments made and falling due on or after 6 April 2000. Tax relief for maintenance payments will be retained where one or more of the parties is aged 65 or over on 5 April 2000. (17)

Mortgage interest relief

Relief on mortgage interest repayments will be removed from 6 April 2000. Mortgage interest relief for those aged 65 and over who take out a loan to buy a life annuity (a home income plan) ends with effect from 9 March 1999, but existing loans will continue to qualify for relief for the remainder of the loan period. (27)

Working Families Tax Credit

From 6 April 2000, there will be a further increase of £1.10 above indexation in the credit for children under 11 years. (20)

Disabled Person's Tax Credit A new "fast-track" to the Disabled Person's Tax Credit will be introduced from October 2000 to help with the retention of staff disabled while working, and whose return to work depends on a reduction in hours or rate of pay. (20)

Table 1.3: Bands of taxable income 2000–2001[1]

1999-00	£ a year	2000-01[2]	£ a year
Starting rate 10 per cent	0–1,500	Starting rate 10 per cent	0–1,530
Basic rate 23 per cent	1,501–28,000	Basic rate 22 per cent	1,531–28,500
Higher rate 40 per cent	over 28,000	Higher rate 40 per cent	over 28,500

[1] The rates of tax applicable to savings income in Section 1A ICTA 1998 remain at 20 per cent for income below the basic rate limit and at 40 per cent above that, apart from the rates applicable to dividends, which for 1999-00 becomes 10 per cent for income below the basic rate limit and 32.5 per cent above that.

[2] Assumptions for the 2000–01 widths derived by applying statutory indexation (as amended by Finance Bill 1999 proposals) based on inflation forecasts consistent with the EFSR.

Income tax 2001-2002

Children's Tax Credit A tax credit of up to £8 per week (£4,160 per year at 10 per cent) will be introduced from 6 April 2001 for families with children. The credit will be tapered away from families where one or both partners is a higher rate taxpayer. (18)

Effects on the Scottish Parliament's tax varying powers – statement regarding Section 76 of the Scotland Act 1998

After the changes outlined above, a one penny change in the Scottish variable rate in 2000–2001 could then be worth approximately plus or minus £230 million, compared with plus or minus £180 million prior to these changes. In the Treasury's view, an amendment of the Scottish Parliament's tax-varying powers is not required as a result of these changes.

Inheritance tax

Threshold The threshold will be increased by statutory indexation to £231,000. (52)

Improving compliance A simpler procedure for obtaining information and stricter penalties for non-compliance will be introduced.(*)

Taxes on capital gains

Capital gains tax rates and annual exempt amount The annual exempt amount will be increased by statutory indexation to £7,100.

Capital gains tax rates will be aligned with those for savings income, charging gains at 20 per cent or 40 per cent depending on the level of income and gains. (53)

Simplifying capital gains in Lloyd's insurance market Rules for individuals in the Lloyd's insurance market will be changed in order to make the calculation of gains simpler and fairer. From 6 April 1999, an individual in a members' agent pooling arrangement (MAPA), will treat his or her share of the syndicates held through the MAPA as if it were a single direct holding. In addition, tax roll-over relief will be extended to include members' interests in syndicates, whether held directly or through a MAPA. (61)

Stamp duty

Rates and thresholds From 16 March 1999, stamp duty rates will be increased on transfers of land and property over £250,000 and less than £500,000 from 2.0 per cent to 2.5 per cent and from 3.0 per cent to 3.5 per cent for land and property over £500,000. (58)

Compliance and administration Interest will be added to repayments of stamp duty and charged on duty paid late, as is the case for other taxes. Penalties will be increased to modern levels and the fixed duties will be raised to £5. Stamp duty will be charged in multiples of £5. These measures will take effect from 1 October 1999.

The Government will clarify the statutory provisions which enable the Treasury to make regulations for the administration of stamp duty reserve tax.

As announced on 29 January 1999, a loophole will be closed by restricting relief for foreign currency bearer instruments to its intended purpose, which is to assist companies borrowing money in other countries.

Measures will be introduced to clarify the stamp duty rules for foreign currency bearer shares and redenomination of the currency of shares in a depositary receipt scheme or clearance service. A relief will also be provided to allow depositary interests in foreign shares to be traded in the UK. (32)

Unit trust and oeics The Government will introduce a clearer and easier framework for stamp duty reserve tax to replace the existing stamp duty regime for unit trusts and open-ended investment companies (oeics) from October 1999. (*)

National insurance 1999-2000

Employers Employers' Class 1B liability will be deductible for tax. (*)

Table 1.4: National insurance contribution rates 1999–2000

Total weekly earnings	Employer NICs		Employee NICs	
	standard rate	contracted-out rate[1]	standard rate	contracted-out rate[1]
Below £66 (LEL)	0	0	0	0
£66 to £83	0	0	10% of earnings between £66 and £500	8·4% of earnings between £66 and £500
£83 to £500	12·2%	9·2%		
Above £500	12·2%	9·2% of earnings between £83 and £500, 12·2% of earnings above £500		

[1] Employees contracted out of SERPS pay lower contributions. The "contracted-out rebate" is currently fixed at 4·6 per cent of earnings between the employee LEL and the UEL. 1·6 per cent is deducted from employees' contributions and 3% from employers' contributions. An employer rebate of 3% is paid in respect of the earning between £66 and £83 though employers pay no NICs in respect of these earnings. Slightly different rebate arrangements apply for employees who contract out into a money-purchase scheme.

Table 1.5: Self-employed national insurance contribution rates 1999–2000

Total weekly profits	Self employed NICs
Below £72.50	0
£72.50 to £145	£6.55 (Class 2) pw
£145 to £500	£6.55 (Class 2) pw plus 6% of profit between £145 to £500 (Class 4)
Above £500	£6.55 (Class 2) pw plus 6% of profit between £145 to £500 (Class 4)

National insurance 2000–2001

Employees From April 2000, the threshold of earnings above which people will pay NICs will increase to £76 per week. A zero rate of NICs will apply on earnings between the previous lower limit and the new threshold, to protect benefit entitlement. The threshold of earnings above which employees will pay no NICs (the upper earnings limit, UEL) will increase to £535 per week. (12)

Employers From April 2000, employer NICs will be extended to those benefits-in-kind which are already subject to income tax. (29)

Self-employed From April 2000, the Class 2 NICs charge (which from April 1999 will be payable when profits reach £72.50 per week) will be reduced from £6.55 to £2 per week. It is assumed that the starting point for Class 2 NICs will be indexed to £73.50 from April 2000. At the same time, the starting point for Class 4 NICs will be aligned with the income tax personal allowance at £85 per week, and the contribution rate increased to 7 per cent. The upper profits limit rises with the UEL, described above. (13)

Table 1.6: National insurance contribution rates 2000–2001

Total weekly earnings	Employer NICs		Employee NICs	
	standard rate	contracted-out rate[1]	standard rate	contracted-out rate[1]
Below £76	0	0	0	0
£76 to £85[2]	0	0	10% of earnings between £76 and £535	8·4% of earnings between £76 and £535
£85 to £535	12·2%	9·2%		
Above £535	12·2%	9·2% of earnings between £85 and £535, 12·2% of earnings above £535		

[1] Employees contracted out of SERPS pay lower contributions. The "contracted-out rebate" is currently fixed at 4·6 per cent of earnings between the employee LEL and the UEL. 1·6 per cent is deducted from employees' contributions and 3% from employers' contributions. An employer rebate of 3% will be paid in respect of the earning between £76 and £85 though employers pay no NICs in respect of these earnings. As now, slightly different rebate arrangements apply for employees who contract out into a money-purchase scheme.

[2] Assumption for this year's income tax personal allowance derived by applying indexation and statutory rounding rules, based on inflation forecasts consistent with the EFSR.

Table 1.7: Self-employed national insurance contribution rates 2000–2001

Total weekly profits	Self employed NICs
Below £73.50	0
£73.50 to £85[1]	£2 (Class 2) pw
£85 to £535	£2 (Class 2) pw plus 7% of profit between £85 to £535 (Class 4)
Above £535	£2 (Class 2) pw plus 7% of profit between £85 to £535 (Class 4)

[1] Assumption for this year's income tax personal allowance derived by applying indexation and statutory rounding rules, based on inflation forecasts consistent with the EFSR.

National insurance 2001–2002

Employees From April 2001, the threshold of earnings below which people will not pay NICs will increase to £87 per week, aligning it with the income tax personal allowance. The UEL will increase to £575 per week. (11)

Employers The rate of NICs paid by employers will be reduced by 0.5 percentage points in April 2001, offsetting the cost to business of the climate change levy (see "Climate change levy" below). (14)

Self-employed The upper profits limit will increase to £575 per week, in line with the UEL. (13)

Table 1.8: National insurance contribution rates 2001–2002

Total weekly earnings	Employer NICs		Employee NICs	
	standard rate	contracted-out rate[1]	standard rate	contracted-out rate[1]
Below £87	0	0	0	0
£87 to £575	11·7%	8·7%	10% of earnings between £87 and £575	8·4% of earnings between £87 and £575
Above £575 (UEL)	11·7%	8·7% of earnings between £87 and £575, 11·7% of earnings above £575		

[1] Employees contracted out of SERPS pay lower contributions. The "contracted-out rebate" is currently fixed at 4·6 per cent of earnings between the employee LEL and the UEL. 1·6 per cent is deducted from employees' contributions and 3% from employers' contributions. An employer rebate of 3% will be paid in respect of the earning between £76 and £85 though employers pay no NICs in respect of these earnings. As now, slightly different rebate arrangements apply for employees who contract out into a money-purchase scheme.

[2] Assumption for this year's income tax personal allowance derived by applying indexation and statutory rounding rule, based on inflation forecasts consistent with the EFSR.

Personal tax avoidance

Measures to prevent parents avoiding tax by placing assets in a bare trust for their children will be introduced. (*)

Loopholes in the anti-avoidance rules relating to inheritance tax and lifetime gifts will be closed, effective from 9 March 1999. (*)

A provision will be introduced to prevent the abuse of extra-statutory concessions which defer a tax charge. (-)

Benefits 1999–2000

Maternity pay Maternity Allowance will be extended to all women earning less than the lower earnings limit for NICs but at least £30 per week, to be paid at 90 per cent of previous earnings. (23)

Income Support Premium for children under 11 years in Income Support will be increased by £4.70 from October 1999. (19)

Continuing Income Support for lone parents starting work From October 1999, lone parents who have been claiming Income Support for at least six months and move into work and are claiming WFTC will be able to claim a "run-on" in their Income Support at the existing level for two weeks. (16)

Employment Credit for the over-50s Workers aged over 50, who have been out of work and claiming benefits (Jobseeker's Allowance, Income Support, Incapacity Benefit or Severe Disablement Allowance) for more than six months (or if their partner has been claiming a dependant's allowance in one of these benefits for them for six months, and neither partner is working), will be eligible for an in-work top-up payment of £60 per week, for 52 weeks, if they move into work for more than 30 hours a week. £40 will be available to those moving into part-time work, of between 16 and 30 hours per week.

A New Deal for the over-50s will provide personalised advice and support, complementing the Employment Credit. The over-50s will be eligible for in-work training grants of up to £750 to help them acquire accredited training. Pathfinders will start in October 1999, with a national roll-out in 2000. (15)

New Deal for 18–24 year olds The Government intends to announce pilots during 1999 to make the initial gateway at the beginning of the New Deal more intensive. The gateway will also be made more intensive for people remaining in the gateway for more than three months.

Pensioners From 1999–2000, the Winter Allowance to every pensioner household will be increased to £100 from its current level of £20. (26)

Benefits 2000-2001

Maternity pay Self-employed women will become entitled to the full rate of Maternity Allowance from April 2000. (23)

Sure Start Maternity Grant From April 2000, the Social Fund maternity payment will be renamed the Sure Start Maternity Grant. The payment for each child will be doubled to £200 and will be paid following contact with a health professional or local Sure Start programme. (22)

Child Benefit Child Benefit will be increased by around 3 per cent in real terms from April 2000, to be worth £15 for the first child and £10 for subsequent children per week. (21)

Income Support Premium for children under 11 years in Income Support will be increased by a further £1.05 over and above indexation in April 2000. (19)

Pensioners In April 2000, the minimum income guarantee for pensioners will be uprated by earnings rather than prices. (25)

BUSINESS TAXES AND SPENDING MEASURES

Tax on business profits

Corporation tax A new 10 per cent rate of corporation tax will be introduced from 1 April 2000, for profits up to £10,000, also benefiting companies with profits up to £50,000. (1)

Tax credits for research and development The Government will introduce new tax credits for spending by small and medium-sized companies on research and development. The new plans will be introduced in 2000 and the Inland Revenue is publishing a technical note on 10 March 1999. (3)

Capital allowances First year allowances for small and medium-sized businesses introduced in 1997 will be extended for one year until 1 July 2000 at a rate of 40 per cent. (2)

Other measures A measure will be introduced to help football clubs adjust to new accounting rules on intangible assets. These rules affect the way in which the cost of players is deducted from profits. The measure will prevent the need for early payments of tax, relating to existing players, which would otherwise have arisen in the transition to the new accounting rules. (55)

Tax relief for donations of equipment or trading stock by businesses is being extended to cover all charitable causes. (51)

Value added tax

Registration threshold The VAT registration threshold will be increased broadly in line with inflation to £51,000 from 1 April 1999. The deregistration threshold will increase from £48,000 to £49,000. Customs and Excise will be working further with business to explore whether it is possible to cushion the impact of VAT registration on growing businesses. (54)

VAT grouping Following consultation during 1998, the requirement for 90 days' notice for applications for group treatment will be removed. Customs and Excise will be able to remove any members from existing VAT groups, mirroring powers to refuse applications. Circumstances in which Customs and Excise will normally invoke their revenue protection powers will be clarified in a business brief. Criteria for including foreign companies in VAT groupings will be redefined. (34)

Modernising VAT and other indirect taxes The rule allowing certain VAT-exempt business activities to be ignored and all input tax to be reclaimed will be withdrawn with effect from 10 March 1999. (33)

From 10 March 1999, the scope of the VAT exemption relating to financial intermediary services, payment and credit transfer services and credit management services will be clarified to restore the position that existed before recent legal challenges. (35)

Legislation will be introduced to make investment gold exempt from VAT from 1 January 2000. It will implement EC Directive 98/80/EC. Industrial gold and jewellery will remain liable to VAT. (*)

The Government will introduce a power to impose a penalty on customers providing incorrect certificates to claim eligibility for reduced rate fuel and power. (*)

The Government will clarify legislation providing a two year time limit for Customs and Excise to penalise VAT-registered businesses not complying with requirements to submit details of sales to VAT-registered businesses in other EU member states. (*)

Membership subscriptions to organisations with political, religious, patriotic, philosophical or philanthropic aims will become exempt from VAT. (36)

Interest payments will be charged at a commercial rate on late payment of Customs duty debts. Traders will be able to claim interest payments for late repayments of a valid duty claim. (*)

Drawback legislation will be further standardised to prevent potential loss of revenue through drawback on non-commercial exports of oil. (*)

North Sea fiscal regime

Compliance costs The timetable for delivery of some petroleum revenue tax (PRT) returns will be relaxed. (-)

Pre-July 1975 gas contracts The Government will ensure that, in line with previous practice, the PRT exemption for gas sold to British Gas under a pre-July 1975 contract can continue following transfer to another company of an interest in a relevant gas field. (*)

Tax avoidance and evasion by business

Direct taxes The Government will extend anti-avoidance legislation which counteracts the artificial techniques that strip value out of subsidiaries prior to sale to avoid tax liabilities. (31)

Loopholes in the rules for North Sea corporation tax and petroleum revenue tax which could be exploited by the sale and leaseback of North Sea assets will be closed. (-)

New rules will prevent companies avoiding tax by channelling UK dividends via controlled foreign companies. (30)

Legislation will be introduced to allow taxpayers and the Inland Revenue to agree in advance how the arm's length principle is to be applied in relation to specific cross-border (or cross-North Sea "ring-fence") transactions . (*)

Following a recent adverse decision by the Privy Council, legislation will be introduced to tax sums paid by landlords to induce tenants to take out a lease, sometimes called reverse premiums. (37)

Value added tax Following consultation, an existing anti-avoidance measure on construction services will be replaced with a new anti-avoidance measure better targeted on abuse. (*)

Anti-avoidance provisions that prevent businesses artificially inflating their recovery of VAT on the construction of non-residential buildings by lease and leaseback will be extended from 10 March 1999. (60)

Loopholes that could allow VAT to be avoided or too much bad debt relief to be claimed when debts are assigned to other parties will be closed from 10 March 1999. (*)

A loophole that could allow businesses to qualify for repayment supplement by lodging their VAT return early will be closed from 9 March 1999. (*)

A loophole that might allow the capital goods scheme to be exploited for tax avoidance will be closed from 10 March 1999. (*)

Provision of personal services Provision of personal services through intermediaries can provide scope for tax avoidance, leave workers unprotected by employment law and result in the loss of benefit entitlement. New legislation will be introduced to tackle this problem. Changes to tax and NICs rules will take effect from 6 April 2000. (28)

Incentives for investors and entrepreneurs

Venture Capital Challenge The Government will introduce a new Venture Capital Challenge of £20 million from the Capital Modernisation Fund (CMF). (The CMF is described under "Public services" below.) This will be invested in new funds for early stage high-technology businesses in partnership with project investors. The funds will operate throughout the UK and will have a strong regional dimension.

Corporate venturing The Government proposes to introduce a tax incentive in Budget 2000 to promote corporate venturing. The Inland Revenue will issue a technical note on 10 March 1999 setting out the proposal in more detail.

Serial entrepreneur-ship The Government will take steps to prevent the incidence of capital gains tax acting as a barrier to investors in the Enterprise Investment Scheme who want to dispose of their investments and reinvest the gains in other EIS companies. Such investors deferring a chargeable gain from an EIS investment by reinvesting it in another EIS company will benefit from the capital gains tax taper on a cumulative basis, calculating taper relief for the deferred gain by reference to the combined ownership period. (*)

Incentives for employees and managers

New all-employee share scheme The Government will introduce a new all-employee share scheme in Budget 2000, to allow employees to buy shares from their pre-tax salary and to receive free shares, with further tax incentives for longer term shareholding. Any gains arising on shares held for three years in the scheme will be tax-free. There will be greater flexibility in the ways in which employers can give shares as well as tax benefits and payroll services. The details are set out in a technical paper issued by the Inland Revenue on 9 March 1999. An advisory group drawn from practitioners, business and other experts will help the Inland Revenue design the details of the new scheme and consider what measures could be specifically introduced to make employee share ownership more attractive to smaller companies. Draft legislation will be published as part of the Pre-Budget Report and the changes will be introduced in Budget 2000.

Enterprise Management Incentives The Government will introduce a new Enterprise Management Incentives scheme in Budget 2000, limited to small higher risk trading companies. The Inland Revenue will issue a technical note on 10 March 1999 setting out the proposed scheme in more detail. The advisory group for the all-employee share scheme will also be closely involved in its design.

Science and new technology

Reforming intellectual property taxation The Inland Revenue is issuing a technical note on 10 March 1999 to look at options to simplify tax treatment of intellectual property and ensure that all related expenditure is relieved, with the aim of introducing a reform in Budget 2000.

Tax relief on mobile telephone licences A new relief will be introduced in 2000 for the cost of such licences. (*)

University Challenge The Government will provide an additional £15 million to fund more high-quality proposals through University Challenge.

Electronic commerce and computers New legislation will allow Customs and Excise and the Inland Revenue to accept tax returns electronically over the Internet. The first services being developed by Customs and Excise will enable businesses to send VAT registrations, returns and payments, with a pilot planned for 1999–2000 and expansion as soon as possible. The Inland Revenue will start accepting Self-Assessment returns and PAYE annual returns as soon as possible.(–)

The Government intends to offer a discount on returns filed via the Internet. Other measures to help small businesses use new technology for administrative purposes are described above under "Administrative help for small businesses".

Later this year, the Driver and Vehicle Licensing Agency will run a pilot scheme for Vehicle Excise Duty relicensing over the Internet or by telephone.

The Government will ensure that computers up to £2,000 in value loaned by employers to their employees will not be taxed as a benefit-in-kind. (4)

Education and training

Individual Learning Accounts The Government will introduce Individual Learning Accounts (ILAs). The first "starter" accounts will open in 1999–2000. For each of these accounts, the Government will provide £150 for spending on education and training, when the holder commits £25.

From 2000, ILAs will offer their holders: discounts of 80 per cent of the cost of certain key courses such as computer literacy; discounts for everyone of 20 per cent on eligible courses, on spending of up to £500 per year; tax relief to employers on contributions to employees' ILAs; and tax relief to employees on their employers' contributions providing that the employer is contributing to the ILAs of their lowest paid employees on similar terms. This will be supplemented by spending within the Department for Education and Employment's Departmental Expenditure Limit on discounts for ILA holders. (5)

Higher rate tax relief on vocational training will be abolished from 6 April 1999, and the remaining relief will be abolished in 2000–2001. (6)

Administrative help for small businesses

Small Business Service The Government will create a Small Business Service (SBS) to co-ordinate advice and support to small and medium-sized businesses across England. It will have a new role to help business comply with regulations and to improve the quality and coherence of delivery of Government support programmes. It will also run the Department of Trade and Industry's Enterprise Fund and the new Venture Capital Challenge for high technology (see above). It will also offer a new automated payroll service for small employers.

Payroll In addition to the new automated payroll service offered by the SBS, the Government will establish new national standards for computer payroll software. Further use of new technology to help small businesses is described above under "Science and new technology".

The limit for Pay As You Earn (PAYE) quarterly payments by employers will be increased to £1,000, allowing more small employers to pay PAYE quarterly rather than monthly. (–)

Business support The Inland Revenue will introduce new business support teams working closely with the SBS to help small businesses and new employers. The service will include the offer of a half-day's one-to-one advice. There will also be a new helpline service for new employers and a range of improved guidance material.

Customs and Excise will conduct a national survey during 1999 to obtain information about current business views to inform service improvements. Support available for newly VAT-registered businesses will be expanded to include a business support programme for new exporters and importers.

Both the Inland Revenue and Customs and Excise will provide support to the Business Links network and will together hold a series of 14 business open days over the next 15 months.

ENVIRONMENTAL TAXES AND SPENDING MEASURES

Climate change levy

A climate change levy on the business use of energy will be introduced from April 2001. The levy will apply to electricity, gas, coal and other solid fuels used by industry, commerce, agriculture and the public sector. A consultation document is published on 9 March 1999 and the rates applying to different fuels will be set in Finance Bill 2000. (38)

The main rate of employer NICs will be reduced by 0.5 percentage points so that the introduction of this levy does not increase the overall burden of tax on business (see "National insurance" above). (14)

Subject to any practical and legal constraints, the Government intends to set significantly lower rates for those energy intensive sectors agreeing targets for improvements in energy efficiency which meet the Government's criteria.

Extra support will also be provided to promote energy efficiency and encourage renewable sources of energy, through energy audits and advice for small and medium-sized firms and a "carbon trust" to promote new low-carbon and energy-efficient technology. (39)

Transport and the environment

Company car taxation The company car tax regime will be reformed fundamentally. From April 2002, the existing charge on 35 per cent of the car's list price, subject to business mileage and age-related discounts, will be replaced with a charge on a percentage price of the car graduated primarily according to the level of the car's carbon dioxide emissions. These reforms will be introduced on a revenue-neutral basis. The Inland Revenue will consult further on the details of how the graduation might work, with a view to bringing forward legislation in Finance Bill 2000. To pave the way, the existing business mileage and age-related discounts are being reduced from April 1999. (44)

Green transport plans From 6 April 1999, the employee benefits tax charge will be removed from: works bus services; subsidies to public bus services for which employees pay the same fare as other members of the public; bicycles and cycling safety equipment; and work-place parking for bicycles. Employers will also be allowed to pay tax free for alternative transport to help employees to get home when normal car-sharing arrangements break down. (40)

In addition, where employees use their own bicycles for business travel, capital allowances and a tax-free allowance of 12 pence per mile for business cycling are being introduced.

The rural transport fund, introduced in Budget 98, will benefit by a further £10 million from the Capital Modernisation Fund, matched by the Department for Environment, Transport and the Regions, over the next two years.

Road fuel duties In line with its commitment to increase road fuel duties by at least 6 per cent in real terms on average a year, the Government proposes to increase duties from 9 March 1999 as shown in Table 1.9. (42)

Table 1.9: Changes to duties on road fuels and other hydrocarbon oils

	Changes in duty (%)	Effect of tax[1] on typical item (increase in pence)	Unit
Leaded petrol	7·35	4·25	litre
Unleaded petrol	7·33	3·79	litre
Higher octane unleaded petrol from 9 March 1999	7·33	4·20	litre
Higher octane unleaded petrol from 1 October 1999	–5·96	–3·67	litre
Diesel	11·60	6·14	litre
Ultra-low sulphur diesel	9·82	4·96	litre
Gas oil	7·33	0·21	litre
Fuel oil	21·56	0·47	litre
AVGAS	7·35	2·13	litre
Road fuel gas	–29·00	–7·20	kg

[1] Tax refers to duty plus VAT, except for gas oil and fuel oil, shown exclusive of VAT

The duty on road-fuel gases will be cut by 6.13 pence per kg. The duty differential between ultra-low sulphur diesel and ordinary diesel will be widened to 3 pence per litre.

The duty differential between diesel and unleaded petrol is also widened to 3 pence per litre. Duty on higher octane unleaded petrol (super-unleaded or Lead Replacement Petrol) will increase by 3.57 pence per litre but will be cut from 1 October 1999 to 2 pence per litre above unleaded petrol. (43)

Duty on gas oil and fuel oil also increases, by 0.21 pence per litre and 0.47 pence per litre respectively from 9 March 1999. (41)

Bus fuel duty rebate The rates of fuel duty rebate paid to local bus operators by the Department of Environment, Transport and the Regions will be increased in line with the changes in fuel duty rates set out above.

Vehicle Excise Duties The normal rate of Vehicle Excise Duty (VED) for cars, taxis and vans will increase by £5 to £155 per year for licences taken out after 9 March 1999. From 1 June 1999, all cars with engines up to 1,100 cc will be eligible for a reduced rate of VED of £100. In Budget 2000, VED rates will be set to secure a revenue-neutral system in 2000-2001 and 2001-2002. A graduated VED system for cars based primarily on carbon dioxide emissions will be introduced in Autumn 2000 for cars first registered from that time. (46)

VED for new classes of lorries with 11.5 tonne axle weights will rise for licences taken out after 9 March 1999. (47)

Most VED rates for lorries have been frozen, pending the results of the review announced in Budget 98. (48)

The maximum reduction in VED for lorries and buses meeting a low emissions standard will be doubled to £1,000. (*)

Plating procedures will be changed, to ease administrative and cost burdens on hauliers. (–)

Land use and water quality

Landfill tax As announced in Budget 98, the standard rate of landfill tax will be increased from £7 per tonne to £10 per tonne from 1 April 1999. The Government intends that the rate will increase by £1 per tonne each year from April 2000 until at least April 2004. (45)

As announced in Budget 98, regulations will be introduced to exempt inert waste used in restoring landfill sites and filling mineral workings from 1 October 1999.

A number of changes will be made to the environmental bodies scheme to clarify the rules and make it easier for landfill operators to support environmental projects, including research and education on recycling.

Extraction of aggregates The Government will shortly publish draft legislation for a tax on the extraction of hard rock, sand and gravel used as aggregates. Before coming to a final decision on whether to implement a tax, the Government will pursue with the quarrying industry the possibility of voluntary environmental improvements. If the industry is unable to agree or deliver a sufficiently tough package, the Government will introduce an aggregates tax.

Water quality and pesticides The Government is continuing work on options to minimise the environmental impact of pesticide use, including a possible tax or charge. It will shortly publish research commissioned by the Department of Environment, Transport and the Regions, and will seek views on the issues discussed there.

OTHER INDIRECT TAXES

Excise duties

Tobacco duties The duties on most tobacco products will be increased by 6.33 per cent, typically 17.5 pence on a packet of 20 cigarettes, equivalent to 5 per cent in real terms, on 9 March 1999. The duty on hand-rolling tobacco will remain unchanged. (49)

Table 1.10: Changes to tobacco duties

	Changes in duty (%)	Effect of tax[1] on typical item (increase in pence)	Unit
Cigarettes	6·33	17·5	packet of 20
Cigars	6·33	7·5	packet of 5
Hand-rolling tobacco	0·00	–	25g
Pipe tobacco	6·33	9·5	25g

[1] Tax refers to duty plus VAT

Alcohol duties There will be no change in duty on alcoholic drinks, with the exception of the duty on sparkling cider with an alcoholic strength exceeding 5.5 per cent but less than 8.5 per cent which will be increased to £1.61 per litre, to align it with the rate on lower-strength sparkling wine, from 9 March 1999. (50)

Future duty changes From Budget 2000, the timing of any changes in duties on alcohol and tobacco will be aligned with the Budget cycle.

Gaming duty The gaming duty bands will be increased on 1 April 1999 by 2.75 per cent in line with inflation during the twelve months to 31 December 1998. (*)

Pools betting duty Pools betting duty will be reduced from 26.5 per cent to 17.5 per cent, with effect from 28 March 1999. This will help the pools companies to combat their declining turnover. The companies have guaranteed to continue their contributions to the Foundation for Sport and the Arts and to the Football Trust until at least March 2002. (56)

Fraud and evasion The Comprehensive Spending Review provided for £35 million additional resources, including over 100 extra Customs officers, to tackle excise duty fraud and evasion. In addition, there will be an independent evaluation of strategy in this area, concentrating on measures to counter the growing threat of tobacco smuggling by organised crime.

Insurance premium tax

The standard rate of insurance premium tax will be increased from 4 per cent to 5 per cent with effect from 1 July 1999. (59)

PUBLIC SERVICES

Capital Modernisation Fund The Comprehensive Spending Review created a £2.5 billion Capital Modernisation Fund (CMF), of £1 billion in 2000–2001 and £1.5 billion in 2001–2002. £250 million will be brought forward to 1999–2000, so that the allocation in the later years is changed to £1 billion in 2000–2001 and £1.25 billion in 2001–2002. The Government announced on 9 March 1999 the first allocations from the CMF.

Table 1.11: Budget 99 measures

	(+ve is an Exchequer yield)			£ million
	1999–00 non-indexed	1999–00 indexed	2000–01 indexed	2001–02 indexed
RAISING PRODUCTIVITY				
1 Corporation tax: new 10 per cent rate for the smallest companies from April 2000	0	0	0	–100
2 Extension of first year capital allowances for SMEs at 40 per cent, for one year	*	*	–175	–150
3 Research and development tax credit	0	0	*	–100
4 Tax relief for employer-loaned computers	–5	–5	–15	–30
5 Individual Learning Accounts: making employer contributions to employee ILAs tax and NICs free	0	0	–10	–10
6 Abolition of Vocational Training Relief (VTR)	*	*	+25	+50
INCREASING EMPLOYMENT OPPORTUNITY				
Tax-benefit reform to promote work incentives				
Income tax:				
7 Indexation of most allowances and limits	–1,050	0	0	0
8 New 10 per cent rate from April 1999	–1,600	–1,500	–1,800	–1,800
9 Basic rate reduced to 22 per cent from April 2000	0	0	–2,250	–2,800
National insurance contributions:				
10 Indexation of thresholds	–45	0	0	0
11 Alignment of threshold with income tax personal allowance, in two stages, beginning April 2000	0	0	–850	–1,800
12 Increases to upper earnings limits for employee contributions in April 2000 and April 2001	0	0	+430	+750
13 Reform of self-employment contribution rates and profits limits from April 2000	0	0	+240	+290
14 Reduction in employer contribution rate by 0.5 percentage points from April 2001	0	0	0	–1,700
Benefits:				
15 New Deal package for the over 50s: Employment Credit	–10	–10	–110	–110
16 Income Support: two week extension for lone parents moving into work	–10	–10	–20	–20
BUILDING A FAIRER SOCIETY				
Measures for families with children				
17 Abolition of married couples allowance from April 2000 for those born after 5 April 1935	0	0	+1,600	+2,050
18 Introduction of Children's Tax Credit from April 2001:	0	0	0	–1,400
19 with increases in Income Support child premia	–220	–220	–550	–550
20 and with increases in Working Families Tax Credit and Disabled Person's Tax Credit	–180	–180	–650	–750
21 Child Benefit: indexation of rates and uprating from April 2000 to £15 per week for first child and £10 per week for subsequent children	0	0	–255	–255
22 Sure Start Maternity Grant	0	0	–20	–20
23 Maternity pay reforms	0	0	0	–15
Fairness to pensioners				
24 Increasing personal allowances for older people	–160	–70	–100	–100
25 Increase minimum income guarantee for pensioners	0	0	–220	–220
26 £100 Winter Allowance from 1999	–640	–640	–640	–640
Securing the tax base				
27 Abolition of mortgage interest relief from April 2000	0	0	+1,350	+1,400
28 Countering avoidance in the provision of personal services	0	0	+475	+375
29 Extension of employer national insurance contributions to all benefits in kind which are subject to income tax from April 2000	0	0	+415	+440

Table 1.11: Budget 99 Measures

	(+ve is an Exchequer yield)			£ million
	1999–00 non-indexed	1999–00 indexed	2000–01 indexed	2001–02 indexed
30 Controlled Foreign Companies (CFCs): taxation of dividends	0	0	0	+20
31 Capital gains on sale of companies	+40	+40	+130	+130
32 Stamp duty: compliance	+25	+25	+25	+25
33 VAT: changes to partial exemption rules	+70	+70	+75	+75
34 VAT: group treatment	+5	+5	+10	+10
35 Enlarging of VAT exemption on financing arrangements	+95	+95	+100	+100
36 VAT: bringing supplies by certain organisations in line with trade unions and professional bodies	–10	–10	*	*
37 Taxation of reverse premiums	+20	+20	+50	+50
Environmental measures				
38 Climate change levy	0	0	0	+1,750
39 Energy efficiency measures and support for renewable energy sources	0	0	0	–50
40 Green transport plans	–5	–5	–5	–5
41 Increase in minor oils duties	+30	+25	+55	+90
42 Hydrocarbon oil duty escalator	+1,675	0	0	0
43 Cut in duty on higher octane unleaded petrol	+20	+20	+60	+40
44 Company car taxation: reduction in business mileage discounts from April 1999	+270	+270	+265	+260
45 Landfill tax: introduction of five year escalator	0	0	+45	+85
Vehicle Excise Duty:				
46 Graduated VED – reduction of charge for small cars and indexation for others	+40	–85	0	0
47 New VED for heavy lorries	+45	+45	+40	+35
48 Freeze other lorry VED	–20	–20	–20	–20
Other				
49 Tobacco – aligning escalator with Budget day, freeze handrolled tobacco	+630	+620	+410	+465
50 Alcohol – aligning revalorisation point with Budget day and freeze	0	*	–10	–10
51 Gifts of equipment by businesses to charities	*	*	–5	–10
52 Inheritance tax: index threshold	–30	0	0	0
53 Capital gains tax: rate adjustment	*	*	–10	–15
54 VAT: indexation of registration and deregistration thresholds	–5	0	0	0
55 Football clubs: assistance for transition to new accounting rules	*	*	–45	+20
56 Revised rate of pools betting duty from 26.5 per cent to 17.5 per cent	–30	–30	–20	–15
57 Removing the income tax charge on mobile phones	–25	–25	–30	–35
58 Stamp duty: 2.5 per cent rate for transfer of land and property above £250,000 and 3.5 per cent above £500,000	+270	+270	+310	+340
59 Increase in the rate of insurance premium tax by 1 percentage point (to 5 per cent)	+210	+210	+290	+300
60 VAT: option to tax land and property rules	+30	+30	+30	+30
61 Lloyd's insurance market: simplifying capital gains	*	*	–5	–5
TOTAL	**–570**	**–1,065**	**–1,385**	**–3,555**

* Negligible

APPENDIX IA: EXPLAINING THE COSTINGS

This appendix explains how the effects of the Budget measures on tax yield are calculated. In the context of these calculations, the tax yield for measures may include amounts for other charges to the Exchequer and, for Customs and Excise, penalties.

The general approach

The revenue effect of a Budget measure is generally calculated as the difference between the tax yield from applying the pre-Budget and post-Budget tax regimes to the levels of total income and spending at factor cost expected after the Budget. The estimates do not therefore include any effect the tax changes themselves have on overall levels of income and spending. They do, however, take account of other effects on behaviour where they are likely to have a significant and quantifiable effect on the yield and any consequential changes in revenue from related taxes. These include estimated changes in the composition or timing of income, spending or other tax determinants. For example, the estimated yield from increasing the excise duty on tobacco includes the change in the yield of VAT on that duty and the change in the yield of VAT and other excise duties resulting from the new pattern of spending. Where the effect of one tax change is affected by implementation of others, the measures are generally costed in the order in which they appear in Table 1.11. There are some exceptions described under the headings 'Income tax allowances' and 'National insurance contributions' in the notes below.

The non-indexed base column in Table 1.11 shows the revenue effect of changes in allowances, thresholds and rates of duty from their pre-Budget levels (these levels include the effect of any measures, such as the real increases in fuel and tobacco duties, previously announced but not yet implemented). The indexed base columns strip out the effects of inflation by increasing the allowances, thresholds and rates of duty in line with prices in this and future Budgets (again taking account of measures previously announced but not yet implemented). Measures announced in this Budget are assumed to be indexed in the same way in future Budgets.

The indexed base has been calculated on the assumption that each year excise duties and VAT thresholds rise in December (January for alcohol and March for fuels) and allowances and thresholds other than VAT and gaming duty bands, rise in April, in line with the increase in the RPI over 12 months to the September following the Budget. The VAT threshold and gaming duty bands are assumed to rise in April in line with the RPI increase over the year to the previous December. For the year to December 1998, the RPI increase was 2.8 per cent. The commitments for real increases in fuel and tobacco duties of 6 and 5 per cent are also built in.

These costings are shown on a National Accounts basis. This aims to recognise tax when the tax liability accrues irrespective of when the tax is received by the Exchequer. It replaces the receipts basis used in previous years and is consistent with other Government publications. However, some taxes under the National Accounts basis are still scored upon receipt, principally due to the difficulty in assessing the period to which the tax liability relates. Examples of such taxes are corporation tax, self assessment income tax, inheritance tax and capital gains tax.

Notes on Individual Budget Measures

Anti-avoidance measures

The yields represent the estimated direct effect of the measures with the existing level of activity. Without these measures, there could be a significant future loss of revenue currently included in the baseline.

New 10 per cent corporation tax rate for the smallest companies

The full effect will not arise until 2002–03 when the cost will be £140 million.

Extension of first year allowances for SMEs

There will be some increase in tax in later years as the balance of unrelieved capital expenditure carried forward is reduced by the higher allowances. The revenue effects include those for companies and unincorporated businesses.

Research and development tax credit

The costs are based on the proposals issued for consultation. The full effect will not arise until 2002–03 when the cost will be £150 million.

Income tax allowances

The income tax measures are costed in the following order: changes to personal allowances, tax bands, tax rates and tax credits. The income tax measures shown in Table 1.11 are therefore costed in the order shown except that the increases to the personal allowances for older people are costed before the indexation of other allowances and limits and the new 10 per cent rate.

The cost includes indexing the personal allowance which was announced in the PBR.

Abolition of married couple's allowance

The full yield from abolition for all married couples would be £2·5 billion in 2001–02.

Children's Tax Credit

The full year equivalent to the cost in 2001–02 is £1·7 billion.

Working Families Tax Credit

The costs represent the increased expenditure on the Tax Credits. The resulting savings on Social Security benefits are included in effect of the Income Support measure.

National insurance contributions

The measures are costed in the order shown in Table 1.11 except that the measure to extend employer national insurance contributions to all benefits in kind subject to income tax is costed before the reduction of the employer contribution rate.

Controlled foreign companies: taxation of dividends

The full effect will not arise until 2003–03 when the cost will be £50 million.

Transition to new accounting rules for football clubs

There are further yields of £15 million in 2002–03 and £10 million in 2003–04 making a net overall effect of nil.

Quarterly payments of PAYE for small employers

Under the new National Accounts basis, the costs of this measure are shown as 'nil'. However the costs in receipt terms as employers defer paying tax by up to two months is estimated as £100 million in 1999–00, £30 million in 2000–01 and £20 million in 2001–02.

Tax relief on mobile telephone licences

The cost in later years is provisionally estimated as £15 million a year.

Excise duties

The cost of changes in excise duty rates under the National Accounts basis depends partly on the extent to which manufacturers and wholesalers anticipate expected increases by releasing their goods early so as to pay duty at pre-Budget rates. Costings for excise duties normally take into account the anticipated level of such forestalling on the timing of accrued liability. This effect can be significant for pre-announced increases, particularly for tobacco products.

The calculation of the expected effect of changes in duty rates on consumer demand for excise goods assumes that any change in duty is passed on in full to consumers from the date of the change in duty rate.

Climate change levy

This will be introduced in April 2001, raising around £1·75 billion in its first full year (2001–02). At the same time the Government intends to cut the main rate of employer national insurance contributions by 0·5 percentage points. Businesses will also benefit from measures aimed at improving energy efficiency and additional support for renewable sources of energy.

Landfill tax

The standard rate of landfill tax will rise by £1 a tonne each year from 2000 to at least 2004.

Higher octane unleaded petrol

This assumes that the cut in duty on 1 October 1999 will encourage take-up of higher octane unleaded petrol (rather than premium unleaded petrol) as a substitute for leaded petrol when that is banned from 1 January 2000.

APPENDIX 1B: TAX CHANGES ANNOUNCED BEFORE THE BUDGET

This appendix sets out a number of tax and national insurance changes which were announced before the Budget, the effects of which are taken into account in the forecasts.

Table 1B.1: Revenue effects of measures announced since Budget 98

	Changes from a non-indexed base 1999-00	Changes from an indexed base		
		1999-00	2000-01	2001-02
Inland Revenue taxes				
1 Subcontractors in the construction industry	−60	−60	−50	−10
2 Extension of flat rate allowances to nurses and other healthcare workers	−15	−15	−15	−5
3 PRP: National Minimum Wage	−5	−5	*	0
4 SDRT: cross border mergers	+10	+10	+10	+10
5 Deep discount securities: amending transitional rules for loan relationships	+10	+10	+25	+30
6 Extension of time limit for tax relief on film expenditure	*	*	−5	−15
Customs and Excise taxes				
7 VAT: exemption for management fees for certain PEPs	−10	−10	−10	−10
8 VAT: foreign exchange transactions	−15	−15	−15	−15
9 VAT: avoidance scheme on business cars	−5	−5	−5	−5
Total	**−90**	**−90**	**−65**	**−20**

* Negligible

Inland Revenue taxes

Tax changes announced before the Budget

In order to achieve greater fairness in the new construction industry scheme, subcontractors are now able to count all their construction income as turnover for the purpose of the turnover test when applying for gross payment certificates. Effect has now been given to this measure under an extra-statutory concession published on 23 October 1998. It will allow many subcontractors running construction operations partly within the scheme to qualify for certificates. (1)

The Government announced on 5 March 1999 that nurses and other health care workers would be added to the list of employment groups that can get a flat rate allowance for the cost of cleaning and maintaining tools and special clothing. (2)

Payments of tax-relieved profit-related pay will be included in earnings that count towards the National Minimum Wage, ensuring that the agricultural sector is treated like other businesses from 28 July 1998. (3)

As announced on 29 January 1999, a loophole in the stamp duty reserve tax (SDRT) in connection with cross-border mergers will be closed with effect from 30 January 1999. The estimates shown represent the direct revenue effects of the measure and are particularly tentative. Much will depend on the extent to which UK companies take over overseas companies in future and how these transactions are structured. Without the new rule, there could be a significant loss of revenue in the future. (4)

On 15 February 1999, the government announced its intention to change the rules on deep discount securities and loan relationships to ensure that deferred charges on such securities remain assessable and that a defect in a definition of discounted securities is corrected. (5)

On 25 March 1998, the Government announced its intention to extend the time limit for 100% write-off of certain expenditure on British films. (6)

Tax relief for the salaries of employees seconded from business to educational establishments was introduced. (*)

An anomaly in PRT rules will be removed, enabling UK companies to compete more fairly for the business of transporting non-UK oil and gas through North Sea pipelines. (–)

Customs and Excise taxes

A court case ruling released on 18 March 1998 found that initial charges for non-self-select Personal Equity Plans (PEP) by PEP managers to PEP investors whose plans are based on shares should be exempt. The table shows the VAT no longer payable on these charges. (7).

A European Court of Justice judgement of 14 July 1998 found that foreign exchange transactions are supplies for VAT purposes. These supplies are exempt but when supplied to a person outside the EU, input tax is recoverable. The table shows input tax now recoverable (but not claims for blocked input tax on previous supplies). (8)

On 16 December 1998 Customs announced that the law had been amended to invalidate tax avoidance schemes exploiting a change to the VAT treatment of business cars which took effect from 1 August 1995. The table shows input tax recovered under the successful schemes. (9)

Table 1B.2: Measures announced in Budget 98 or earlier which take effect after this Budget

		£ million yield (+) / cost (−) of measure			
		Changes from a non-indexed base	Changes from an indexed base		
		1999-00	1999-00	2000-01	2001-02
	Inland Revenue taxes				
1	Construction industry scheme	+350	+350	nil	+60
2	Working Families Tax Credit	−375	−375	−1,200	−1,300
3	Disabled Person's Tax Credit	−10	−10	−30	−35
4	Corporation tax: 1 per cent cut in main rate from April 1999	*	*	−700	−1,000
5	Corporation tax: 1 per cent cut in small companies rate from April 1999	*	*	−90	−120
6	Abolish ACT and introduce quarterly payments of corporation tax	+1,600	+1,600	+2,000	+3,100
7	Abolish quarterly accounting for gilts	−600	−600	*	+100
8	Married couples allowance—cutting relief from 15 per cent to 10 per cent from April 1999. 65s and over compensated	+800	+800	+1,020	+1,120
9	Individual Savings Accounts	+60	+60	+10	−60
10	Company car fuel scales increased	+175	+175	+275	+400
11	Professional businesses: withdrawal of cash basis	*	*	+40	+40
12	Reform of policy holder taxation	neg	neg	+100	+100
13	Controlled foreign companies-tighten rules	+50	+50	+100	+100
14	Transfer pricing: modernise legislation	+20	+20	+50	+50
	Customs and Excise taxes				
15	6 per cent increase in road fuel duties	+1,730	+1,500	+2,925	+4,255
16	5 per cent increase in tobacco duties	+10	+10	+370	+750
17	Landfill tax: Standard rate to £10 per tonne – exemption for waste used in site restoration	+105	+95	+100	+100
	Total	**+3,915**	**+3,675**	**+4,970**	**+7,660**

Negligible

Inland Revenue taxes

The changes to the construction industry scheme will take effect from 1 August 1999. (1)

The Working Families Tax Credit and Disabled Person's Tax Credit replace Family Credit and Disability Working Allowance from 5 October 1999. (2, 3)

The reforms of corporation tax announced in the 1998 Budget to promote enterprise mostly come into effect in April 1999.

- The main and small companies rates are reduced from 1 April 1999 by 1 per cent to 30 per cent and 20 per cent respectively.

- ACT is abolished on dividends paid after 5 April 1999 and quarterly instalment payments for large companies are introduced for accounting periods ending on or after 1 July 1999.

– The scheme under which companies account quarterly for income tax on gilt interest received gross is abolished from 1 April 1999.

The revenue effects are uncertain and they largely depend on annual changes in corporation tax liability. When the transition is complete in 2003–04, the Exchequer cost is expected to be £1.6 billion a year (4, 5, 6, 7).

Tax relief on the married couple's allowance will be restricted from 15 per cent to 10 per cent from April 1999 and the 65s and over eligible for the age-related allowances will be fully compensated. (8)

The Individual Savings Account (ISA) will start on 6 April 1999. No new subscriptions to PEPs may be made and no new TESSAs can be taken out after 5 April 1999. The figures shown are the estimated revenue effects associated with the introduction of ISAs (including the residual cost of PEPs and TESSAs), measured against the baseline of continuing with PEPs and TESSAs with their current tax reliefs. (9)

The Chancellor announced in Budget 98 that scale charges for fuel provided for private motoring in company cars would increase by 20 per cent above revalorisation from 6 April 1998, and in each of the following four years. (10)

From 6 April 1999, practices which permit some professional businesses to pay tax on a more favourable ("cash") basis will be withdrawn, in order to spread impact for those affected. (11)

Certain changes were announced in the Budget 98 to the rules for taxing gains from certain life insurances. Their purpose was to make the existing rules more effective in protecting tax revenue. The changes related to policies held in trust, overseas life assurance business, personal portfolio bonds and a requirement for certain overseas life insurers to have a tax representative in the United Kingdom. The revenue effects have been revised to incorporate changes made to the original proposals following consultation with the insurance industry. When the changes are complete, the annual yield is expected to be £120 million. (12)

The transfer pricing and controlled foreign company rules are being modernised and brought within the self assessment regime for companies which applies to company accounting periods ending on or after 1 July 1999. (13, 14)

Customs and Excise taxes

In the context of the above table, the indexed yield shows the revenue effect of the changes compared with revalorisation of the duty rates only.

The Chancellor said in the July 1997 Budget that road fuel duties would be increased on average by at least 6 per cent in real terms in future Budgets. (15)

The Chancellor said in the July 1997 Budget that tobacco duties would be increased on average by at least 5 per cent in real terms in future Budgets – one measure aimed at reducing tobacco consumption and dissuading young people from starting smoking. (16)

The Chancellor said in Budget 98 that the standard rate of landfill tax would be increased to £10 a tonne from April 1999. Following consultation, from October 1999 there will be an exemption for inert materials used in site restoration. (17)

APPENDIX IC: TAX ALLOWANCES AND RELIEFS

This appendix provides estimates of the revenue cost of some of the main tax allowances and reliefs. The larger the reliefs, the higher rates of tax have to be in order to finance Government expenditure, other things being equal.

Tax reliefs can serve a number of purposes. In some cases they may be used to assist or encourage particular individuals, activities or products. They may thus be an alternative to public expenditure. In this case they are often termed "tax expenditures". There may, for instance, be a choice between giving tax relief as an allowance or deduction against tax, or by an offsetting cash payment.

Many allowances and reliefs can reasonably be regarded (or partly regarded) as an integral part of the tax structure – called "structural reliefs". Some do no more than recognise the expense incurred in obtaining income. Others reflect a more general concept of "taxable capacity": the personal allowances are a good example. To the extent that income tax is based on ability to pay, it does not seek to collect tax from those with the smallest incomes. But even with structural reliefs of the latter kind, the Government has some discretion about the level at which they are set.

Many other reliefs combine both structural and discretionary components. Capital allowances, for example, provide relief for depreciation at a commercial rate as well as an element of accelerated relief. It is the latter element which represents additional help provided to business by the Government and is a "tax expenditure".

The loss of revenue associated with tax reliefs and allowances cannot be directly observed, and estimates have to be made. This involves calculating the amount of tax that individuals or firms would have had to pay if there were no exemptions or deduction for certain categories of income or expenditure, and comparing it with the actual amount of tax due. The Government regularly publishes estimates of tax expenditures and reliefs for both Customs and Excise and Inland Revenue taxes. Largely because of the difficulties of estimation, the published tables are not comprehensive but do cover the major reliefs and allowances.

The estimates in Table 1C.1 below show the total cost of each relief. The classification of reliefs as tax expenditures, structural reliefs and those elements combining both is broad brush and the distinction between the expenditures and structural reliefs is not always straightforward. In many cases the estimated costs are extremely tentative and based on simplifying assumptions. The figures make no allowance for the fact that changes in tax reliefs may cause people to change their behaviour. This means that figures in table 1C.1 are not directly comparable with those of the main Budget measures.

Estimation of behavioural effects is notoriously difficult. The sizes of behavioural change will obviously depend on the measure examined and possible alternative behaviours. For example, removing the tax privileges of one form of saving may just lead people to switch to another tax privileged form of saving.

Table 1C.1 also gives details of reliefs relating to VAT, which is collected by Customs and Excise. It shows the estimated yield forgone by not applying the standard rate of VAT ($17^1/_2$ per cent) to goods and services which are currently zero-rated, reduced-rated, exempt or outside the scope of VAT. Estimates of the scale of structural reliefs for local authorities and equivalent bodies are also shown. Again, the figures are estimates and must be treated with caution. In line with the treatment of Inland Revenue taxes, they make no allowance for changes in behaviour.

The estimated costs of reliefs and allowances given in Table 1C.1 cannot be added up to give a meaningful total. The combined yield of withdrawing two related allowances would therefore be higher than the sum of individual costs. Similarly the sum of the costs of component parts of reliefs may differ from the total shown.

More details on individual allowances and reliefs can be found in the HM Treasury publication *"Tax Ready Reckoner and Tax Reliefs"*.

Table 1C.1: Estimated costs of principal tax expenditures and structural reliefs

	Estimated cost for 1997–98	£million Estimated cost for 1998–99
Tax Expenditures		
Income tax		
Relief for:		
Occupational pension schemes	8,900	8,500
Contributions to personal pensions (including retirement annuity premia and FSAVCs)	2,500	2,600
Life assurance premiums (for contracts made prior to 14 March 1984)	130	120
Private medical insurance premiums for the over 60s	90	5
Mortgage interest	2,750	1,900
Approved profit sharing schemes	150	150
Approved discretionary share option schemes	100	110
Approved savings-related share option schemes	380	420
Personal Equity Plans	800	1,000
Venture Capital Trusts	60	80
Enterprise Investment Scheme	20	80
Profit related pay	1,700	1,500
Exemption of:		
First £30,000 of payments on termination of employment	1,100	1,100
Interest on National Savings Certificates including index-linked Certificates	275	240
Tax Exempt Special Savings Account interest	400	400
Premium Bond prizes	90	110
SAYE	90	100
Income of charities	825	850
Foreign service allowance paid to Crown servants abroad	100	100
First £8,000 of reimbursed relocation packages provided by employers	300	300
Capital gains tax		
Exemption of gains arising on disposal of only or main residence	750	900
Retirement relief	230	300
Re-investment relief	75	neg
Inheritance tax		
Relief for:		
Agricultural property	105	115
Business property	100	110
Heritage property and maintenance funds	60	60
Exemption of transfers to charities on death	250	270

Value Added Tax

Zero-rating of:

Food	7,900	8,100
Construction of new dwellings (including refunds to DIY builders)	2,100	2,150
Domestic Passenger Transport	1,650	1,700
International Passenger Transport	1,300	1,350
Books, newspapers and magazines	1,250	1,300
Children's clothing	950	1,000
Water and sewerage services	1,000	1,000
Drugs and supplies on prescription	700	750
Supplies to charities	150	150
Ships and aircraft above a certain size	350	350
Vehicles and other supplies to disabled people	150	150
Lower rate on domestic fuel and power	1,750	1,900

Structural Reliefs

Income tax

Personal allowance	29,400	30,900

Income tax and corporation tax

Double taxation relief	5,200	5,200

Corporation tax

Reduced rate of corporation tax on policy holders' fraction of profits	250	300

National Insurance Contributions

Contracted-out rebate occupational schemes of which:	7,770	8,000
Occupational schemes deducted from National Insurance Contributions received	5,680	5,950
Occupational schemes (COMPS) paid by Contributions Agency direct to scheme	–	80
Personal pensions	2,090	1,970

Value Added Tax

Refunds to:

Local authorities and Northern Ireland government of VAT incurred on non-business purchases	3,250	3,330
The BBC and ITN of VAT incurred on non-business purchases	200	200
Central Government, Health Authorities and NHS Trusts on contracted-out services and projects under the private finance initiative	1,550	1,750

Reliefs with Tax Expenditure and Structural Components

Income tax

Married couple's allowance	2,800	2,900
Age-related allowances	1,000	1,100
Additional personal allowance for one parent family	210	220
Relief for maintenance payments	90	90

Exemption of:

British government securities where owner not ordinarily resident in the United Kingdom	800	900
Child benefit (including one parent benefit)	700	700
Long-term incapacity benefit	430	430
Industrial disablement benefits	70	70
Attendance allowance	250	260
Disability living allowance	300	300

War disablement benefits	100	100
War widows pension	60	60
Income tax and corporation tax		
Capital allowances	19,000	20,200
Corporation tax		
Small companies' reduced rate of corporation tax	1,200	1,250
Capital gains tax		
Indexation allowance and rebasing to March 1982	1,700	1,850
Taper relief	Nil	100
Exemption of:		
Annual exempt amount (half of the individuals' exemption for trustees)	3,000	1,500
Gains accrued but unrealised at death	725	750
Petroleum revenue tax		
Uplift on qualifying expenditure	170	200
Relief for exploration and appraisal expenditure	70	30
Oil allowance	430	270
Safeguard: a protection for return on capital cost	350	270
Tariff receipts allowance	90	70
Exemption for gas sold to British Gas under pre-July 1975 contracts	100	140
Inheritance tax		
Nil rate band for chargeable transfers not exceeding the threshold	5,200	5,600
Exemption of transfers on death to surviving spouses	900	1,000
Stamp duties		
Exemption of transfers of land and property where the consideration does not exceed the threshold	270	240
National Insurance Contributions		
Reduced contributions for self-employed not attributable to reduced benefit eligibility	3,400	3,300
Value Added Tax		
Exemption of:		
Rent on domestic dwellings	2,650	2,750
Rent on commercial properties	1,000	1,050
Private education	900	950
Health services	500	500
Postal services	450	500
Burial and cremation	100	100
Finance and insurance	100	100
Betting and gaming and lottery	900	950
Small traders	100	100

A

THE ECONOMY

The UK economy remains well placed to steer a course of stability:

- recent developments have been much as anticipated in the Pre-Budget Report. Forecasts for GDP growth and inflation are unchanged;

- the benefits of early policy action to tackle inflationary pressures are becoming clear. Domestic interest rates peaked at historically low levels, and have fallen significantly since last October;

- this will boost confidence and private sector cashflow against a backdrop of underlying strength in household and company finances;

- the economy is well placed for stronger growth into 2000, with domestic demand picking up, helped by the planned increase in government capital spending, and as the drag from net trade unwinds;

- this would be a much better outcome compared to the instability of previous cycles, when boom has led to bust;

- but uncertainties remain, highlighted by ongoing risks to the world economic outlook.

INTRODUCTION[1,2]

A1 This annex sets out the economic background to the Budget. It provides overviews of domestic and world economic prospects for the next three years, followed by a more detailed account of the UK outlook.

A2 Projections for GDP growth are again presented as opportunity ranges, illustrating the potential for higher sustainable growth and employment based on improved supply-side performance of the UK economy. The ranges do not represent general forecast uncertainties: key short-term risks are examined later in this annex and average errors on past forecasts are shown in Table A7. A detailed explanation of the opportunity ranges was provided in the November 1997 Pre-Budget Report – Box A1 sets out the key points. Projections for the public finances (Annex B) are based on the lower end of the opportunity ranges.

---

[1] The forecast is consistent with UK output, income and expenditure data to the fourth quarter of 1998 released by the Office for National Statistics on 23 February 1999. Because full national accounts are not yet available for the fourth quarter last year, some figures for 1998 in the charts and tables are estimates. A full set of charts and tables relating to the economic forecast is available on the Treasury's internet site (http://www.hm-treasury.gov.uk), and copies can be obtained on request from the Treasury's Public Enquiry Unit (0171 270 4558).

[2] The forecast is based on the assumption that the exchange rate moves in line with an uncovered interest parity condition, consistent with the interest rates underlying the economic forecast. Potential 'Year 2000 problem' impacts are excluded from the forecast, as in the 1998 Pre-Budget Report (page 97).

Box A1: Opportunity ranges for GDP growth

The Economic and Fiscal Strategy Report sets out the Government's strategy to improve longer-term economic performance. The New Deal programmes and tax and benefit reforms are likely to raise potential output over a number of years by raising the sustainable rate of employment. The range of measures being pursued to improve the UK's productivity performance should raise the economy's potential growth rate more permanently, though the timing and magnitude of improvements is uncertain.

For this reason, projections for GDP growth at the low end of the opportunity ranges make no allowance for any underlying improvement in supply-side performance. They are consistent with a projected trend growth rate of $2\frac{1}{4}$ per cent a year, in line with average growth over the post-war period. This assumption is transparent and cautious, and underpins the projections of the public finances.

The upper ends of the opportunity ranges for GDP growth are based on the assumption that improved labour market performance leads to a $\frac{1}{2}$ percentage point decline in the sustainable rate of unemployment (or NAIRU) in both 1999 and 2000, and a further $\frac{1}{4}$ percentage point reduction in 2001. It is further assumed that these benefits are fully and immediately translated into higher employment and output, though in practice the effects would partly show up in lower wages and prices for a period.

The projections for GDP growth within the opportunity ranges should be seen as illustrating the span of plausible outcomes offered by improved supply-side performance. Projections at the low end, meanwhile, constitute a more detailed consideration of prospects, though based on the particular assumption of no underlying supply-side improvement. As a result, a 'central view' for GDP growth cannot be found by taking the average of the projections at the lower and upper ends of the ranges. Actual outcomes will depend on both the success of Government policies and the actions of the private sector. In particular, responsible wage bargaining offers the opportunity to promote jobs.

Irrespective of the precise path the economy takes over the shorter term, the opportunity ranges illustrate a substantive point. Very small improvements in trend economic growth, much smaller than those shown here, if sustained over the medium to long term, offer the prospect of very large improvements in UK economic welfare. Annex A of the EFSR illustrates how the long-term sustainability of the public finances could be strengthened, creating the potential for improved public services.

UK OVERVIEW

Recent economic developments

A3   Key indicators show that the Pre-Budget Report forecast is broadly on track. GDP grew by 0·2 per cent in the fourth quarter of 1998, in line with the Pre-Budget Report forecast, although manufacturing output fell by more than was expected, down 1·3 per cent. This was balanced by firmer than expected service sector output growth, up 0·6 per cent in the fourth quarter, and the continued buoyancy of labour market activity.

A4   Indeed, the labour market was surprisingly strong through the second half of 1998, with growth in employment showing a marked upturn compared to the first half of the year. Increased labour market participation has largely accounted for the flattening of the previously downward trend in unemployment to date, though both the ILO and claimant count measures show further modest falls on the latest readings.

A5   Total domestic demand has remained relatively firm, though this partly reflects strong inventory accumulation. Household consumption grew by 0·4 per cent in the fourth quarter of last year, despite weak December retail sales, and the latest monthly evidence signals continued expansion into 1999. The EC/GfK measure of consumer confidence moved further above normal levels in February, and retail sales volumes in the three months to January, spanning the Christmas and New Year sales trading periods, were up 0·4 per cent compared to the previous three months.

A6   Net trade was weaker than expected towards the end of last year, as was manufacturing output. Export volumes to non-EU countries have fallen sharply, reflecting the pattern of global growth. With growth in import volumes again outstripping that of exports, where the overall trend is flat to falling, net trade reduced GDP growth by more than 1 percentage point in the fourth quarter of last year.

A7   The more forward-looking business survey indicators have begun to rise from the lows recorded last autumn, as world economic turbulence has receded and interest rates have fallen. They suggest an easing in pressures in the manufacturing sector and continued growth in services, though below trend, as expected.

Box A2: Improving knowledge of the economy

The national accounts provide an essential framework for monitoring the economy. To ensure that methodologies are as robust and relevant as possible, a number of developments are planned, including improvements to the quality and coherence of GDP estimates at constant prices:

- expanded data collection for capital expenditure, inventories, purchases by industry and a wider range of prices for deflation;

- the development of constant price input-output tables to ensure greater coherence between the expenditure and output measures of real GDP, progressively improving estimates of growth starting with the 2000 Blue Book;

- the development of a monthly index of service sector output, beginning with an index of distribution.

This process should, in time, be aided by savings released as a result of the recently completed Efficiency Review.

Nevertheless, official statistics will never give an entirely up-to-date and complete picture of the economy, not least because of time lags in data collection and processing. So the Treasury also makes extensive use of:

- a wide range of survey data compiled by private sector organisations. This information is typically more timely and provides certain indicators not otherwise available;

- information obtained through direct contact with regional and business organisations, both private and public. This includes a programme of regular regional visits undertaken by Treasury officials, regular participation in various business discussion groups, and ad-hoc business contacts.

These additional sources are invaluable in forming assessments of economic developments and prospects.

A8 RPI excluding mortgage interest payments (RPIX) inflation of $2^1/_2$ per cent in the fourth quarter of 1998 was exactly as forecast. Earnings decelerated in the second half of last year, pay settlements have fallen back recently and producer output price inflation is historically low. This confirms the possibility of RPIX inflation dipping temporarily below $2^1/_2$ per cent, before returning to its target level later this year, as forecast in the Pre-Budget Report.

Main features of the forecast

A9 The global downturn is having a significant impact on the UK economy. Lower exports to Asia have accounted for around half of the $£2^1/_4$ billion widening of the UK trade in goods deficit in the year to the fourth quarter of 1998, and reduced demand from the major oil producing nations has also played a significant part. Overall, net trade reduced UK growth by $1^3/_4$ percentage points last year, and slower growth expected in 1999 is mainly due to weaker growth in UK export markets.

A10 Growth in UK export markets is now expected to fall to $5^3/_4$ per cent this year and 6 per cent in 2000, down from $7^1/_4$ per cent in 1998 and $10^1/_2$ per cent in 1997. This represents a further downward revision since the Pre-Budget Report forecast, and around $1^1/_2$ percentage points lower than expectations at the time of the March 1998 Budget in both years. This accounts for most of the downward revision to UK growth in 1999 compared to that projected a year ago. Domestic activity and spending has also been affected by the external shock to confidence following world financial turbulence last year.

A11 However, a combination of the timely policy loosening, underlying private sector financial strength, increased government capital spending, and an easing in trade conditions, is expected to underpin stronger growth, back towards trend rates, into 2000. Downside risks remain, including ongoing risks to the world economic outlook, though this is balanced by much firmer domestic consumer confidence.

Table A1: Summary of forecast

			Forecast	
	1998	**1999**	**2000**	**2001**
GDP growth (per cent)	$2^1/_4$	1 to $1^1/_2$	$2^1/_4$ to $2^3/_4$	$2^3/_4$ to $3^1/_4$
RPIX inflation (per cent, Q4)	$2^1/_2$	$2^1/_2$	$2^1/_2$	$2^1/_2$

A12 Following revisions to the first and third quarters of 1998, GDP is now estimated to have grown by 2·3 per cent in 1998 as a whole. These revisions entirely account for the undershoot relative to the Pre-Budget Report projection. As expected, growth in household consumption slowed markedly compared to the previous year, though company spending, as usual, has lagged the cycle and so total domestic demand has shown greater resilience to date. Net trade was very weak due to the sharp slowdown in world trade growth and the delayed impact of sterling's earlier rise.

A13 Growth in household spending is expected to remain restrained in the near term, accompanied by a slowing in business investment reflecting weaker profits, and there is likely to be an additional drag on growth as firms attempt to correct the build up of excess inventories last year. However, the forces necessary for the economy to gather pace into 2000 are likely to build, as explained in more detail later in this annex, accompanied by some easing in trade conditions through 1999. Overall, GDP is projected to grow by 1 to $1^1/_2$ per cent in 1999, with domestic demand contributing 2 to $2^1/_2$ percentage points, and net trade reducing growth by $1^1/_4$ percentage points.

A14   The GDP forecast is unchanged from the Pre-Budget Report, although the forecast detail is a little different. Net trade and hence manufacturing output were weaker than expected in the fourth quarter of 1998. With European growth slowing recently, export volumes to EU countries have fallen and there has probably also been an upturn in import volumes from the Asian crisis economies. As a matter of arithmetic, these undershoots relative to the Pre-Budget Report forecast in the fourth quarter of 1998 feed through to lower projected annual growth of both export volumes and manufacturing output in 1999, with a larger negative contribution to GDP growth for the year as a whole.

A15   In line with most independent forecasts, manufacturing output is expected to firm into 2000. By the first quarter it is forecast to be around 1 per cent up on a year earlier. Within total GDP, weaker net trade is offset by stronger domestic demand in 1999 as a whole, though growth through the year is little changed since the Pre-Budget Report.

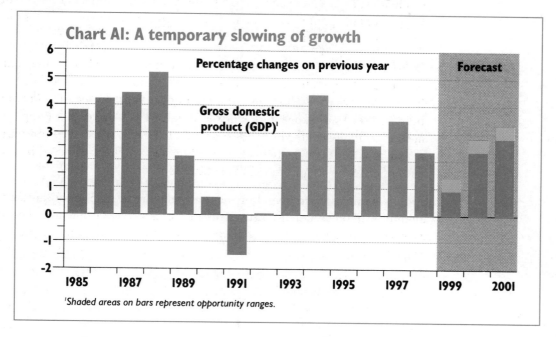

Chart A1: A temporary slowing of growth

Shaded areas on bars represent opportunity ranges.

A16   The projected GDP path would be a much better outcome for the UK economy than has been experienced in recent cycles. There are good reasons to expect this, despite adverse world developments.

A17   Although some evidence of excess labour market tightness remains, inflation is clearly less of a concern today compared to past cycles. The output gap, a key indicator of domestic price pressures, is estimated to have peaked at around $^3/_4$ per cent at the end of 1997, as opposed to more than 4 per cent in 1988. This was largely due to a more timely, and better coordinated, tightening of monetary and fiscal policy[2]. This means that only a relatively mild and necessary slowing of growth has been required in order to lock in economic stability for the years ahead, maintaining low inflation once the favourable impact of falling import prices unwinds (see Box A3).

A18   As a result, interest rates peaked at $7^1/_2$ per cent, an historically low level compared to the cyclical peaks of 15 per cent or more seen over the previous 30 years. Furthermore, the subsequent easing of domestic monetary policy has been rapid. The Bank of England's Monetary Policy Committee has reduced interest rates by 2 percentage points since last October, rather faster than financial markets expected.

---

[2] See *Delivering Economic Stability: Lessons from Macroeconomic Policy Experience*, Pre-Budget Report Publications, November 1998.

> ## Box A3: The output gap: how large was the cyclical peak?
>
> As in the Pre-Budget Report forecast, the economy is judged to have moved above trend during the first half of 1997. The subsequent GDP path implies that the output gap peaked at around $^3/_4$ per cent of GDP at the end of the year, with the economy estimated to have moved back to around trend at the end of 1998. A two-year half cycle would be very short by historical standards and, as a result, the estimated cyclical peak is not very sensitive to the assumed trend rate for GDP growth. To infer a larger peak output gap, it is necessary to assume that the economy first moved above trend much earlier. The Pre-Budget Report set out why, on the basis of a range of indicators, this does not seem plausible.
>
> Moreover, a variety of key manufacturing indicators, for example, capacity utilisation and output prices, continue to suggest that the sector may already be operating with ample spare capacity. More generally, margins have come under pressure, skilled labour shortages have eased and earnings growth has fallen back. Such factors support the view that the economy as a whole may now have moved back close to potential, following a relatively small peak last year.

A19   In addition, the private sector remains in relatively sound financial health, with nothing approaching the deterioration which occurred prior to the 1990s' recession. Then, both households and companies moved into substantial financial deficit as spending boomed, leading to a significant worsening of the private sector balance sheet. This, combined with double digit interest rates for four years, led directly to sharp falls in private consumption in the early 1990s. For companies, the link between depressed financial health and falling investment spending most probably reflected weak liquidity and the associated tightening of credit conditions.

A20   Although there is no definitive measure of financial health, a number of relevant indicators are shown in Box A4. They suggest that the private sector is better placed to maintain moderate spending growth. Household consumption growth is expected to recover gradually during the course of this year, reaching trend rates in 2000. In addition, world trade growth is expected to strengthen modestly next year, as the Asian crisis economies begin to stabilise. The further drag on growth from net trade is expected fully to unwind through this year with the gradual easing in sterling. GDP is forecast to grow by $2^1/_4$ to $2^3/_4$ per cent in 2000.

A21   As in previous forecasts, stronger growth into next year and beyond is expected to be supported by the planned expansion in public sector capital expenditure, in line with the CSR commitments. General government investment is expected to contribute around $^1/_4$ percentage point to GDP growth in each of the next three years. In addition, Budget 99 continues to lock in the structural improvement in the public finances over the past two years while at the same time providing a boost to the economy of some £6 billion, thus supporting monetary policy while the economy is in its below trend phase.

A22   On the basis of the slowing in growth to date, and lower growth in 1999, in line with the Pre-Budget Report forecast, output is now projected to fall to around 1 per cent below trend by the end of this year, with the gap narrowing in 2000. This allows stronger growth in 2001, when GDP growth is projected to grow by $2^3/_4$ to $3^1/_4$ per cent, consistent with achieving the Government's inflation target in the medium term.

A23   As in the Pre-Budget Report, RPIX inflation is expected to dip temporarily below the Government's $2^1/_2$ per cent inflation target during the course of this year. Continuing negative imported inflation is expected to combine with an easing in domestic costs for a period. With the economy only returning to its trend level by the end of 2001, the easing in domestic pressures is likely to intensify, though this is expected to be broadly offset by a stabilisation and subsequent recovery in import prices, returning RPIX inflation close to target by the end of this year.

Box A4: Private sector financial position

A range of indicators suggests that the financial position of the private sector is secure, relative to previous cycles.

The household sector has been in financial surplus throughout the current upswing, remaining in balance despite the decline in the saving ratio over the past year. Non-financial corporations have recorded deficits since mid 1997 associated with strong growth in capital spending, but the deterioration is much less marked than 10 years ago.

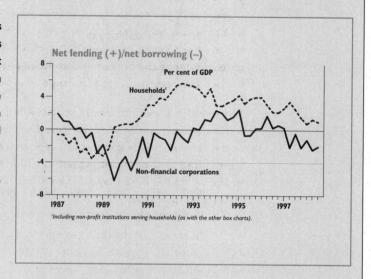

Private sector balance sheets, represented here by the ratio of total financial assets to loans outstanding, have strengthened over recent years, though household net wealth is sensitive to equity values. Improved company net worth has been mirrored by a continued decline in company gearing (loans relative to outstanding share capital).

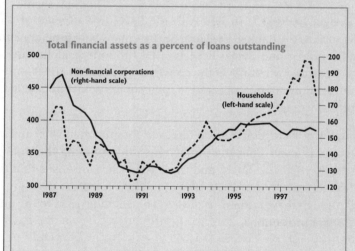

Company liquidity is particularly robust at present, providing a useful cushion against the weaker short-term profits outlook. Household liquidity has strengthened in recent years, though there has also been a structural shift towards lower holdings of liquid cash balances over time.

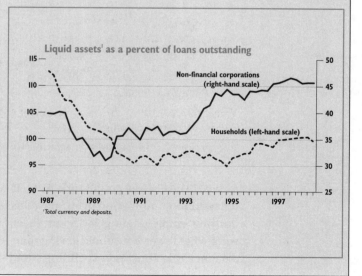

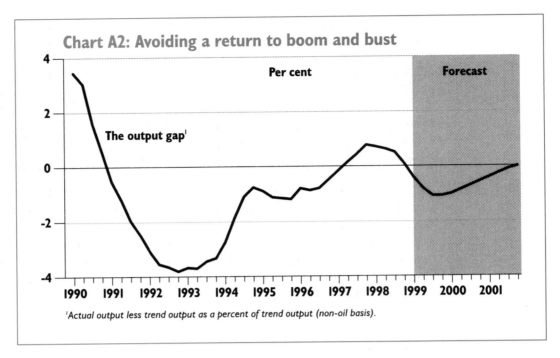

Chart A2: Avoiding a return to boom and bust

Per cent

Forecast

The output gap¹

¹Actual output less trend output as a percent of trend output (non-oil basis).

Forecast risks

A24   The Budget forecast is in line with the latest assessments of a number of leading organisations such as the Bank of England, the International Monetary Fund and the National Institute for Economic and Social Research. Of the independent forecasts surveyed each month by the Treasury, two thirds of the growth projections for 1999 and 2000 currently lie in a relatively narrow range of plus or minus ¹/₂ percentage point either side of the low end of the Budget opportunity range.

A25   Although the average of outside forecasts for growth in 1999 and 2000 is around ¹/₄ to ¹/₂ percentage point lower than the projections underpinning the public finances, outside views appear to have firmed lately, and there is a clear consensus that the economy is well placed for stronger growth into 2000. Half of the new forecasts show growth of 2 per cent or more in 2000, though there remain, as always, considerable risks to the outlook lying on both sides of the Budget projections.

Table A2: Budget and independent¹ forecasts

	Percentage changes on a year earlier unless otherwise stated					
	1999			2000		
		Independent			Independent	
	March Budget	Average	Range	March Budget	Average	Range
Gross domestic product	1 to 1¹/₂	0·6	−0·5 to 2·1	2¹/₄ to 2³/₄	1·8	0·2 to 2·6
RPIX (Q4)	2¹/₂	2·2	1·5 to 3·1	2¹/₂	2·2	1·2 to 2·9
Current account (£ billion)	−10	−5·8	−15·0 to 0·5	−10¹/₂	−6·8	−17·0 to 3·9

¹ 'Forecasts for the UK Economy: A Comparison of Independent Forecasts', February 1999.

A26   Households' confidence in their own financial situation has moved to record levels, reflecting a combination of strong gains in household net financial wealth, low inflation, still buoyant employment growth and recent reductions in mortgage rates. This may encourage somewhat lower household saving than projected. While some uncertainties remain, there is a chance that consumer spending could strengthen more quickly than anticipated.

A27   On the downside, company spending is hard to predict. Considerable world uncertainties remain and so the recovery in business confidence could still falter. While survey measures of investment intentions remain positive for the service sector, they have deteriorated in manufacturing. So despite the low real cost of capital and underlying financial strength, there is a risk that business investment could be weaker than expected, following strong growth in recent years. There is also the possibility of a more significant downward inventory correction than allowed for in the Budget projections (see paragraph A53). The 'Year 2000 problem', meanwhile, raises the possibility of stronger growth in company spending in 1999, but poses a downside risk to world and UK output in 2000.

A28   The trade outlook is also uncertain, partly because the deterioration to date has generally been less marked than might have been expected. It is difficult to gauge the extent to which the Asian crisis economies have been able to increase export volumes to the UK, or in third markets, or how successful they might be in the period ahead. The deterioration in Eurozone growth prospects poses a new risk, though slower growth in UK export markets has been factored into the latest forecast. Against that, CBI export optimism has turned up decisively and sterling has eased.

WORLD OVERVIEW

A29   The world economic outlook remains mixed, although world financial markets have stabilised since last autumn. Turbulence in Brazil, and the continued weakness of commodity prices will impact on growth in many developing countries. However, there are some signs that recessions in the Asian crisis countries are bottoming out. Prospects for G7 growth as a whole are little changed from the Pre-Budget Report, but the imbalance between strong growth in the United States and greater weakness elsewhere has increased. Global inflationary pressures remain very subdued. Table A3 summarises the outlook.

Table A3: The world economy

| | Percentage changes on a year earlier | | | |
| | | Forecast | | |
	1998[1]	1999	2000	2001
Major 7 countries[2]				
Real GDP	2	1½	1¾	2¼
Consumer price inflation[3]	1¼	1¼	1¾	1¾
World trade in manufactures	4½	5¼	5¾	6¾
UK export markets[4]	7¼	5¾	6	6¼

[1] *Estimates.*

[2] *G7: US, Japan, Germany, France, UK, Italy and Canada.*

[3] *Final quarter of each period. For UK, RPIX.*

[4] *Other countries' imports of manufactures weighted according to their importance in UK exports.*

G7 activity

A30   For the G7 overall, growth is expected to slow from 2 per cent in 1998 to $1^1/_2$ per cent this year, before picking up to $1^3/_4$ per cent in 2000. But prospects remain fragile. The outlook for growth in the Eurozone has deteriorated since the autumn, though this has been offset by an ongoing rapid expansion in the US. With Japan still in recession, the balance of global output and demand is becoming increasingly uneven. This increases the vulnerability of the world economy to any sharp slowdown in the United States. However, there has been no repeat of the world financial market volatility that occurred last autumn.

A31   The weaker economic outlook for the Eurozone in 1999 reflects a greater than expected impact from global turbulence, deteriorating business sentiment and still fragile consumer demand, though growth should pick up in 2000. Japan remains in recession with business and consumer confidence low. However, progress is now being made with financial sector reform.

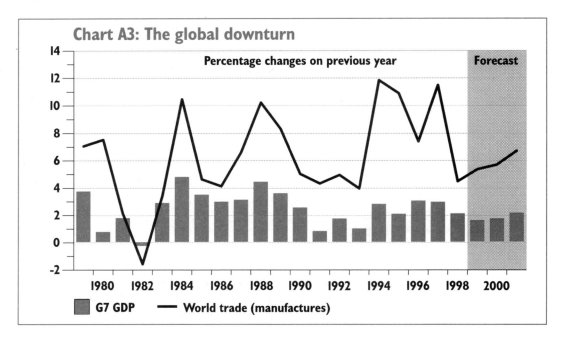

Chart A3: The global downturn

Percentage changes on previous year

Forecast

G7 GDP   —— World trade (manufactures)

A32   By contrast, the US economy has continued to expand at well above trend rates, with GDP up nearly 4 per cent in 1998. Last autumn's interest rate cuts, together with a recovery in equity prices, helped sustain consumer confidence at high levels. Growth is expected to slow in 1999, but forecasts have been revised upwards significantly.

Recent developments in developing countries

A33   The Brazilian real fell sharply after the government abandoned its US dollar currency peg on 15 January. Brazilian GDP is now likely to contract sharply this year, though the wider financial market contagion from the devaluation has been relatively limited. The spreads on Argentinian and Mexican bonds over US Treasury bonds remained well below levels reached immediately after the Russian crisis. Nevertheless, activity in Latin America as a whole is expected to slow significantly this year.

A34   GDP fell sharply in the Asian crisis countries in 1998, but there is now some evidence that the recessions are beginning to bottom out, notably in Korea. The weakness in commodity prices has adversely affected a number of developing country commodity producers in the Middle East and elsewhere.

World inflation and commodity prices

A35   Global inflationary pressures are very weak. Spare capacity at a global level has contributed to historically low G7 consumer price inflation, estimated at $1^{1}/_{4}$ per cent in 1998, and sharp falls in commodity prices. Oil prices fell by about 35 per cent during the course of 1998, at one stage reaching their lowest level for around 12 years, while non-oil commodity prices fell by 17 per cent. Non-oil commodity prices are expected to pick up gently through 1999. Moderate world activity and subdued commodity prices are expected to keep G7 consumer price inflation low, forecast at $1^{1}/_{4}$ per cent in the fourth quarter of 1999.

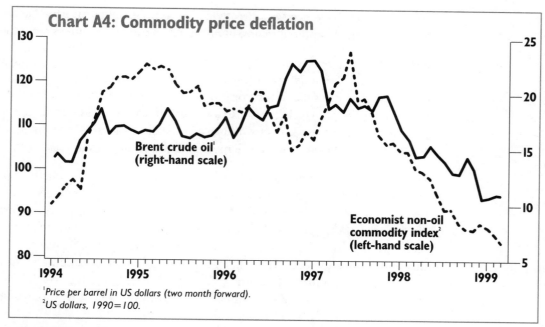

Chart A4: Commodity price deflation

Brent crude oil¹
(right-hand scale)

Economist non-oil
commodity index²
(left-hand scale)

¹Price per barrel in US dollars (two month forward).
²US dollars, 1990=100.

World trade

A36   Growth of world trade in manufactures is estimated to have slowed sharply to 4½ per cent in 1998, partly a result of the collapse in intra-Asian trade. Trade growth should pick up this year as the Asian crisis economies begin to stabilise, although lower growth in Latin America will offset this to some extent. Growth in world trade is expected to recover to 5¼ per cent this year.

A37   UK export markets are estimated to have grown more rapidly than world trade in 1998, at 7¼ per cent. However, with slower growth in the G7, and the weaker outlook for Europe in particular, UK export market growth is expected to slow to 5¾ per cent this year, slightly weaker than forecast in the November Pre-Budget Report.

FORECAST IN DETAIL

Trade and the balance of payments

A38   As widely expected, the UK's balance of trade in goods and services turned negative last year. From a position of near balance in 1997, a deficit of £7¼ billion was recorded for 1998 as a whole, more than accounted for by a widening of the deficit on trade in goods. As a result, the current account moved from a surplus of £6¼ billion in 1997 to an estimated deficit of £2¼ billion, or ¼ per cent of GDP, in 1998, despite the UK's surplus on trade in services rising to a record high of nearly £13½ billion. The current account deficit was about £½ billion larger than projected in the Pre-Budget Report, more than explained by stronger than expected import volumes.

A39   Although sterling has eased significantly since last spring, exchange rates tend to affect trade volumes with a lag, and so the effects of sterling's earlier appreciation continued to be felt through the year. The impact of the financial market turmoil in Asia also took its toll. Trade with Asia, and particularly lower exports, accounted for around half of the widening of the trade in goods deficit in the year to the fourth quarter of 1998. Although the value of UK imports from the region increased by much less, this probably masked a significant increase in import volumes, as the Asian economies became better placed to take advantage of their devaluations in 1997. UK exports may also have been displaced from third countries, some of which have been hit directly by world financial market turbulence, including other emerging markets and the major oil producing nations.

A40   In the short term, prospects for the traded goods sector remain quite weak. Asian demand for UK goods and services is likely to remain muted which, together with the deterioration in European growth prospects and recent events in Latin America, will act to restrain export growth in 1999. As a result, despite the projected pick up in world trade growth, UK export markets growth is likely to fall further this year. In addition, there may be some further delayed, albeit more moderate, adjustment to the rise in sterling since 1996.

A41   However, key business survey readings relating to manufacturing export orders and confidence have shown some stabilisation and recovery in recent months. They suggest some easing in trade conditions, implying a gradual strengthening in exports growth into 2000, as UK export markets growth picks up and the benefits of the decline in sterling since last spring feed through. Import volume growth is expected to slacken further in 1999, with domestic demand subdued, recovering thereafter as UK activity strengthens. Overall, net trade is forecast to exert a broadly neutral influence on GDP growth through this year and beyond, though this implies a negative impact on growth in 1999 as a whole, with net exports well down on levels recorded last year.

Table A4: Trade in goods and services

| | Percentage changes on previous year | | | | | £ billion |
| | Volumes | | Prices[1] | | | Goods and services balance |
	Exports	Imports	Exports	Imports	Terms of trade[2]	
1998	$2^3/_4$	$7^3/_4$	$-4^1/_4$	-6	$1^3/_4$	$-7^1/_4$
Forecast						
1999	$^1/_4$ to $^3/_4$	$3^3/_4$ to $4^1/_4$	$-^1/_2$	$-1^1/_2$	1	$-13^1/_4$
2000	$4^1/_2$ to 5	$4^1/_2$ to 5	$2^1/_4$	$2^1/_4$	0	$-13^1/_2$
2001	6 to $6^1/_2$	$5^1/_2$ to 6	3	3	0	$-13^3/_4$

[1] Average value indices.

[2] Ratio of export to import prices.

A42   The exchange rate and the Asian crisis have been important factors in putting downward pressure on trade prices. Import prices fell by 6 per cent last year, rather more than the fall in export prices. However, import prices are likely to gradually recover later this year as the easing of the exchange rate feeds through and combines with the effects of firmer world activity. This implies continued, but moderating, downward pressure on domestic inflation for a period, but with import price inflation turning positive and then gradually moving back into line with domestic inflation in the first half of 2000.

A43   The deficit in trade in goods and services is forecast to widen to around £13$^1/_4$ billion in 1999, stabilising around this level as growth in both exports and imports move closer together. The investment income surplus is also expected to fall back as a result of reduced profitability of UK subsidiaries overseas. Overall, the current account deficit is forecast to widen to £10 billion, or 1$^1/_4$ per cent of GDP, in 1999, remaining around this level through the forecast period. This is a relatively modest deficit by historical standards.

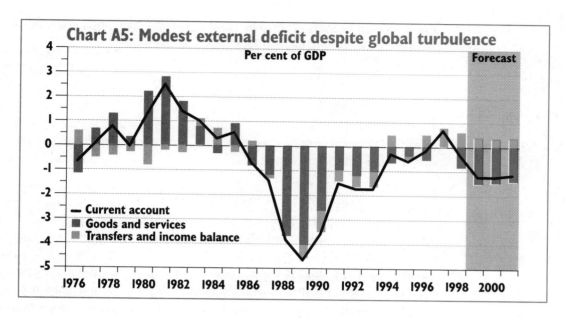

Chart A5: Modest external deficit despite global turbulence

Per cent of GDP

Forecast

- Current account
- Goods and services
- Transfers and income balance

The household sector

A44   Household consumption rose by 2³/₄ per cent in 1998, down from rates of 3³/₄ to 4 per cent in the previous two years. While the quarterly profile of consumption has been somewhat erratic, the broad picture, based on a variety of indicators, has been of an underlying slowing in demand through the year. Quarterly growth averaged just under ¹/₂ per cent in 1998. Expenditure on goods has been weaker, perhaps reflecting a discrete adjustment to the strength in purchases of durables last year, in turn partly associated with the 'windfall payments'. Spending on non-durable goods has also eased, but consumption of services has remained much more buoyant.

A45   Growth in consumer spending would have been weaker, were it not for the cyclical fall in saving. Real household disposable income is estimated to have risen by ¹/₂ per cent in 1998, with the effect on spending cushioned by a fall in the saving ratio to 7 per cent, down from rates of over 9 per cent in preceding years. Growth in nominal disposable income was below estimated growth of nearly 7 per cent in wages and salaries. This reflected an increase in income tax payments related to the implementation of self-assessment, and a rise in net interest payments. As a proportion of gross disposable income, household net interest payments are estimated to have risen from 2·9 per cent in 1997 to 3·9 per cent last year, despite households' holdings of interest bearing deposits almost matching their loan liabilities.

A46   The increase in self-assessment tax payments in 1998 probably represented a permanent increase in the tax base. However, this does not imply that the impact on disposable income growth last year will be repeated. Indeed, the evidence on self-assessment receipts in January suggests that growth in overall taxes on income has fallen back to more normal rates.

A47   The outlook for household saving reflects a balance of factors. On the one hand, precautionary motives for saving have risen, given the slowing in the wider economy. On the other, inflation is low, protecting the real value of existing household wealth. Moreover, a variety of indicators do suggest that households are well placed to maintain spending growth in the period ahead. Box A4 showed that households are not over-borrowed and net financial wealth remains at historically high levels, consistent with the strength of household confidence in their own financial situation.

Table A5: Household sector[1] expenditure and income

| | Percentage changes on previous year | | | |
| | | Forecast | | |
	1998	1999	2000	2001
Household consumption[2]	2¾	2 to 2½	2½ to 3	2¾ to 3¼
Real household disposable income	½	2½ to 3	2½ to 3	2½ to 3
Saving ratio (level, per cent)	7	7½	7½	7½

[1] Including non-profit institutions serving households.

[2] At constant prices.

A48   Overall, prospects for consumption remain good, though spending is likely to remain restrained in the near term. However, those factors depressing disposable incomes last year are expected to unwind, implying stronger real income growth. On balance, the forecast assumes no significant change in the household saving ratio which, with real disposable income growth picking up, implies that underlying growth in spending has already bottomed out. Nevertheless, for 1999 as a whole, household consumption growth is expected to slow to 2 to 2½ per cent. It is forecast to rise to 2½ to 3 per cent in 2000 and 2¾ to 3¼ per cent in 2001.

Companies and investment

A49   Private non-financial corporations (NFCs), which account for the bulk of business investment, secured a strong rise in gross saving from 7 per cent of GDP in 1990 to more than 10 per cent in 1996. This first led to a move into financial surplus, and then supported rapid growth in total business investment, averaging 8¾ per cent a year in the three years to 1997, partly accounting for the return to financial deficit that year. This trend continued in 1998, with business investment growth rising further to 11 per cent. However, the scale of company net borrowing, at around 2 per cent of GDP, remained much more modest than in the late 1980s.

A50   The strong pick up in business investment in recent years is likely to be interrupted in 1999, as weaker demand continues to erode corporate profitability. This is consistent with survey evidence, particularly in manufacturing, where indicators of confidence, profits and capacity utilisation fell quite markedly in the second half of 1998. Manufacturing investment has already turned, falling in each of the past three quarters, and investment growth in the service sector is likely to be moderate in the period ahead. Overall, business investment is expected to grow by 1 to 1¾ per cent in 1999 as a whole.

Table A6: Gross fixed capital formation

| | Percentage changes on previous year | | | |
| | | Forecast | | |
	1998	1999	2000	2001
Whole economy[1]	8	2 to 2½	2¾ to 3¼	3½ to 4
of which:				
Business[2,3]	11	1 to 1¾	1½ to 2	2½ to 3
Private dwellings[3]	5¼	½ to 1	2¾ to 3¼	2¼ to 2¾
General government[3,4]	−1	11	12¼	12¾

[1] Includes costs associated with the transfer of ownership of land and existing buildings.

[2] Private sector and public corporations' (except National Health Service Trusts) non-residential investment. Includes investment under the Private Finance Initiative.

[3] Excludes purchases less sales of land and existing buildings.

[4] Includes National Health Service Trusts.

A51 The period of more moderate investment growth is, however, expected to be temporary. Having repaired their balance sheets in recent years, companies are better placed to respond to the improved business conditions expected later this year, helped by the low real cost of capital. This is in marked contrast to 10 years ago, when heavy borrowing prior to the downturn eroded company finances at a time of falling demand and rising capital costs. The ratio of financial assets to loans outstanding provides an indication of binding financial constraints on companies in the short run. For all NFCs, this ratio was squeezed significantly in the late 1980s, as was company liquidity, but companies appear much better placed this time around (see Box A4). Despite the impact of tougher world economic conditions, business investment is likely to be stronger into 2000, with growth of $1^1/_2$ to 2 per cent projected for the year as a whole.

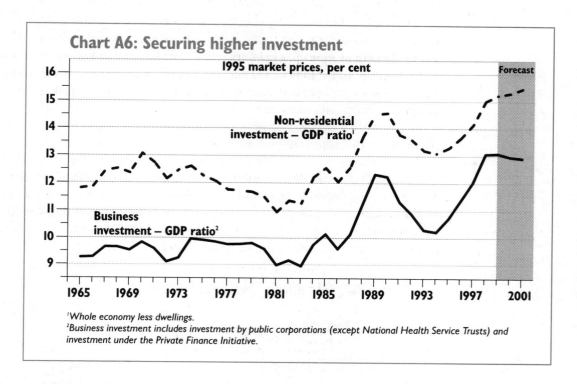

Chart A6: Securing higher investment

1995 market prices, per cent

Forecast

Non-residential investment – GDP ratio[1]

Business investment – GDP ratio[2]

[1]Whole economy less dwellings.
[2]Business investment includes investment by public corporations (except National Health Service Trusts) and investment under the Private Finance Initiative.

A52 Whole economy investment is expected to rise faster than business investment as the Government's CSR commitment to raise public investment takes effect. General government investment is expected to grow at double-digit rates from now on, reversing the sharp falls of recent years. This boost to investment is well timed to support stronger economic growth. Sustaining improved investment performance and fostering a higher ratio of investment to GDP is a key factor in closing the productivity gap with other industrialised countries.

A53 Inventory accumulation averaged $^1/_2$ per cent of GDP per quarter last year, well above its average over the last cycle. Although these data are less reliable than other national accounts series, the build up was mirrored in business survey evidence. It is likely that firms will run down excess inventories in the coming period, providing a temporary restraint on growth during 1999. While there is a risk that the correction could be larger than expected, it is important not to over-emphasise the influence of inventory accumulation on overall activity. Inventory accumulation has tended to coincide with the growth cycle in the past, as opposed to driving it.

The labour market

A54   A variety of indicators, including high vacancies and relatively low unemployment inflows, show that labour market activity has remained surprisingly robust. The key feature has been the strong upturn in employment growth during the second half of 1998. In the fourth quarter, LFS employment was up 122,000 on the previous quarter and around 250,000 on the second quarter, close to the rapid gains recorded in early 1997.

A55   A recent switch to part-time working has meant that the continued, though more moderate, economic expansion has remained relatively jobs-rich. This partly reflects still firm service sector growth. However, although part-time employment accounted for around two thirds of the total employment growth in the fourth quarter of 1998, a 175,000 expansion in full-time jobs accounted for the larger part of employment gains through the year as a whole. Total hours worked have risen more than $^1/_2$ per cent over the past year.

A56   The counterpart has been a cyclical slowing in productivity growth which, on a non-oil basis, is estimated to have fallen from around 2 per cent in the second half of 1997 to under $1^1/_4$ per cent in the fourth quarter of 1998. Productivity growth tends to fall in downswings as companies hold onto some excess labour due to the costs of changing employment levels. With company finances in relatively good shape and unemployment low, firms are likely to continue to hoard trained employees through the temporary period of slower growth. Survey measures of employment expectations remain relatively optimistic in the service sector, and less pessimistic for manufacturing than in past downturns. Government policies to move people from welfare into work and make work pay, as described in Chapter 4 of the Economic and Fiscal Strategy Report, will help minimise dislocations associated with lower growth.

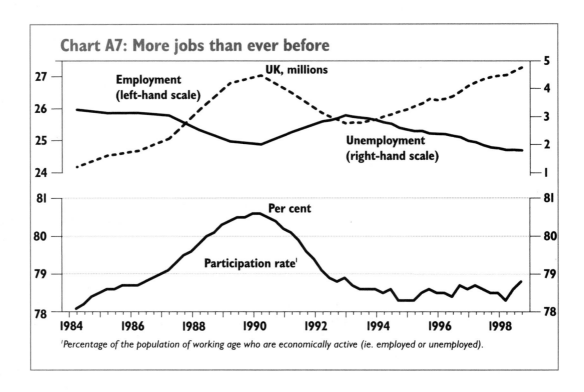

Chart A7: More jobs than ever before

¹Percentage of the population of working age who are economically active (ie. employed or unemployed).

A57   Recent increases in labour market participation have been significant. In the fourth quarter of 1998, the economic inactivity rate among people of working age was $^1/_2$ percentage point down on six months earlier, though this looks to have been from an erratically high level. Overall, the decline in working age inactivity added around 70,000 to the labour force through the course of 1998, almost halting the downward trend in unemployment in the second half. This was a key change from the previous year when rising inactivity had reinforced the downward trend in unemployment.

A58   Indeed, with the population of working age continuing to rise, it is the recent acceleration in employment that has prevented unemployment from rising. Both unemployment measures continue to show modest declines on the latest readings and the ILO unemployment rate now stands at around $6^1/_4$ per cent, down from about 8 per cent two years ago and $10^1/_2$ per cent in early 1993. However, in addition to 1·8 million currently ILO unemployed, there are a further 2·3 million working age people who want a job but are either not seeking or unavailable for work, evidence of the need for the Government's policies to make work pay. So despite apparent labour market tightness, amongst working age people there are still over 4 million, equivalent to $11^1/_2$ per cent, who are without work and want a job.

A59   Moreover, the recently re-instated Average Earnings Index points to an easing in labour market pressures, with whole economy earnings growth slowing from around $5^3/_4$ per cent in the second quarter of 1998 to $4^1/_2$ per cent in the fourth quarter. Private sector earnings growth has eased to a similar degree, though in both cases this has been partly a result of lower bonuses. This suggests that earnings growth has fallen back in response to the slowing of the economy, despite output remaining above potential and evidence of labour market tightness. Additional factors that may have contributed include the fall in headline RPI inflation, increased uncertainties following the shock to confidence last autumn, and the concentration of recent employment growth in part-time jobs (which is likely to have depressed overall average earnings).

A60   Firm evidence of a fall back in wage settlements is also emerging. For example, CBI data show that manufacturing settlements in the three months to January averaged 3 per cent, down $^1/_2$ percentage point on the previous three months. Service sector settlements were down 0·7 percentage points over the same period, to around $3^3/_4$ per cent. The decline in average earnings growth and settlements is encouraging. Economic stability depends on wage responsibility across the public and private sectors.

Inflation

A61   RPIX inflation averaged 2·6 per cent in 1998 as a whole and was exactly at its $2^1/_2$ per cent target between August and November last year. This favourable inflation outturn benefited from sharp falls in import prices, masking stronger growth in UK labour costs and an expansion in domestic retail margins. This was reflected in services price inflation (excluding rent and utilities) of $4^3/_4$ per cent, more than double the rate of goods price inflation, despite some recent signs of easing.

A62   Import prices have fallen for ten consecutive quarters, primarily the result of sterling's previous appreciation, but with additional pressure from the sharp falls in the prices of raw materials. Brent oil prices reached a 12 year low in late 1998. But despite lower import costs, producer profits have been squeezed by strong competition from cheap imports, particularly from Asia, and the build up of inventories last year. As a result, producer output prices (excluding excise duties) of manufactures fell by 0·8 per cent in the year to January and survey price expectations are also at historically low levels.

A63   As in the Pre-Budget Report forecast, RPIX inflation is expected to dip temporarily below target during 1999. In the short term, import prices are likely to remain weak, forcing domestic manufacturers to cut prices further. For a period, this is expected to combine with moderating domestically-generated inflation to reduce RPIX inflation. This domestic easing is likely to intensify with the output gap projected to turn negative in early 1999, and output remaining below trend until late 2001. Growth in earnings has already fallen back since last spring, accompanied by a significant easing in wage settlements in recent months.

A64   Retail margins are also likely to be squeezed as those factors that boosted them in recent years unwind. Retailers have benefited from strong consumer demand, enabling them to pass on only part of the drop in import prices. However, import prices are expected first to stabilise and then gradually recover later this year, as the easing in sterling begins to feed through. Non-oil commodity prices are also expected to pick up gently through 1999, as the Asian crisis economies stabilise. This is likely to offset the decline in domestically-generated inflation, bringing RPIX inflation back to target by the end of this year.

A65   Inflation, as measured by the GDP deflator, is likely to be similar to RPIX inflation in 1998-99. The rise in the terms of trade over the past two years, with import prices falling more sharply than export prices, has tended to boost the GDP deflator relative to RPIX inflation. However, this effect has been offset by abnormally low consumers' expenditure deflator (CED) inflation relative to RPIX, reflecting coverage differences. CED inflation is assumed to move broadly back in line with RPIX inflation during 1999, and the terms of trade effect should diminish as the effect of the previous exchange rate appreciation unwinds. So GDP deflator inflation is expected to remain close to $2^{1}/_{2}$ per cent in financial year 1999-2000.

A66   The Harmonised Index of Consumer Prices (HICP) is the inflation measure adopted by the European Central Bank for assessing its price stability objective. UK HICP inflation has recently been running at around $1^{1}/_{2}$ per cent, 1 percentage point or more below RPIX inflation. Half of this differential can be explained by coverage differences, primarily the exclusion of some housing components from the HICP; the remainder is due to the different formulae by which the two indices aggregate individual prices. This formula effect will persist, but the differential due to coverage differences is expected to narrow over the forecast period.

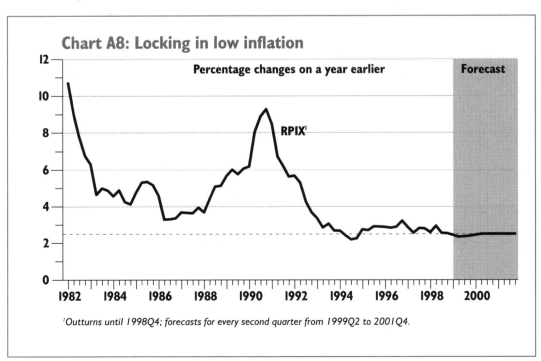

Chart A8: Locking in low inflation

Percentage changes on a year earlier

Forecast

RPIX[1]

[1]Outturns until 1998Q4; forecasts for every second quarter from 1999Q2 to 2001Q4.

Table A7: Summary of economic prospects[1]

| | Percentage changes on a year earlier unless otherwise stated | | | | Average errors from past forecasts[3] | |
| | | | Forecast[2] | | | |
	1998	1999	2000	2001	1999	2000
Output at constant market prices						
Gross domestic product (GDP)	2¼	1 to 1½	2¼ to 2¾	2¾ to 3¼	½	1
Manufacturing output	¼	−1½ to −1	1½ to 2	2¼ to 2¾	½	2½
Expenditure components of GDP at constant market prices[4]						
Domestic demand	3½	2 to 2½	2¼ to 3 [5]	2¾ to 3¼	¼	1
Household consumption[6]	2¾	2 to 2½	2½ to 3	2¾ to 3¼	½	1¼
General government consumption	1½	3	2¼	2	¾	1¼
Fixed investment	8	2 to 2½	2¾ to 3¼	3½ to 4	1	2½
Change in inventories[7]	¼	−¼	−¼ to 0	0 to ¼	¼	¼
Export of goods and services	2¾	¼ to ¾	4½ to 5	6 to 6½	1½	2¼
Imports of goods and services	7¾	3¾ to 4¼	4½ to 5	5½ to 6	1¾	2½
Balance of payments current account						
£ billion	−2¼	−10	−10½	−10¼	7½	10
per cent of GDP	−¼	−1¼	−1¼	−1	¾	1
Inflation						
RPIX (Q4)	2½	2½	2½	2½	¾	1¼
Producer output prices (Q4)[8]	−¾	−¼	1½	2½	¾	1
GDP deflator at market prices (financial year)	2½	2½	2½	2½	¾	1¼
Money GDP at market prices (financial year)						
£ billion	848	880 to 885	925 to 936	975 to 989	10¼	15½
percentage change	4½	3¾ to 4¼	5¼ to 5¾	5¼ to 5¾	1¼	1¾

[1] The forecast is consistent with UK output and expenditure data to the fourth quarter of 1998, released by the Office of National Statistics on 23 February 1999.

[2] Growth ranges for GDP components do not necessarily sum to the ½ percentage point ranges for GDP growth because of rounding and the assumed invariance of the levels of public spending within the opportunity ranges.

[3] Average absolute errors for current year and year-ahead projections made in spring forecasts over the past ten years. The average errors for the current account are calculated as a percent of GDP, with £ billion figures calculated by scaling the errors by forecast money GDP in 1999 and 2000.

[4] Further detail on the expenditure components of GDP is given in Table A8.

[5] Reflects rounding down at lower end of range and rounding up at upper end of range, with unrounded range only marginally exceeding ½ percentage point.

[6] Includes households and non-profit institutions serving households.

[7] Contribution to GDP growth, percentage points.

[8] Excluding excise duties.

Table A8: Gross domestic product and its components

	£ billion at 1995 prices, seasonally adjusted									
	Household consumption[1]	General government consumption	Fixed investment	Change in inventories	Domestic demand	Exports of goods and services	Total final expenditure	*Less* imports of goods and services	*Plus* statistical discrepancy[2]	GDP at market prices
1998	501·9	145·1	140·5	4·3	791·9	242·8	1034·7	264·3	3·3	773·7
1999	511·4 to 513·9	149·6	143·3 to 144·0	2·4 to 3·2	806·9 to 810·8	243·4 to 244·5	1050·2 to 1055·3	274·3 to 275·6	4·7	780·6 to 784·4
2000	524·7 to 529·9	153·0	147·3 to 148·7	0·8 to 2·4	826·0 to 834·2	254·5 to 257·0	1080·5 to 1091·2	286·4 to 289·2	4·7	798·8 to 806·7
2001	538·7 to 546·4	156·1	152·5 to 154·7	1·7 to 4.0	849·3 to 861·4	269·8 to 273·7	1119·1 to 1135·1	302·4 to 306·8	4·7	821·3 to 833·0
1998 1st half	250·3	72·2	69·3	1·5	393·4	121·4	514·8	130·2	1·1	385·6
2nd half	251·6	72·9	71·2	2·8	398·6	121·4	520·0	134·1	2·2	388·0
1999 1st half	254·1 to 255·0	74·3	71·5 to 71·7	1·9 to 2·1	401·9 to 403·3	120·8 to 121·2	522·7 to 524·6	136·0 to 136·5	2·3	389·0 to 390·4
2nd half	257·3 to 258·9	75·2	71·8 to 72·2	0·6 to 1·0	405·0 to 407·5	122·6 to 123·3	527·5 to 530·8	138·3 to 139·1	2·3	391·6 to 394·0
2000 1st half	260·6 to 262·9	76·5	72·9 to 73·6	0·1 to 0·7	410·1 to 413·7	125·5 to 126·5	535·6 to 540·2	141·3 to 142·5	2·3	396·6 to 400·0
2nd half	264·1 to 267·0	76·6	74·4 to 75·2	0·8 to 1·6	415·9 to 420·5	129·0 to 130·4	544·9 to 550·9	145·0 to 146·6	2·3	402·2 to 406·7
2001 1st half	267·7 to 271·4	78·0	75·7 to 76·7	0·2 to 1·3	421·7 to 427·5	132·9 to 134·7	554·6 to 562·2	149·1 to 151·1	2·3	407·8 to 413·4
2nd half	271·0 to 275·1	78·1	76·9 to 78·0	1·4 to 2·6	427·5 to 434·0	136·9 to 139·0	564·4 to 572·9	153·3 to 155·6	2·3	413·5 to 419·7
	Percentage changes on previous year[3,4]									
1998	2¾	1½	8	¼	3½	2¾	3¼	7¾	½	2¼
1999	2 to 2½	3	2 to 2½	–¼	2 to 2½	¼ to ¾	1½ to 2	3¾ to 4¼	¼	1 to 1½
2000	2½ to 3	2¼	2¾ to 3¼	–¼ to 0	2¼ to 3[5]	4½ to 5	3 to 3½	4½ to 5	0	2¼ to 2¾
2001	2¾ to 3¼	2	3½ to 4	0 to ¼	2¾ to 3¼	6 to 6½	3½ to 4	5½ to 6	0	2¾ to 3¼

[1] *Includes households and non-profit institutions serving households.*

[2] *Expenditure adjustment.*

[3] *For change in inventories and the statistical discrepancy, changes are expressed as a percent of GDP.*

[4] *Growth ranges for GDP components do not necessarily sum to the ½ percentage point ranges for GDP growth because of rounding and the assumed invariance of the levels of public spending within the opportunity ranges.*

[5] *Reflects rounding down at lower end of range and rounding up at upper end of range, with unrounded range only marginally exceeding ½ percentage point.*

B

THE PUBLIC FINANCES

The public finances have been transformed over the past two years. The current budget has moved into surplus this year, and the debt burden is falling. Chapter 2 of the EFSR briefly summarised these developments and the prospects for the public finances. This annex presents more detail. It includes:

- estimates of the fiscal balances for 1998–99 and comparisons with the forecasts made in last year's Budget and last November's *Pre-Budget Report*;

- projections for the public finances over the next five years, starting with the key assumptions on which the projections are based and then describing in turn the prospects for budget balances, debt, public expenditure and receipts; and

- some more detailed analyses of sectoral borrowing and funding. Historical series for different measures of the main fiscal aggregates, and a description of the accounting conventions used in presenting the public finances, are given at the end of the annex.

The key points are:

- It is estimated that the current budget will be £4 billion in surplus in 1998–99. This compares with an average deficit of over 4 per cent of GDP between 1991–92 and 1996–97. Net borrowing, which peaked five years ago at almost 8 per cent of GDP, has also moved into surplus. Net debt, which doubled over the first half of the 1990s, has been falling as a percentage of GDP since mid-1997.

- The Budget continues to lock in this improvement for the future. On the assumption that the economy grows at the lower end of the opportunity ranges given in Annex A, the current budget is projected to remain in surplus. While fiscal policy provides support for the economy during its below trend phase, the structural position continues to improve.

- As economic growth picks up, the current budget is projected to move increasingly into surplus in the medium term. Net borrowing remains low, despite higher public investment (set to double as a percentage of GDP over this Parliament), and the debt burden continues to fall.

- The fiscal rules are met with some margin to spare.

- Both the budget deficit and debt burden were well within Maastricht reference levels in calendar 1998. It is expected that the Maastricht criteria will continue to be met with comfort.

THE POSITION IN 1998–99

B1   Over the first ten months of 1998–99, there was a budget surplus of £7½ billion, compared with net borrowing of £3½ billion in the first ten months of 1997–98. This large improvement was largely in the central government balance, although local authorities and public corporations both repaid debt.

Table B1: Net borrowing in April–January

	£ billion		
	1997–98	1998–99	Change
Central government	4·8	−4·8	−9·6
Local government	−0·1	−0·3	−0·2
Public corporations	−1·3	−2·5	−1·2
Public sector	**3·4**	**−7·6**	**−10·9**

B2 For 1998–99 as a whole, it is estimated that there will be a net repayment of £1 billion. This estimate is still uncertain; the levels of both spending and receipts towards the end of the financial year are always hard to predict. A provisional estimate of the outturn will be published by the Office for National Statistics on 20 April 1999.

B3 It is estimated that the current budget will be in surplus by £4 billion ($^{1}/_{2}$ per cent of GDP) in 1998–99. The first estimate of the outturn will be published by the Office for National Statistics on 27 May 1999. This year's surplus compares with a deficit of £22$^{1}/_{2}$ billion (3 per cent of GDP) in 1996–97. An estimated $^{3}/_{4}$ per cent of this 3$^{1}/_{2}$ per cent of GDP improvement is accounted for by above-trend economic growth. About $^{3}/_{4}$ per cent is accounted for by tax measures in the 1997 and 1998 Budgets. The remainder mainly reflects comparatively slow growth of public spending, as the Government has kept within the plans it inherited for the first two years.

Table B2: Change in current budget surplus between 1996–97 and 1998–99[1]

	Per cent of GDP
Outturn for 1996–97	**–3**
Effect of tax changes[2]	$^{3}/_{4}$
Estimated effect of economic cycle	$^{3}/_{4}$
Other (chiefly public spending)	2
Forecast for 1998–99	**$^{1}/_{2}$**

[1]Excluding windfall tax and associated spending.
[2]Tax changes (relative to an indexed base) in 1997 and 1998 Budgets.

B4 Table B3 compares these latest estimates for 1998–99 with the forecasts that were made in the 1998 Budget and the 1998 PBR. Comparisons with the 1998 Budget forecasts are complicated by the introduction of the new European System of National Accounts (ESA95) in September 1998. To facilitate comparison, the 1998 Budget forecasts are adjusted for classification changes, so as to put them on the same basis as the estimated outturns.

Table B3: Comparison with 1998 forecasts[1]

	£ billion	
	1997–98	1998–99
Surplus on current budget:		
1998 FSBR (old basis)	–1·3	3·6
1998 FSBR (ESA95 basis)	**–4·8**	**–0·1**
1998 PBR	–4·4	5·5
1999 FSBR	**–5·1**	**4·1**
Net investment:		
1998 FSBR (old basis)	6·2	6·7
1998 FSBR (ESA95 basis)	**4·6**	**5·0**
1998 PBR	3·8	4·0
1999 FSBR	**4·0**	**3·1**
Net borrowing		
1998 FSBR (old basis)	7·5	3·1
1998 FSBR (ESA95 basis)	**9·4**	**5·1**
1998 PBR	8·2	–1·5
1999 FSBR	**9·1**	**–1·0**

[1] Excluding windfall tax and associated spending.

B5   On constant definitions, the improvement in the public finances has been greater than expected at the time of the last Budget. The estimated current budget surplus of £4 billion in 1998–99 compares with a forecast of balance in the last Budget. Receipts, especially from income tax and social security contributions, have been higher than expected, while expenditure, especially on social security, has been lower. Forecast surpluses have been revised downwards slightly since the PBR. This mainly reflects lower receipts than expected from corporation tax. The estimated net debt repayment of £1 billion compares with a forecast of net borrowing of £5 billion in the last Budget.

B6   The debt burden has fallen more quickly than expected in last year's Budget. From a peak of 44.7 per cent of GDP in mid-1997, the net debt ratio fell below 40 per cent at end-January 1999. Borrowing is usually high in the last two months of the financial year, and the ratio may be a little above 40 per cent at end-March.

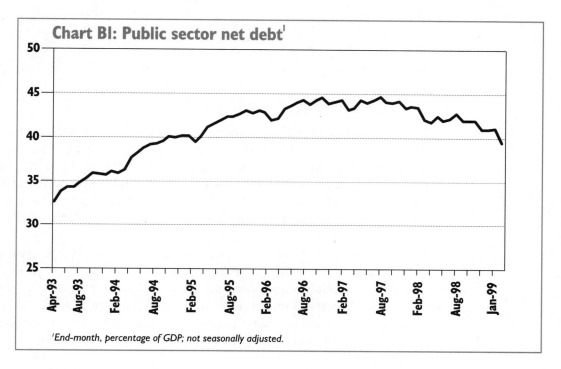

Chart BI: Public sector net debt[1]

[1]*End-month, percentage of GDP; not seasonally adjusted.*

B7   The estimated net wealth of the public sector fell from around 70 per cent of GDP in the late 1980s to just 15 per cent of GDP at end-1997 – in part because of rising debt and in part because privatisations and historically low levels of public investment reduced the stock of government assets. But, with the current budget now in surplus, net wealth is likely to have stabilised in 1998 as a percentage of GDP.

PROSPECTS

ASSUMPTIONS

B8   The projections:

- assume that the economy follows the path described in Annex A. In the interests of caution, the lower end of the opportunity range for GDP growth has been used;

- take account of the effects of the Budget measures, but assume that there are no further tax changes beyond the escalators for fuel and tobacco duties[1] and the indexation of rates and allowances;

[1]Announced in the March and November 1996 Budgets and increased in the July 1997 Budget.

- assume that Departmental Expenditure Limits (DEL) are in line with the plans set out in the July 1998 Comprehensive Spending Review (CSR); and

- incorporate new projections of Annually Managed Expenditure (AME) and assume that the AME margin is the same as in the CSR.

Table B4: Economic assumptions for public finance projections

| | Percentage changes on previous year | | | | | |
	1998–99	1999–00	2000–01	2001–02	2002–03	2003–04
Output (GDP)	$1^3/_4$	1	$2^1/_2$	$2^3/_4$	$2^1/_2$	$2^1/_4$
Prices						
RPIX	$2^3/_4$	$2^1/_4$	$2^1/_2$	$2^1/_2$	$2^1/_2$	$2^1/_2$
GDP deflator	$2^1/_2$	$2^1/_2$	$2^1/_2$	$2^1/_2$	$2^1/_2$	$2^1/_2$
RPI (September)[1]	$3^1/_4$	$1^1/_4$	3	$2^3/_4$		
Rossi (September)[1]	$2^1/_4$	2	2	2		
Money GDP (£ billion)	848	880	925	975	1023	1072

[1] Used for projecting social security expenditure over the following financial year.

B9 Ten of the eleven key assumptions and conventions audited by the National Audit Office (NAO) and used for last year's Budget projections (see page 109 of the March 1998 FSBR and the NAO report *Audit of Assumptions for the Budget*, 19 March 1998, HC 616) are unchanged. In accordance with these assumptions and conventions, oil prices are assumed flat at $11 a barrel (in real terms), equity prices are projected to grow from current levels in line with money GDP, and interest rates are projected in line with market expectations.

B10 A new, more cautious, planning assumption is used for projecting expenditure on social security. Previously, the projections were based on the assumption that claimant unemployment would remain constant. This assumption is a long-standing convention that was endorsed by the National Audit Office (NAO) before the 1997 Budget and has been retained in subsequent forecasts. While simple and transparent, such an assumption does not provide a consistently cautious basis for projecting social security expenditure at every point in the cycle.

B11 It has been decided to base the projections of social security expenditure in this Budget on the average of outside forecasts of unemployment compiled in *Forecasts of the UK Economy* (latest edition, HM Treasury, February 1999). When such an average shows a rise, that will be used as the basis for fiscal planning. This does not reflect the Government's views on the prospects for unemployment. It is a deliberately cautious approach for the purpose of fiscal planning. When unemployment is projected to fall by outside forecasters, the flat assumption will again be used[2]. This approach has been endorsed by the NAO, whose report, *Audit of the Unemployment Assumption for the March 1999 Budget Projections*, is published as a House of Commons Paper (HC 294).

[2] More precisely, the average of outside forecasts is used if this average shows the claimant count higher at the end of the following year than it is currently. So that the average is not affected by extreme observations, the highest and lowest 10 per cent of outside forecasts are excluded from the sample. Full details are given in the NAO report.

BUDGET DEFICITS

B12   Table B5 shows projections for the current and capital budgets in £ billion and Table B6 shows them as a percentage of GDP.

B13   While the estimated current budget surplus for 1998–99 has been revised down since the PBR in the light of lower than expected receipts, the forecasts for the next two years have been revised up. This reflects downward revisions to the projections of public spending. Lower interest rates and inflation will reduce debt interest, while spending on social security is turning out substantially lower than projected in last July's Comprehensive Spending Review.

B14   With economic growth assumed to be lower in 1999-2000, receipts (excluding windfall tax) are projected to rise only slightly as a percentage of GDP. As a result, the current budget surplus falls slightly next year, after several years of improvement. But the structural position continues to improve – Table B7.

Table B5: Current and capital budgets

					£ billion		
	Outturn	**Estimate**			**Projections**		
	1997–98	**1998–99**	**1999–00**	**2000–01**	**2001–02**	**2002–03**	**2003–04**
Current budget							
Current receipts	315·7	334·2	345	364	385	405	425
Current expenditure	304·3	313·5	329	346	362	379	398
Depreciation	14·0	14·6	15	15	16	16	17
Surplus on current budget (including windfall tax)	–2·6	6·2	1	3	7	9	11
Surplus on current budget[1]	**-5·1**	**4·1**	**2**	**4**	**8**	**9**	**11**
Capital budget							
Gross investment	22·0	21·7	24	26	29	32	35
less asset sales	–4·0	–3·8	–4	–4	–4	–4	–4
less depreciation	–14·0	–14·6	–15	–15	–16	–16	–17
Net investment	4·0	3·4	5	7	10	12	15
Net borrowing (including windfall tax)	6·6	–2·8	4	5	2	3	4
Net borrowing[1]	**9·1**	**–1·0**	**3**	**3**	**1**	**3**	**4**

[1] *Excluding windfall tax receipts and associated spending.*

B15   From 2001–02 onwards, with the economy growing at or slightly above trend, the projected current budget surpluses gradually build up. Current expenditure rises in line with GDP, while receipts rise slightly faster because of real fiscal drag (the tendency under a progressive income tax system for receipts to grow faster than incomes as incomes grow), the impact of past Budget measures and real increases in excise duties. Over the economic cycle (1997–98 to 2002–03), the surpluses average $\frac{1}{2}$ per cent of GDP; so that the golden rule is met with a margin to spare – Table B7.

B16   Net borrowing is expected to become positive again next year, partly reflecting the reduction in the current budget surplus and partly an increase in public investment. Although net investment is projected to more than double as a share of GDP between 1998–99 and 2001–02, net borrowing remains low as a percentage of GDP.

B17   Table B6 also shows the definition of the budget deficit – general government net borrowing on an ESA79 basis – used in the Excessive Deficits Procedure of the Maastricht Treaty. The reference level of 3 per cent of GDP is achieved very comfortably. There was a surplus on the Maastricht measure of 0·6 per cent of GDP in 1998. A small deficit of 0·3 per cent of GDP is forecast for 1999.

Table B6: Current and capital budgets

				Per cent of GDP			
	Outturn	Estimate			Projections		
	1997–98	1998–99	1999–00	2000–01	2001–02	2002–03	2003–04
Current budget							
Current receipts	38·9	39·4	39·2	39·4	39·5	39·6	39·7
Current expenditure	37·5	37·0	37·4	37·4	37·1	37·1	37·1
Depreciation	1·7	1·7	1·7	1·6	1·6	1·6	1·6
Surplus on current budget (including windfall tax)	–0·3	0·7	0·1	0·3	0·7	0·9	1·0
Surplus on current budget[1]	**–0·6**	**0·5**	**0·3**	**0·4**	**0·8**	**0·9**	**1·0**
Capital budget							
Gross investment	2·7	2·6	2·7	2·9	3·0	3·2	3·3
less asset sales	–0·5	–0·4	–0·4	–0·4	–0·4	–0·4	–0·3
less depreciation	–1·7	–1·7	–1·7	–1·6	–1·6	–1·6	–1·6
Net investment	0·5	0·4	0·6	0·8	1·0	1·2	1·4
Net borrowing (including windfall tax)	0·8	–0·3	0·5	0·5	0·2	0·3	0·4
Net borrowing[1]	**1·1**	**–0·1**	**0·3**	**0·4**	**0·1**	**0·3**	**0·4**
Public sector net debt	**42·5**	**40·6**	**39·4**	**38·2**	**36·8**	**35·6**	**34·6**
Memos:							
Net taxes[2]	36·6	37·2	36·6	36·7	37·0	37·0	37·1
Maastricht deficit[3]	0·6	–0·6	0·3	0·2	0·2	0·1	0·3
General government gross debt	49·6	47·6	46·6	45·3	43·5	42·2	41·0

[1] *Excluding windfall tax receipts and associated spending.*

[2] *Total tax receipts and social security contributions net of tax credits.*

[3] *General government net borrowing on an ESA79 basis. The Maastricht definition does not exclude the windfall tax and associated spending.*

Table B7: Budget balances[1]

				Per cent of GDP			
	Outturns	Estimate			Projections		
	1997–98	1998–99	1999–00	2000–01	2001–02	2002–03	2003–04
Budget balances							
Surplus on current budget	–0·6	0·5	0·3	0·4	0·8	0·9	1·0
Average surplus since 1997–98	–0·6	–0·1	0·0	0·1	0·3	0·4	0·5
Net borrowing	1·1	–0·1	0·3	0·4	0·1	0·3	0·4
Cyclically-adjusted budget balances							
Surplus on current budget	–0·7	0·2	0·6	1·0	1·1	0·9	1·0
Average surplus since 1997–98	–0·7	–0·2	0·1	0·3	0·4	0·5	0·6
Net borrowing	1·1	0·1	0·0	–0·2	–0·1	0·3	0·4

[1] *Excluding windfall tax receipts and associated spending.*

PUBLIC SECTOR DEBT

B18   Table B8 sets out projections for two measures of debt. Public sector net debt (used to judge the sustainable investment rule) is approximately the stock counterpart of public sector borrowing, while general government gross debt is the Maastricht measure. Both measures rose sharply over the first half of the 1990s as a result of the high levels of government borrowing and slow growth in money GDP, but peaked as a percentage of GDP in 1997. Public sector net debt is projected to fall from under 41 per cent of GDP at the end of the current financial year to under 35 per cent in five years time. General government gross debt was 51 per cent of GDP at end-1998 – comfortably below the Maastricht criterion of 60 per cent – and is projected to fall to 42 per cent of GDP.

Table B8: Public sector debt[1]

	Outturn 1998	Estimate 1999	2000	2001	Projections 2002	2003	2004
Public sector net debt							
£ billion	353	350	355	363	367	373	380
–per cent of GDP[2]	42·5	40·6	39·4	38·2	36·8	35·6	34·6
General government gross debt							
£ billion	403	404	410	419	424	431	439
–per cent of GDP[3]	50·8	48·8	47·7	46·3	44·5	43·1	41·9

[1] End-March.

[2] GDP centred on end-March.

[3] Maastricht basis.

RECEIPTS

B19   In total, the Budget measures have little effect on taxes on an accruals basis in 1999–2000 and 2000–01, and reduce tax accruals by £2$^{1}/_{2}$ billion in 2001–02. The reduction in 2001–02 mainly reflects the lower rates of income tax.

B20   Table B9 gives projections of receipts, as a percentage of GDP, over the medium term. A more detailed breakdown, in £ billion, for 1998–99 and 1999–2000 is given in table B10. Excluding the windfall tax, total receipts are estimated to rise by 6 per cent in 1998-99, which is rather faster than forecast money GDP growth of 4$^{1}/_{2}$ per cent. This relatively strong growth of receipts mostly reflects the effects of past Budget measures, together with the normal tendency for the receipts-to-GDP ratio to rise when GDP is growing. The growth of receipts is forecast to slow to 4 per cent next year. The slowdown in the economy (with money GDP growing by 3$^{3}/_{4}$ per cent) is expected to affect corporation tax receipts in particular, following several years of rapid growth. The 1998 Budget measures, which included the introduction of quarterly tax instalments for large companies, will bring forward the response of corporation tax to the slowdown in the economy. The ratio of corporation tax to GDP increased from 2·3 per cent in 1993–94 to 3·7 per cent in 1997–98. It is forecast to fall back to 3.4 per cent over the next two years, and then to remain at about 3·5 per cent thereafter.

B21   The growth of receipts picks up from 2000–01 as the economy demonstrates stronger growth. Excluding Budget measures, the underlying receipts-to-GDP ratio rises by about 0·1 per cent a year on average over the next five years, largely reflecting the effects of real fiscal drag on income tax receipts and the fuel and tobacco escalators.

Table B9: Current receipts

	Outturn	Estimate			Projections		
	1997–98	1998–99	1999–00	2000–01	2001–02	2002–03	2003–04
Income tax (gross of tax credits)	9·8	10·3	10·3	10·4	10·5	10·6	10·7
Income tax credits[1]	–0·4	–0·2	–0·3	–0·5	–0·7	–0·8	–0·8
of which: Working Families' Tax Credit	0·0	0·0	–0·1	–0·5	–0·6	–0·6	–0·6
Corporation tax	3·7	3·5	3·4	3·4	3·6	3·6	3·5
Windfall tax	0·3	0·3	0·0	0·0	0·0	0·0	0·0
Value added tax	6·2	6·1	6·1	6·1	6·1	6·1	6·0
Excise duties[2]	4·1	4·2	4·1	4·4	4·4	4·5	4·6
Social security contributions	6·3	6·5	6·3	6·2	6·2	6·2	6·2
Other taxes and royalties[3]	6·4	6·5	6·6	6·7	6·9	6·9	6·9
Net taxes and social security contributions[4]	**36·6**	**37·2**	**36·6**	**36·7**	**37·0**	**37·0**	**37·1**
Other receipts and accounting adjustments[5]	2·3	2·2	2·6	2·7	2·5	2·6	2·5
Current receipts (including windfall tax)[6]	38·9	39·4	39·2	39·4	39·5	39·6	39·7
Current receipts (excluding windfall tax)[6]	**38·6**	**39·2**	**39·4**	**39·5**	**39·6**	**39·6**	**39·7**
Memo:							
Current receipts (£bn)[6]	315·7	334·2	345	364	385	405	425

Per cent of GDP

[1] *Mainly MIRAS (up to April 2000), and tax reliefs under the Working Families' Tax Credit (from October 1999) and the Children's Tax Credit (from April 2001) schemes.*

[2] *Fuel, alcohol and tobacco duties.*

[3] *Includes Council Tax and money paid into the National Lottery Distribution Fund, as well as other central government taxes. Net of bus fuel duty rebate. Includes Climate change levy.*

[4] *Includes VAT and 'own resources' contributions to EU budget. Net of income tax credits. Cash basis.*

[5] *Includes tax credits (and accruals adjustments), and nets off VAT and 'own resources' contributions to EU budget.*

[6] *Accruals basis.*

Table B10: Current receipts: further details

	£ billion		
	Outturn 1997–98	Estimate 1998–99	Forecast 1999–00
Inland Revenue			
Income tax (gross of tax credits)	79·8	87·5	90·8
Income tax credits	–2·9	–2·0	–2·8
Corporation tax[1]	30·4	29·8	29·9
Windfall tax	2·6	2·6	0·0
Petroleum revenue tax	1·0	0·5	0·1
Capital gains tax	1·5	2·4	3·2
Inheritance tax	1·7	1·8	2·0
Stamp duties	3·5	4·7	5·7
Total Inland Revenue (net of tax credits)	**117·5**	**127·3**	**128·9**
Customs and Excise			
Value added tax	50·6	51·7	54·0
Fuel duties	19·4	21·5	23·1
Tobacco duties	8·4	8·3	7·0
Spirits duties	1·5	1·6	1·6
Wine duties	1·4	1·5	1·6
Beer and cider duties	2·8	2·8	2·9
Betting and gaming duties	1·6	1·5	1·5
Air passenger duty	0·5	0·8	0·8
Insurance premium tax	1·0	1·2	1·4
Landfill tax	0·4	0·3	0·4
Customs duties and levies	2·3	2·0	1·8
Total Customs and Excise	**89·8**	**93·4**	**96·2**
Vehicle excise duties	4·5	4·6	4·6
Oil royalties	0·5	0·3	0·2
Business rates[2]	14·9	15·2	15·6
Social security contributions	51·1	54·9	55·7
Council Tax	11·0	11·8	12·8
Other taxes and royalties[3]	8·0	7·7	7·9
Net taxes and social security contributions[4]	**297·2**	**315·2**	**321·8**
Interest and dividends	4·2	4·2	3·7
Gross operating surpluses and rent	17·6	18·3	18·4
Other receipts and accounting adjustments[5]	–3·2	–3·5	1·0
Current receipts	**315·7**	**334·2**	**344·3**
Memo:			
North Sea revenues[6]	3·3	2·6	1·2

[1] Includes advance corporation tax (net of payment):

	11·5	11·0	0·7

  Also includes North Sea corporation tax after ACT set off, and corporation tax on gains.

[2] Includes district council rates in Northern Ireland.

[3] Net of bus fuel duty rebate . Includes money paid into the National Lottery Distribution Fund.

[4] Includes VAT and 'traditional own resources' contributions to EU budget. Net of income tax credits. Cash basis.

[5] Includes accruals adjustments and tax credits scored as public expenditure, and nets off VAT and 'own resources' contributions to EU budget.

[6] North Sea corporation tax (before ACT set-off), petroleum revenue tax and royalties.

Comparison with last Pre-Budget forecast

B22   Total receipts are estimated to be £1·7 billion lower in 1998-99 than forecast at the time of the PBR, and are forecast to be £3·0 billion lower in 1999–2000.

Table B11: Changes in current receipts since the PBR

	£ billion	
	1998–99	1999–00
Income tax (gross of tax credits)	0·5	–1·9
Income tax credits	0·0	0·0
Corporation tax	–1·6	–0·2
Windfall tax	0·0	0·0
Value added tax	–0·9	–1·0
Excise duties[1]	–0·4	–2·4
Social security contributions	0·1	–1·3
Other taxes and royalties[2]	–0·2	1·8
Net taxes and NICs	–2·5	–5·0
Other receipts and accounting adjustments	0·8	1·9
Current receipts	**–1·7**	**–3·0**

[1] Fuel, alcohol and tobacco duties.

[2] Includes Council Tax and money paid into the National Lottery Distribution Fund, as well as other central government taxes. Net of bus fuel duty rebate (previously netted off excise duties).

Income tax receipts

B23   Higher receipts from self assessment and PAYE have boosted current year income tax receipts, which have been revised up by £1/2 billion since the PBR. The introduction of self assessment contributed to the rapid growth of income tax receipts last year. Self assessment receipts have risen a little further in 1998–99, suggesting that self assessment has led to a permanent step increase in the tax base. The lower forecast of income tax payments for 1999–2000 mostly reflects the introduction of the 10p lower rate of income tax.

Corporation tax

B24   Following weaker than expected receipts of advance corporation tax (ACT) and mainstream payments, corporation tax in 1998–99 is likely to fall short of the PBR forecast by about £1 1/2 billion. This partly reflects lower dividends for some companies and higher than expected set off of previous ACT payments. With the abolition of ACT in April 1999, the impact on forecasts is relatively small.

VAT receipts

B25   VAT receipts have been slightly weaker than expected since the PBR, and the estimate for the current year has been revised down by £0·9 billion. The latest figures suggest a slight fall in the ratio of VAT receipts to consumer spending in 1998–99, following a slight increase in 1997–98. The projections continue to assume a modest downward trend in the VAT ratio – an assumption audited by the NAO. Compared with a flat VAT ratio, this cautious assumption reduces receipts by over £1 billion by 2003–04.

Excise duties

B26   Excise duties are expected to fall short of the PBR estimate by about £0.4 billion this year and £2·4 billion in 1999–2000.

B27   Bringing forward the tobacco duty escalator from December to March increases tax accruals. Tax accruals measure receipts at the time the product is finally sold, and this is the basis on which total current receipts are shown in Tables B9 and B10. The timing of cash receipts is also likely to change, which affects the cash figures for excise duties shown in the two tables. With the December escalator, a high proportion of the year's tobacco duty was collected in December as manufacturers anticipated the annual tax increases by accelerating clearances. In the absence of such forestalling, there is likely to be a temporary dip in cash receipts in 1999–2000. An offsetting accruals adjustment is included in the 'accounting adjustments'.

B28   The forecast of receipts from tobacco duty also takes account of new evidence, available since the PBR, that cigarette smuggling and the loss of revenue associated with it, has been growing rapidly. It is very hard to predict the extent of the future loss of receipts from smuggling. The Government is taking measures to tackle the problem – see Chapter 1.

B29   Forecast receipts from excise duties are also lower by about £ $^1/_2$ billion a year because of the switch to consumption of cleaner fuels associated with the rapidly growing availability of ultra low sulphur diesel and, from the end of this year, the ban on leaded petrol.

Social security contributions

B30   Social security (national insurance) contributions have grown strongly since the PBR and the estimate for receipts in the current year has been revised up slightly. Nonetheless, the forecast for 1999–2000 has been revised down by £1·3 billion since the PBR. This partly reflects upward revisions to the costings of the 1998 Budget reforms.

Other taxes and receipts

B31   Overall, the yield from other taxes and receipts since the PBR has been much as expected. The forecast for 1999–2000 has been revised up significantly however. This reflects in part higher forecasts of capital taxes and stamp duty following a recovery in equity prices since November, together with upward revisions to business rates.

Total taxes

B32   Chart B2 shows the tax/GDP ratio, measured as total taxes and social security contributions, net of tax credits, as a percentage of GDP (see the conventions section at the end of this Annex). It is forecast to fall by a $^1/_2$ percentage point next year. Apart from the windfall tax, which increased the tax ratio in 1998–99, this fall largely reflects the effects of the economic slowdown, especially on corporation tax receipts. Thereafter, the tax ratio is projected to rise (on average) by a little over 0.1 percentage points a year, mainly reflecting real fiscal drag.

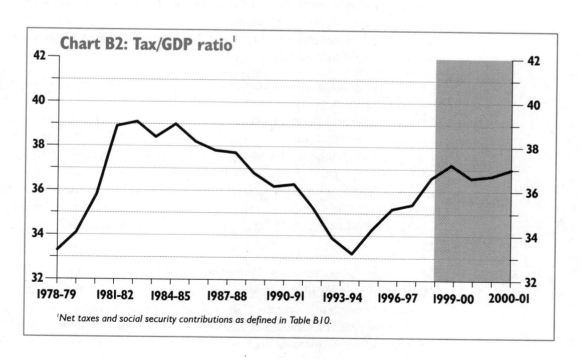

Chart B2: Tax/GDP ratio[1]

[1]Net taxes and social security contributions as defined in Table B10.

PUBLIC EXPENDITURE

Current year   **B33**   Table B12 shows forecasts for general government expenditure for the current year – the last of the old control regime – and changes against the PBR forecast. Control Total spending is estimated to be some £2 billion lower than planned, mainly because of lower expenditure on social security benefits (see table B19 for further details by department). This underspend is £3/4 billion greater than estimated in the PBR, again reflecting lower social security spending.

Table B12: General government expenditure[1]

		£ billion	
	Outturn 1997–98	Estimate 1998–99	Change since PBR 1998–99
Control Total	**263·5**	**273·4**	**–0·8**
Welfare to Work spending	0·1	0·7	–0·4
LA spending under the capital receipts initiative	0·2	0·7	0
Cyclical social security	12·8	12·3	0·1
Central government gross debt interest	29·7	29·5	0
Accounting and other adjustments	13·4	13·0	–0·1
Privatisation proceeds	–1·8	–0·1	0
GGE	**317·9**	**329·5**	**–1·1**

[1] Adjusted for classification change since the Pre-Budget Report.

PROSPECTS

B34   Table B13 shows the projections for public expenditure for the three years, 1999–2000 to 2001–02, covered by the Comprehensive Spending Review (CSR). These projections cover the whole public sector, using the aggregate Total Managed Expenditure (TME). TME is split into Departmental Expenditure Limits (DEL), for which three-year plans are set, and Annually Managed Expenditure (AME).

B35   Excluding classifications changes, DEL is unchanged from the CSR apart from bringing forward £1/4 billion of expenditure under the Capital Modernisation Fund from 2001–02 to 1999–2000. However the components of AME have been reviewed. Since the PBR there has been a downward revision to next year's forecast of social security benefit expenditure. This is in spite of the change in the unemployment assumption, and reflects consistently lower outturns over the past two years which have changed the view of future trends. Debt interest is lower, reflecting both lower interest rates and RPI inflation. The AME margin has been set at its CSR level. The overall effect is to reduce AME by £4·7 billion, £4·2 billion and £5·4 billion in 1999–00, 2000–01 and 2001–02 respectively. This decrease feeds directly through into lower TME.

B36   Current expenditure for 1999–2000 to 2001–02 is now lower than in the CSR (after adjusting for classification changes), because of the forecast reductions made to AME. The average real growth rate over the CSR period is 2 1/4 per cent, as set by the CSR in July 1998. As shown in the CSR, the ratio of net investment to GDP doubles between 1998–99 and 2001–02. (The levels of net investment are lower than shown in the CSR, but this mainly reflects ESA95 classification changes, which have substantially increased the estimated level of depreciation.)

B37   Chart B3 shows the ratio of TME to GDP. The ratio rises very slightly over the next three years, reflecting the higher levels of public investment.

Table B13: Total Managed Expenditure

	Forecast 1998–99	Forecast 1999–00	Forecast 2000–01	Forecast 2001–02	Changes since PBR		
					Forecast 1999–00	Forecast 2000–01	Forecast 2001–02
Departmental Expenditure Limits	168·0	179·2	189·7	199·5	0·2	0·0	–0·2
Annually Managed Expenditure							
Social Security Benefits[1]	93·5	99·1	101·5	106·4	0·3	1·0	0·6
Housing Revenue Account subsidies	3·7	3·4	3·5	3·5	–0·1	0·0	0·0
Common Agricultural Policy	2·6	2·4	2·7	2·9	–0·2	0·2	0·1
Export Credits Guarantee Department	–0·2	0·5	0·8	0·8	0·0	0·0	0·0
Net Payment to EC Institutions[2]	3·5	2·7	2·6	2·9	–0·1	–0·1	–0·1
Self-financing Public Corporations	–0·2	–0·1	–0·2	–0·3	0·1	0·1	0·1
Locally Financed Expenditure	16·1	17·0	18·3	19·8	0·0	0·1	0·2
Net Public Service Pensions	5·1	6·2	6·1	6·2	–0·1	–0·4	–0·7
National Lottery	1·4	2·6	2·7	2·8	0·0	0·0	0·0
Central government gross debt interest	29·5	26·0	27·6	27·1	–2·4	–0·8	–0·9
Accounting and other adjustments	8·3	9·3	11·7	12·9	–0·2	–1·6	–1·6
AME Margin		1·0	2·0	3·0	–2·0	–2·5	–3·0
Annually Managed Expenditure	163·4	170·0	179·1	187·8	–4·7	–4·2	–5·4
Total Managed Expenditure of which:	331·4	349·2	368·8	387·3	–4·4	–4·2	–5·6
Public sector current expenditure	313·5	328·9	346·1	362·0	–3·8	–3·3	–4·5
Public sector net investment	3·4	5·5	7·5	9·6	–0·7	–0·9	–1·1
Public sector depreciation	14·6	14·8	15·2	15·7	0·0	0·0	0·0

[1] Adjusted since the PBR to take account of the new NAO-audited assumption for unemployment-related social security spending, which raises social security spending by an estimated £1 billion in 1999–2000, £2 billion in 2000–01 and £2¼ billion in 2001–02.

[2] Net payments to EC institutions exclude the UK's contribution to the cost of EC aid to non-Member States (which is attributed to the aid programme). Net payments therefore differ from the UK's net contribution to the EC Budget, latest estimates for which are (in £ billion)

	1998–99	1999–00	2000–01	2001–02
Figures from 1999–2000 are trend estimates	4·0	3·2	3·4	3·8

B38 The CSR plans extend only to 2001-02. The spending totals for the last two years of the projection period are illustrative. They assume that real current expenditure continues to grow by 2¼ per cent a year and net investment continues to rise as a share of GDP (from 1 per cent in 2001–02 to 1½ per cent in 2003–04).

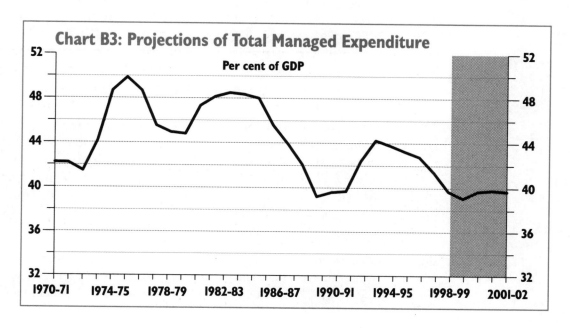

Chart B3: Projections of Total Managed Expenditure
Per cent of GDP

Social security   **B39**   The growth in real spending on social security benefits has slowed during the 1990s, and in 1997–98 spending fell by 1 per cent. Real expenditure is expected to be about constant in the current year, but is projected to rise by $2^3/_4$ per cent on average over the three CSR years. As noted above, this projection is based on an assumption of unemployment following the average of outside forecasts. This assumption has been audited by the NAO.

Debt interest   **B40**   Central government gross debt interest is estimated at £29·5 billion, or $3^1/_2$ per cent of GDP, for 1998-99. It is expected to fall quite sharply next year in response to a lower average level of interest rates and lower inflation. The forecasts are lower than those shown in the PBR as interest rates are assumed to be lower. (The audited assumption is that interest rates move in line with market expectations of future rates, which have come down substantially.) This reduces interest payments both on existing debt, and on debt which is refinanced at the current market rate. It also reduces the all-items RPI inflation rate, which is used to calculate the uplift on indexed gilts.

Accounting adjustments   **B41**   The main accounting adjustments – those items within TME but outside DEL which are not shown separately in table B13 – are shown in table B14. The total increases because of the introduction from October 1999 of the Working Families' Tax Credit.

Table B14: Accounting and other adjustments[1]

	£ billion			
	1998–99	1999–00	2000–01	2001–02
1 Non-trading capital consumption	7·1	7·3	7·6	7·8
2 VAT refunded on general government expenditure	5·1	5·3	5·5	5·8
3 EC contributions	–6·2	-5·8	-5·7	-5·8
4 Income tax credits	2·0	2·9	5·3	5·5
of which Working Families' and Disabled Persons' Tax Credit:	*0·0*	*1·3*	*5·1*	*5·4*
5 Other spending in AME	0·3	0·2	0·2	0·3
6 Adjustments for public corporations	2·9	3·4	3·8	3·9
7 Intra-public sector debt interest	-2·2	-2·0	-2·0	-1·9
8 Capital transfer receipts	-0·2	-0·2	-0·2	-0·2
9 Financial transactions in DEL and AME	-0·5	-1·9	-2·8	-2·5
10 Other accounting adjustments	0·1	0·0	0·0	0·0
Total	**8·3**	**9·3**	**11·7**	**12·9**

[1] *Explanatory notes for each line of the accounting and other adjustments are included in the conventions section.*

FORECAST ERRORS AND RISKS

B42   The fiscal balances are the difference between two large aggregates of spending and receipts, and forecasts of them are inevitably subject to wide margins of error. Over the past five years, the average absolute error (i.e. the average error irrespective of whether the errors have been positive or negative) for one-year ahead forecasts of net borrowing has been over 1 per cent of GDP, or plus or minus $£8^1/_2$ billion at today's prices. The error tends to grow as the forecast horizon lengthens (see table B13 on page 122 of the PBR). Much of this error arises from errors in the forecasts of GDP.

B43   Short-term forecasts of the public finances are critically dependent on the path of the economy, as most tax revenues and some public expenditure (especially social security) vary automatically with the economic cycle. If GDP growth were 1 per cent higher or lower than assumed over the coming year, net borrowing might be lower or higher by 0.4 per cent of GDP in the first year (equivalent to about £3½ billion) and lower or higher by a further 0.3 per cent of GDP (£2½ billion) in the second year.

B44   Such errors in short-term growth forecasts may have only a *temporary* effect on the public finances. For a given path of trend output, higher or lower growth in the short term will be followed by lower or higher growth later on, and the public finances may be little affected on average over the cycle. However, errors in estimating the cyclical position of the economy in relation to its trend – the output gap – will have a *permanent* effect on prospects.

B45   It is for this reason that Chapter 2 of the EFSR illustrates the effect of uncertainty over the cyclical position of the economy by showing a cautious case in which the output gap is 1 per cent higher than the central view. On this assumption, the Government would still remain on track to meet the golden rule.

CAPITAL SPENDING AND PRIVATE FINANCE INITIATIVE

Capital spending   **B46**   On national accounts definitions, public sector capital expenditure has been falling in recent years. However, these definitions exclude capital spending by the private sector under the Private Finance Initiative (PFI), which also benefits public services and is discussed in the next section.

Table B15: Public sector capital expenditure

	£ billion			
	1998–99	1999–00	2000–01	2001–02
CG spending and LA support in DEL	11·0	12·3	14·3	16·5
Locally financed spending	0·7	0·6	0·7	0·7
National Lottery	1·1	2·2	2·3	2·4
Public corporations[1]	4·2	4·3	4·3	4·5
Other capital spending in AME	1·0	0·7	0·9	1·0
Allocation of Reserve	0·0	0·1	0·2	0·2
Public sector gross investment[2]	**18·0**	**20·3**	**22·7**	**25·4**
Less depreciation	−14·6	−14·8	−15·2	−15·7
Public sector net investment[2]	**3·4**	**5·5**	**7·5**	**9·6**
Proceeds from the sale of fixed assets[3]	3·8	3·8	3·8	3·8

[1] *Public corporations' capital expenditure is partly within DEL and partly within AME.*

[2] *This and previous lines are all net of sales of fixed assets.*

[3] *Projections of total receipts from the sale of fixed assets by public sector. These receipts are taken into account in arriving at public sector gross and net investment, which are net of sales of fixed assets.*

Private Finance Initiative   **B47**   Under the Private Finance Initiative (PFI) the public sector purchases services from a private sector partner. In addition to requiring capital investment to be undertaken by the private sector, its ability to be innovative and manage risks appropriately allocated to it can result in a specified level of service at a price that represents value for money.

B48   The PFI has now become an established method of delivering many public services which require significant investment in capital assets. Projects with a combined capital value of around £4 billion have been signed since the General Election in such diverse areas as schools, colleges, hospitals, local authorities, defence, IT and property management. Approval of a PFI scheme depends on a thorough assessment of the lifetime costs of both providing and maintaining the underlying asset and the running costs of delivering the required service. The PFI provides considerable investment opportunities for the private sector, while, in return, the contractual relationship with the public sector ensures the ongoing delivery of cost effective and quality services.

B49 The Government is committed to developing PFI and other partnership arrangements with the private sector to enhance further the delivery of public services and ensure the delivery of a higher sustainable level of public sector investment. The Government wants to exploit all commercial potential and spare capacity in public sector assets through a sensible balance of risk and reward. A review of the progress made in the delivery of PFI and other Public Private Partnerships was announced in November 1998. Its purpose is to assist the Government to maintain the momentum for improvement in PFI and to extend this to other Public Private Partnerships, such as the Wider Markets Initiative which was launched in July 1998.

B50 Table B16 shows a breakdown by Department of the estimated public sector investment resulting from both signed contracts and those expected to be signed over the next three years. From 1999-000 to 2001-02, some £11 billion of new investment is expected as a result of PFI. Under PFI, the public sector contracts for services not assets, and capital investment is only one of the activities undertaken by the private sector in order to supply these services. The figures in Table B16 therefore do not reflect the total value of the contracts.

Table B16: Private Finance Initiative: estimated capital spending by the private sector

	£ million			
	1998–99	1999–00	2000–01	2001–02
Defence	320	105	405	150
Foreign Office and Overseas Development	24	29	4	2
Agriculture[1]	18	56	21	8
Trade and Industry	51	88	21	7
Environment, Transport and the Regions[2]	686	986	886	735
Education and Employment[3]	11	23	28	9
Home Office	67	257	331	266
Legal Departments	18	37	15	9
Culture, Media and Sport	1	18	11	2
Health	310	610	740	690
Social Security	87	264	166	20
Scotland	263	557	371	60
Wales	24	89	50	19
Northern Ireland	17	48	62	21
Chancellor's Departments	38	36	22	20
Local authorities[4]	250	600	1,000	1,000
Total	**2185**	**3803**	**4133**	**3018**

[1] Includes Forestry Commission.

[2] In June 1998 the Deputy Prime Minister announced that the CTRL deal was being restructured. The figures above reflect the current most likely profile for private sector investment although the profile may change as a result of on-going negotiations.

[3] Excludes PFI/PPP activity in the further and higher education sectors which are classified to the private sector. For further and higher education, the total estimated capital value of major PFI/PPP projects which have signed or are expecting to sign is £24 million in 1998–99 and £129 million in 1999–2000.

[4] PFI activity in local authority schools is included here. Also includes local authority information for Scotland and Wales.

B51 Table B17 shows a forecast of the estimated payments by the public sector flowing from new private investment over the next twenty five years. Actual expenditure will depend on the details of the payment mechanism for each contract.

Table B17: Private Finance Initiative: estimated payments under PFI contracts

£ million		£ million	
1999–00	1456	2013–14	3423
2000–01	1947	2014–15	3373
2001–02	2532	2015–16	3139
2002–03	3019	2016–17	3159
2003–04	3338	2017–18	3188
2004–05	3608	2018–19	2722
2005–06	3548	2019–20	2696
2006–07	3659	2020–21	2692
2007–08	3714	2021–22	2624
2008–09	3641	2022–23	2556
2009–10	3539	2023–24	2592
2010–11	3511	2024–25	2545
2011–12	3569	2025–26	2363
2012–13	3562	2026–27	2091

Asset sales **B52**   Table B18 shows estimated receipts from asset and loan sales for 1998–99, and projections to 2001–02. Planned sales of fixed assets by central government are set out in their Departmental Investment Strategies, and total £1 billion per year over the next three years.

B53   The figures for sales of financial assets include proceeds from the sale of British Energy debt and from the Public Private Partnerships for Belfast port, National Air Traffic Services and the Defence Evaluation and Research Agency.

Table B18: Loans and sales of assets

£ billion					
	Outturn	Estimate		Projections	
	1997–98	1998–99	1999–00	2000–01	2001–02
Sales of fixed assets					
Ministry of Defence: sale of married quarters	0·7				
Department of Social Security: PRIME and Newcastle estate	0·1	0·4			
Other Central Government	0·8	1·3	1·0	1·0	1·0
Local Authorities	2·5	2·2	2·8	2·8	2·8
Total sales of fixed assets	**4·1**	**3·8**	**3·8**	**3·8**	**3·8**
Loans and sales of financial assets					
Sale of Housing Corporation and Housing for Wales loan portfolios	0·7				
Sale of student loans portfolio	1·0	1·0	2·1		
Other loans and sales of financial assets	0·3	–1·5	0·0	–0·7	–1·1
Total loans and sales of financial assets	**2·0**	**–0·5**	**2·1**	**–0·7**	**–1·1**
Total receipts from sales of assets	**6·1**	**3·3**	**5·9**	**3·0**	**2·7**

DEPARTMENTAL PROGRAMMES

B54   Table B19 analyses the Control Total by department, showing changes from previous plans as published in the March 1998 *Financial Statement and Budget Report*. It also shows total changes from plans inherited from the previous Government, published in the March 1997 *Public Expenditure Statistical Analyses*. Central government support for local authorities and the financing requirements of nationalised industries have been attributed to the appropriate departments; departmental groupings are defined at the end of the annex.

Table B19: Control Total by department

			£ million[1]			
	Outturn	Estimated Outturn	Changes since[2] March 1998		Changes since[2] March 1997	
	1997–98	1998–99	1997–98	1998–99	1997–98	1998–99
Education and Employment	14290	14360	–400	1300	330	960
Health	35320	37640	–20	470	400	1970
of which NHS	*34680*	*36860*	*0*	*350*	*340*	*1770*
DETR	12380	11990	–210	–100	–320	–80
DETR – Local government[3]	31370	32760	0	0	0	860
Home Office	6730	7020	–90	120	–90	180
Legal departments	2640	2670	–50	30	–30	30
Defence	20920	22550	–230	300	–220	300
Foreign Office	1080	1120	–10	60	10	40
International Development	2240	2430	–20	140	50	130
Trade and Industry	2820	2700	–230	50	–220	100
Agriculture, Fisheries and Food	3510	3420	–110	50	–240	40
Culture, Media and Sport	910	920	0	10	20	0
Social Security	79230	81740	–390	–1920	–560	–1340
Scotland	14420	14940	–140	310	40	490
Wales	6820	7110	–140	140	–80	230
Northern Ireland	8140	8540	–140	130	–90	280
Chancellor's departments	3100	3190	–80	140	10	110
Cabinet Office	930	1350	–40	50	–110	10
European Communities	2050	3460	270	1020	–200	1070
LASFE	14300	14600	600	600	1100	1100
Reserve				–3000	–2300	–5000
Carry forward of underspending			750	–750	2250	–2250
Allowance for shortfall		–1200	400	–1200	0	–1200
Control Total	**263200**	**273400**	**–200**	**–2000**	**–200**	**–2000**

[1] *All figures are rounded to the nearest £10 million except for the Reserve, Control Total and Local Authority self-financed expenditure (LASFE) which are rounded to the nearest £100 million.*

[2] *Previous plans adjusted for transfer and classification changes and for the carry forward of £750 million from the 1997–98 underspend into the 1998–99 Control Total.*

[3] *Includes payments of Revenue Support Grant and National Non-domestic Rates to English local authorities. These finance, at local authorities' discretion, a range of local services, including education, social services and other environmental services.*

B55   In the July 1997 Budget the Government announced that it would work within the previous Government's plans for the first two years of the Parliament. Taking 1997–98 and 1998–99 together, it is estimated that spending will undershoot these plans by £2 billion.

B56   The main differences from the March 1997 plans are as follows:

- The extra resources for the NHS and schools announced since the General Election are reflected in the lines for local government and the territorial departments as well as those for Education and Health.

- The increases in the Education and Employment line also reflect a re-profiling of the sale of student loans and take up of end-year flexibility.

- A substantial underspend is expected on social security expenditure, which largely reflects lower than expected claimants.

- The increase in 1998–99 for net payments to European Community Institutions is largely due to a change introduced in 1998 to the financing practice for the EC Budget. Adjustments to be made in respect of the UK's gross contributions to the 1998 EC Budget, which under earlier practice would have been made in 1999, were drawn forward into 1998.

Table B20: Departmental Expenditure Limits – Current and Capital Budgets 1996–97 to 2001–02

| | £ billion | | | | | |
| | Outturns | | Estimate | | Plans | |
	1996–97	1997–98	1998–99	1999–00	2000–01	2001–02
Current Budget						
Education and Employment	13·4	14·0	13·7	14·5	15·8	16·8
Health	33·4	35·1	37·6	39·9	42·7	45·5
of which: NHS	*32·8*	*34·5*	*36·9*	*39·2*	*41·9*	*44·5*
DETR – Main programmes	4·2	4·1	4·1	4·4	4·6	4·8
DETR – Local Government and Regional Policy	31·2	31·1	32·4	33·9	35·4	36·9
Home Office	5·9	6·2	6·6	7·4	7·5	7·6
Legal Departments[1]	2·5	2·6	2·6	2·7	2·7	2·6
Defence	20·7	20·1	20·9	20·8	21·3	21·4
Foreign and Commonwealth Office	1·0	1·0	1·0	1·0	1·1	1·1
International Development	1·9	1·9	2·1	2·0	2·5	2·7
Trade and Industry[2]	2·8	2·7	2·7	2·9	3·1	3·1
Agriculture, Fisheries and Food[3]	1·8	1·4	1·2	1·1	1·0	1·0
Culture, Media and Sport	0·9	0·8	0·8	0·9	0·9	1·0
Social Security (administration)	3·4	3·4	3·5	3·3	3·4	3·4
Scotland[1]	11·4	11·5	11·7	12·2	12·8	13·3
Wales	5·4	5·6	5·9	6·3	6·7	7·0
Northern Ireland	4·8	4·9	5·2	5·3	5·5	5·5
Chancellor's Departments	2·7	2·7	2·9	3·0	3·1	3·1
Cabinet Office	1·0	0·8	1·2	1·2	1·1	1·1
Welfare to Work[4]		0·0	0·4	1·2	1·0	1·0
Invest to Save Budget (unallocated)				0·0	0·0	0·1
Capital Modernisation Fund (unallocated)				0·0	0·0	0·0
Reserve[4,5]				1·1	1·7	2·2
Allowance for shortfall			−1·5			
Total Current Budget	**148·3**	**149·8**	**155.1**	**165·3**	**174.0**	**181·6**
Capital Budget						
Education and Employment	0·8	0·7	1·0	1·2	1·7	2·1
Health	0·4	0·2	0·0	0·5	0·5	0·6
of which: NHS	*0·2*	*0·1*	*−0·1*	*0·4*	*0·5*	*0·6*
DETR – Main programmes	5·5	5·5	5·2	5·2	5·9	7·1
DETR – Local Government and Regional Policy	0·1	0·3	0·4	0·3	0·1	0·0
Home Office	0·5	0·5	0·4	0·4	0·4	0·4
Legal Departments[1]	0·1	0·1	0·1	0·1	0·1	0·1
Defence	0·7	0·9	1·6	1·5	1·5	1·5
Foreign and Commonwealth Office	0·1	0·1	0·1	0·1	0·1	0·1
International Development	0·2	0·2	0·2	0·3	0·3	0·4
Trade and Industry[2]	0·5	0·4	0·4	0·4	0·4	0·5
Agriculture, Fisheries and Food[3]	0·3	0·3	0·1	0·2	0·2	0·2
Culture, Media and Sport	0·1	0·1	0·1	0·1	0·1	0·1
Social Security (administration)	0·1	0·0	−0·3	0·0	0·1	0·1
Scotland[1]	1·5	1·4	1·6	1·7	1.7	1·9
Wales	1·0	0·9	0·9	0·8	0·8	0·8
Northern Ireland	0·5	0·5	0·5	0·5	0·6	0·6
Chancellor's Departments	0·2	0·2	0·1	0·2	0·0	0·1
Cabinet Office	0·2	0·2	0·2	0·3	0·2	0·2
Welfare to Work[4]		0·1	0·3	0·3	0·4	0·3
Invest to Save Budget (unallocated)				0·0	0·0	0·0
Capital Modernisation Fund (unallocated)				0·1	0·7	0·8
Reserve[4,5]				0·1	0·2	0·2
Total Capital Budget	**13·0**	**12·6**	**12·9**	**14·0**	**15·8**	**18·1**
Departmental Expenditure Limits	**161·3**	**162·3**	**168.0**	**179·2**	**189·7**	**199·5**
Total education spending[6]	36·2	37·4	38·3	41·3	44·8	48·0

[1] The Crown Office is included in the Lord Chancellor's Department figures up to 1998–99, and in the Scotland figures from 1999–2000, reflecting a machinery of government change. See Chapter 22 of the CSR White Paper for further details.

[2] Includes the capital expenditure of the Export Credits Guarantee Department.

[3] Includes spending on BSE related programmes.

[4] Figures are consistent with those published in the Pre-Budget Report, except that the DEL Reserve for 1998–99 has been set to zero.

[5] Reserve has been arbitrarily apportioned between current and capital, with 10% allocated to capital. Figures for 1998–99 have been set to zero.

[6] Central government spending on education falling within DEL plus locally financed education spending (in AME).

PUBLIC BORROWING BY SECTOR

Central **B57**   The monthly outturns for central government borrowing are measured from the cash
government flows into and out of central government's funds and accounts, after consolidation. Table B21
transactions on a sets out the 1997–98 outturn and 1998–99 and 1999–2000 forecasts for central government
cash basis borrowing in terms of this cash flow presentation, which is used in the ONS monthly press release

Table B21: Central government transactions

| | £ billion | | | |
| | 1997–98 | 1998–99 | | 1999–00 |
	Outturn	**Last Budget forecast[2]**	**Latest estimate**	**Forecast**
Cash receipts				
Inland Revenue[1]	117·6	126·1	127·5	130.3
Customs and Excise[1]	89·8	95·6	93·4	96.2
Social security	49·3	52·0	53·3	54·0
Interest and dividends	9·5	8·7	9·4	8·7
Other	20·9	19·9	20·2	18·7
Total cash receipts	**287·0**	**302·3**	**303·8**	**307.9**
Cash outlays				
Investment payments	27·7	27·6	27·1	24·6
Privatisation proceeds	−1·8	0·0	−0·1	−0·4
Net departmental outlays	263·7	277·5	272·7	288·5
Total cash outlays	**289·6**	**305·1**	**299·8**	**312·8**
Net cash requirement (own account)[3]	2·6	2·8	−4·1	4·9
less Financial transactions:				
Net lending to private sector and rest of world	0·4	−0·2	−0·5	1·2
Net acquisition of UK company securities	1·6	0·0	0·1	0·4
Accounts receivable/payable	−0·4	−1·8	−0·3	−4.0
Adjustment for interest on gilts	2·4	2·5	2·4	1·4
Other financial transactions	0·4	0·8	0·4	0·4
Net borrowing	**7·0**	**4·0**	**−1·9**	**4·2**

[1] *Payments to the Consolidated Fund.*

[2] *Restated on ESA95 basis.*

[3] *Total cash outlays (excluding on-lending to local government and public corporations) minus total cash receipts. Previously known as Central Government borrowing requirement on own account (CGBR(O)).*

B58   In 1998–99 estimates for both net borrowing and the own account net cash
requirement are substantially lower than the forecasts in the last Budget. The cash forecast is
almost £7 billion lower, partly because of lower cash outlays (down £5½ billion) and partly
higher cash receipts (up £1½ billion). The reduction in net borrowing is slightly smaller than
that to the cash requirement because of changes to the financial transactions – particularly a
reduction in accounts receivable, reflecting lower accruals of tax relative to cash for tobacco
duty and business rates.

B59   For 1999–2000, the forecast for net borrowing is £6 billion higher than in the current
year; but with changes to the financial transactions, own account net cash requirement is £9
billion higher. Net lending includes a larger sale of student loans in 1999–2000 than 1998–99.
The adjustment for interest on gilts is down because lower inflation in 1999–2000 reduces the
uplift on index-linked gilts. Higher accruals of tax relative to cash are forecast in 1999–2000,
particularly for tobacco duty and business rates.

Financing policy **B60** Table B22 updates the financing arithmetic for 1998–99 to allow for the latest central government net cash requirement forecast, and sets out the financing arithmetic for 1999–2000.

B61 The gilts issuance programme for 1998–99 was revised in November 1998, following the November PBR. However at that stage, gilt sales in 1998–99 had already reached £6·5 billion, against a revised gilts financing requirement in the PBR of £6·4 billion. The Government announced that, although there would be no further issuance of conventional gilts in 1998–99, the remaining index-linked auctions would take place as planned. If this resulted in excess gilt sales, such sales were necessary in order to meet the commitment to a minimum issuance of £2·5 billion (cash) of index-linked gilts in 1998–99 (and in future years) in support of the move to index–linked auctions. The latest view of the financing arithmetic in Table B22 shows forecast excess gilt sales of £2·3 billion in 1998–99. These excess sales will be unwound in 1999–2000 by a residual adjustment which reduces the initial requirement for gilt sales in that year.

B62 The requirement for gilt sales in 1999–2000 is further reduced by the increase in the level of the stock of Treasury bills and other short-term debt which will be required if, as planned, the Debt Management Office (DMO) take over responsibility for cash management in that year. However this is more than offset by the additional requirement in 1999–2000 to finance investment in the foreign currency reserves which has previously been financed by issuance of Euro Treasury bills. The main details of the debt management plans for 1999–2000 are contained in the remits to the UK Debt Management Office and National Savings announced on 9 March. Full details, including the remits, will be published in the 1999–2000 Debt Management Report.

Table B22: Financing requirement forecasts for 1998–99 and 1999–2000

					£ billion
			1998–99		1999–00
	March 1998 Original Remit	June 1998 EFSR	November 1998 PBR	March 1999 Budget	March 1999 Budget
Central government net cash requirement	3·7	3·5	–2·1	–2·7	6·2
plus expected net financing for reserves[1]	0·0	0·0	0·0	0·0	2·4
plus expected gilt redemptions	16·7	16·8	16·8	16·9[2]	14·8
plus residual unwinding excess gilt sales from previous financial year	–5·1	–8·2	–8·2	–8·2	–2·3
Financing requirement	15·2	12·1	6·5	6·1	21·0
less net National Savings inflow	1·0	0·5	0·1	0·2	0·1
less increase in T-bills and other short-term debt[3]	0·0	0·0	0·0	0·0	3·6
Gilt sales required	14·2	11·6	6·4	5·8	17·3
of which:					
assumed gilt sales:					
index-linked gilts				2·6	3·5
short conventional gilts (3-7 years)				0·0	5·0
medium conventional gilts (7-15 years)				2·5	3·0
long conventional gilts (>15 years)				3·1	5·8
reduction in short-term borrowing in-year to offset excess gilt sales				–2·3	

[1] The reserves require financing in 1999–2000 to replace 3.5 billion Euro currently raised by issues of Euro Treasury bills, estimated at the current exchange rate.

[2] Includes ESA95 reclassification of Bank of England holdings.

[3] The stock of Treasury bills and other short-term debt will need to increase during 1999–2000 to accommodate the DMO's cash management operations.

B63 Table B25 shows a full analysis of public sector receipts and expenditure by economic category with a breakdown between central government, local authorities and public corporations.

B64 Tables B23 and B24 summarise the information on local authorities' and public corporations' transactions that appear in Table B25. It is estimated that both public corporations and local authorities will make a small debt repayment this year, as they did in 1997–98. Their net borrowing is projected to be close to zero in 1999–2000.

B65 Table B26 presents forecasts of the net cash requirement by sector, giving details of the various financial transactions that do not affect net borrowing (the change in the sector's net financial indebtedness) but do affect its need to raise cash.

Table B23: Local authority transactions

| | £ billion | | |
	Outturn	Estimate	Forecast
	1997–98	1998–99	1999–00
Receipts			
Council Tax[1]	10·8	11·8	12·8
Current grants from central government	59·9	60·1	62·2
Other receipts[2]	9·7	10·4	10·0
Capital grants from central government	2·7	3·0	2·8
Total receipts	**83·1**	**85·4**	**87·9**
Expenditure			
Current expenditure on goods and services	57·2	59·3	61·0
Current grants and subsidies	14·7	14·1	15·1
Interest	4·4	4·3	4·1
Capital expenditure before depreciation	6·5	7·2	7·6
Total expenditure	**82·8**	**85·0**	**87·8[3]**
Net borrowing	**−0·3**	**−0·3**	**−0·1**

[1] Net of rebates and Council Tax benefit.

[2] Includes interest receipts, rent and gross operating surplus.

[3] Assumes no allocation from the Reserve.

Table B24: Public corporations' transactions

| | £ billion | | |
	Outturn	Estimate	Forecast
	1997–98	1998–99	1999–00
Receipts			
Gross operating surplus (including subsidies)	4·4	4·8	4·3
Other current grants	1·3	1·2	1·2
Capital grants from general government	1·7	1·6	1·3
Total receipts	**7·4**	**7·7**	**6·8**
Expenditure			
Interest, dividends and taxes on income	2·8	2·9	2·7
Capital expenditure before depreciation	4·4	4·2	4·3
Total expenditure	**7·2**	**7·0**	**7·0[1]**
Net borrowing	**−0·1**	**−0·7**	**0·2**

[1] Assumes no allocation from the Reserve.

Table B25: Public sector transactions by sub-sector and economic category

		£ billion				
		1998–99				
		General government			**Public corporations**	**Public sector**
	Line	Central government	Local authorities	Total		
Current receipts						
Taxes on income and wealth	1	123·6	0·0	123·6	–0·4	123·2
Taxes on production and imports	2	116·4	0·0	116·4	0·0	116·4
Other current taxes	3	3·2	12·3	15·5	0·0	15·5
Taxes on capital	4	1·8	0·0	1·8	0·0	1·8
Social contributions	5	55·0	0·0	55·0	0·0	55·0
Gross operating surplus	6	3·5	8·6	12·1	4·8	17·0
Rent and other current transfers	7	0·7	0·0	0·7	0·5	1·2
Interest and dividends from private sector and abroad	8	3·2	0·8	4·0	0·2	4·2
Interest and dividends from public sector	9	6·2	–3·9	2·3	–2·3	0·0
Total current receipts	10	**313·6**	**17·7**	**331·4**	**2·8**	**334·2**
Current expenditure						
Current expenditure on goods and services	11	95·9	59·3	155·2	0·0	155·2
Subsidies	12	4·7	0·8	5·5	0·0	5·5
Net social benefits	13	93·9	13·3	107·2	0·0	107·2
Net current grants abroad	14	–0·9	0·0	–0·9	0·0	–0·9
Current grants (net) within public sector	15	60·1	–60·1	0·0	0·0	0·0
Other current grants	16	16·9	0·0	16·9	0·0	16·9
Interest and dividends paid	17	29·5	0·4	30·0	–0·4	29·6
Apportionment of DEL Reserve and AME margin	18	0·0	0·0	0·0	0·0	0·0
Total current expenditure	19	**300·1**	**13·8**	**313·8**	**–0·4**	**313·5**
Depreciation	20	3·8	6·3	10·2	4·4	14·6
Surplus on current budget	21	**9·7**	**–2·3**	**7·4**	**–1·2**	**6·2**
Capital expenditure						
Gross domestic fixed capital formation	22	4·4	6·0	10·5	4·2	14·6
Less depreciation	23	–3·8	–6·3	–10·2	–4·4	–14·6
Increase in inventories	24	0·1	0·0	0·1	0·0	0·1
Capital grants (net) within public sector	25	4·6	–3·0	1·6	–1·6	0·0
Capital grants to private sector	26	2·6	1·2	3·8	0·0	3·8
Capital grants from private sector	27	0·0	–0·5	–0·5	0·0	–0·6
Apportionment of DEL Reserve	28	0·0	0·0	0·0	0·0	0·0
Net capital expenditure	29	**7·9**	**–2·7**	**5·3**	**–1·9**	**3·4**
Public sector net borrowing	30	**–1·9**	**–0·3**	**–2·2**	**–0·7**	**–2·8**

Table B25: Public sector transactions by sub-sector and economic category

	£ billion					
	1999–2000					
	General government					
Line	Central government	Local authorities	Total	Public corporations	Public sector	
						Current receipts
1	125·1	0·0	125·1	–0·4	124·7	Taxes on income and wealth
2	123·8	0·0	123·8	0·0	123·8	Taxes on production and imports
3	3·1	12·8	15·9	0·0	15·9	Other current taxes
4	2·0	0·0	2·0	0·0	2·0	Taxes on capital
5	56·1	0·0	56·1	0·0	56·1	Social contributions
6	4·4	8·8	13·2	4·3	17·5	Gross operating surplus
7	0·7	0·0	0·7	0·4	1·1	Rent and other current transfers
8	2·8	0·6	3·5	0·2	3·7	Interest and dividends from private sector and abroad
9	5·9	–3·7	2·1	–2·1	0·0	Interest and dividends from public sector
10	**323·8**	**18·6**	**342·4**	**2·4**	**344·9**	**Total current receipts**
						Current expenditure
11	102·5	61·0	163·5	0·0	163·5	Current expenditure on goods and services
12	4·6	0·8	5·4	0·0	5·4	Subsidies
13	100·5	14·3	114·8	0·0	114·8	Net social benefits
14	–1·2	0·0	–1·2	0·0	–1·2	Net current grants abroad
15	62·2	–62·2	0·0	0·0	0·0	Current grants (net) within public sector
16	18·4	0·0	18·4	0·0	18·4	Other current grants
17	26·0	0·4	26·3	–0·3	26·0	Interest and dividends paid
18	2·1	0·0	2·1	0·0	2·1	Apportionment of DEL Reserve and AME margin
19	**315·1**	**14·2**	**329·3**	**–0·3**	**328·9**	**Total current expenditure**
20	4·0	6·5	10·5	4·4	14·8	Depreciation
21	**4·8**	**–2·2**	**2·7**	**–1·6**	**1·1**	**Surplus on current budget**
						Capital expenditure
22	5·2	6·4	11·6	4·3	15·9	Gross domestic fixed capital formation
23	–4·0	–6·5	–10·5	–4·4	–14·8	*Less* depreciation
24	0·0	0·0	0·0	0·0	0·0	Increase in inventories
25	4·1	–2·8	1·3	–1·3	0·0	Capital grants (net) within public sector
26	3·6	1·2	4·9	0·0	4·9	Capital grants to private sector
27	0·0	–0·6	–0·6	0·0	–0·6	Capital grants from private sector
28	0·1	0·0	0·1	0·0	0·1	Apportionment of DEL Reserve
29	**9·0**	**–2·2**	**6·8**	**–1·3**	**5·5**	**Net capital expenditure**
30	**4·2**	**–0·1**	**4·1**	**0·2**	**4·3**	**Public sector net borrowing**

Table B26: Net cash requirement[1]

	1998–99				1999–2000			£ billion
	Central govern-ment	Local auth-orities	Public corpor-ations	Public sector	Central govern-ment	Local auth-orities	Public corpor-ations	Public sector
Net borrowing	**–1·9**	**–0·3**	**–0·7**	**–2·8**	**4·2**	**–0·1**	**0·2**	**4·3**
Financial transactions								
Net lending to private sector and abroad	0·5	–0·1	0·0	0·5	–1·2	–0·1	0·0	–1·3
Cash expenditure on company securities (including privatisation proceeds)	–0·1	0·0	0·0	–0·1	–0·4	0·0	0·0	–0·4
Accounts receivable/ payable	0·3	0·0	0·0	0·3	4·0	–0·4	0·0	3·6
Adjustment for interest on gilts	–2·4	0·0	0·0	–2·4	–1·4	0·0	0·0	–1·4
Miscellaneous financial transactions	–0·4	0·1	–0·2	–0·5	–0·4	0·0	0·0	–0·4
Net cash requirement	**–4·1**[2]	**–0·3**	**–0·9**	**–5·2**	**4·9**[2]	**–0·5**	**0·2**	**4·5**

[1] *Excluding windfall tax and associated spending, the public sector net cash requirement is forecast at –£3.4 billion (-0.4 per cent of GDP) for 1998-99 and £3.0 billion (0.3 per cent of GDP) for 1999-2000. It is projected at £5 billion (0·5 per cent of GDP) for 2000–01 and £3 billion (0·3 per cent of GDP) for 2001–02.*

[2] *Own account.*

HISTORICAL SERIES

B66   Tables B27 and B28 set out historical data for the main fiscal aggregates.

Table B27: Historical series of public sector balances, receipts and debt

| | Per cent of GDP | | | | | | | | |
	Current budget[1]	Net borrowing[1]	Net cash requirement[1]	General government net borrowing[2]	Net taxes and social security contributions	Current receipts	Public sector net debt[3]	General government gross debt[4]	Net wealth[5]
1970–71	7·0	−0·6	1·2	−2·0		42·8	69·6	78.2	41·7
1971–72	4·5	1·0	1·5	−0·7		41·2	65·2	73.8	48·1
1972–73	2·2	2·9	3·7	2·2		38·6	58·5	67·1	60·0
1973–74	1·0	4·5	5·7	4·1		39·7	58·4	67.0	76·8
1974–75	−0·6	6·4	8·8	4·0		42·3	54·9	63·5	78·0
1975–76	−1·3	7·1	9·1	4·8		42·8	56·5	65·1	66·5
1976–77	−1·0	5·6	6·4	4·2		43·1	55·2	63·8	63·9
1977–78	−1·1	4·3	3·8	3·6		41·3	51·9	60·5	58·6
1978–79	−2·1	4·8	5·1	4·0	33·3	40·2	48·7	57·3	64·9
1979–80	−1·4	3·9	4·8	2·8	34·1	40·9	44·8	53·4	71·8
1980–81	−2·6	4·6	5·2	3·6	35.8	42·7	46·7	55·3	77·1
1981–82	−1·0	2·1	3·4	3·1	38·9	46·0	46·9	55·5	74·7
1982–83	−1·3	3·0	3·2	3·1	39·1	45·5	45·4	54·0	67·1
1983–84	−1·8	3·8	3·2	3·8	38·4	44·6	45·8	54·4	65·5
1984–85	−2·5	4·2	3·1	3·8	39·0	43·9	46·0	54·6	61·4
1985–86	−1·0	2·3	1·6	2·6	38·2	43·3	44·2	52·8	61·0
1986–87	−1·3	2·1	0·9	2·6	37·8	41·8	41·7	50·3	66·6
1987–88	−0·2	0·9	−0·8	1·3	37·7	41·1	37·5	46·1	69·1
1988–89	1·9	−1·5	−3·0	−1·0	36·8	40·7	31·1	39·7	76·4
1989–90	1·7	−0·4	−1·4	−0·1	36·2	40·0	28·1	36·7	71·9
1990–91	0·8	0·7	−0·1	1·5	36·3	39·0	26·7	35·3	60·4
1991–92	−1·7	3·6	2·3	3·1	35·2	38·8	27·8	36·4	53·5
1992–93	−5·7	7·8	5·9	7·4	33·9	36·5	32·6	41·2	40·7
1993–94	−6·2	7·9	7·1	7·9	33·2	35·9	37·7	46·9	28·1
1994–95	−4·8	6·3	5·3	6·5	34·3	36·9	41·2	50·4	25·3
1995–96	−3·5	4·9	4·4	4·8	35·2	37·9	43·3	53·2	19·9
1996–97	−3·0	3·7	3·0	3·9	35·4	37·7	44·3	53·6	18·1
1997–98	−0·6	1·1	0·4	0·6	36·6	38·9	42·5	50·8	14·8
1998–99	0·5	−0·1	−0·4	−0·6	37·2	39·4	40·6	48·8	13·7
1999–00	0·3	0·3	0·3	0·4	36·6	39·2	39·4	47·7	15·5

[1] Excluding windfall tax receipts and associated spending.

[2] On UK national accounts definition prior to 1991–92 and Maastricht basis thereafter.

[3] At end-March, GDP centred on end-March.

[4] Maastricht basis, at end-March, GDP centred on end-September. Treasury estimates prior to 1992–93.

[5] At end-December; GDP centred on end-December.

Table B28: Historical series of government expenditure

	£ billion (1997–98 prices)				Per cent of GDP			
	Current expenditure	Net capital expenditure	General government expenditure	Total Managed Expenditure	Current expenditure	Net capital expenditure	General government expenditure	Total Managed Expenditure
1970–71	143·4	29·0	183·2	188·5	32·1	6·5	41·0	42·2
1971–72	150·2	25·3	188·8	192·3	32·9	5·5	41·4	42·2
1972–73	157·5	24·5	196·5	199·6	32·7	5·1	40·8	41·5
1973–74	173·4	27·5	211·6	220·7	34·7	5·5	42·4	44·2
1974–75	191.9	28·8	238·0	242·1	38·6	5·8	47·8	48·7
1975–76	196·3	28·5	238·1	246·2	39·8	5·8	48·2	49·9
1976–77	201.8	23·4	231·9	247·4	39·7	4·6	45·6	48·7
1977–78	198·6	16·4	221·0	237·2	38·1	3·1	42·4	45·5
1978–79	204·5	14·3	231·5	241·7	38·0	2·7	43·1	44·9
1979–80	210·9	13·6	237·9	247·4	38·2	2·5	43·1	44·8
1980–81	217·6	10·6	245·3	252·1	40·9	2·0	46·1	47·3
1981–82	227·0	5·9	248·9	256·5	42·6	1·1	46·7	48·1
1982–83	232·6	9·2	254·5	264·6	42·6	1·7	46·6	48·5
1983–84	239·5	10·9	257·6	273·3	42·4	1·9	45·6	48·3
1984–85	245·8	9·6	262·9	277·4	42·5	1·7	45·5	48·0
1985–86	246·6	8·0	261·8	274·3	41·0	1·3	43·5	45·6
1986–87	250·5	5·0	261·3	275·6	39·9	0·8	41·6	43·9
1987–88	253·6	5·0	262·3	276·9	38·5	0·8	39·8	42·1
1988–89	247·7	2·9	255·8	269·7	36·0	0·4	37·2	39·2
1989–90	249·0	9·2	268·1	277·1	35·6	1·3	38·3	39·6
1990–91	250·3	10·5	268·9	277·5	35·8	1·5	38·5	39·7
1991–92	265·2	13·3	281·4	292·6	38·4	1·9	40·8	42·4
1992–93	279·2	14·6	297·2	307·0	40·2	2·1	42·8	44·2
1993–94	287·8	12·1	306·4	312·7	40·3	1·7	42·9	43·8
1994–95	298·0	11·3	314·7	322·6	40·0	1·5	42·2	43·3
1995–96	302·4	10·2	321·6	326·7	39·6	1·3	42·1	42·8
1996–97	304·9	5·6	316·9	324·3	38·9	0·7	40·4	41·4
1997–98	304·3	4·0	317·5	322·3	37·5	0·5	39·1	39·7
1998–99	305·8	3·3	321·5	323·3	37·0	0·4	38·9	39·1
1999–00	313	5	330	332	37·4	0·6	39·4	39·7

CONVENTIONS USED IN PRESENTING THE PUBLIC FINANCES

Box B1: New format for the public finances

The last Economic and Fiscal Strategy Report (EFSR) in June 1998, set out a new format for presenting the public finances that corresponded more closely to the two fiscal rules. The three principal measures are:

- the surplus on *current budget* (relevant to the golden rule);
- public sector *net borrowing*; and
- the public sector *net debt ratio* (relevant to the sustainable investment rule).

These measures are based on the national accounts and are consistent with the new European System of Accounts 1995 (ESA95).

The fiscal rules are similar to the criteria for deficits and debt laid down in the Maastricht treaty but there are important definitional differences:

- UK fiscal rules cover the whole public sector, whereas Maastricht includes only general (*ie* central and local) government;
- the fiscal rules apply over the whole economic cycle, not to individual years;
- the UK debt measure is net of liquid assets, whereas Maastricht uses gross debt; and
- until February 2000 the Maastricht deficit remains on the old, more cash-based, European System of Accounts 1979 (ESA79).

NATIONAL ACCOUNTS

The national accounts record most transactions, including most taxes (although not corporation tax), on an accruals basis, and impute the value of some transactions where no money changes hands (for example, non-trading capital consumption). The principal fiscal balances are described below.

The **current budget** (formerly known as the current balance) measures the balance of current account revenue over current expenditure. The definition of the current balance presented in Tables B[5 -7] is very similar to the national accounts concept of net saving. It differs only in that it includes inheritance tax (mainly death duties) in current rather than capital receipts.

Public sector net borrowing (formerly known as the financial deficit in the UK national accounts) is the balance between expenditure and income in the consolidated current and capital accounts. It differs from the public sector net cash requirement because it is measured on an accruals basis and because certain financial transactions (notably net lending and privatisation proceeds, which affect the level of borrowing but not the public sector's net financial indebtedness) are excluded from public sector net borrowing but included in the public sector net cash requirement.

General government net borrowing, which excludes net borrowing of public corporations, is the most internationally comparable measure of the budget deficit. It is reported to the European Commission under the Maastricht Treaty, using the definitions in ESA79. This Maastricht definition differs from that in the UK national accounts in that it scores interest on a predominantly cash basis. The capital uplift on index-linked gilts is scored at the time of the gilt's redemption (as in the net cash requirement), rather than on an accrued basis over the lifetime of the gilt. Interest on national savings certificates is scored when withdrawn, rather than when it accrues (as in both the UK national accounts and the public sector net cash requirement). The Maastricht definition also excludes discounts at issue on gilts, which are amortised over the life of the gilt in the UK national accounts.

CASH BASIS

The cash approach measures the actual cash transactions between the public sector and the rest of the economy. It is the starting point for monthly estimates of net borrowing. Table B26 shows, for central government, the determinants of the net cash requirement and the financial transactions that are deducted to reach net borrowing. The cash basis also corresponds closely to the way public expenditure is currently planned, controlled and accounted for, though this will change with the introduction of Resource Accounting and Budgeting next year.

Box B2: New monthly data

In July 1998, the monthly First Release on the public finances was expanded to include monthly estimates of *net borrowing* (previously the release showed only the public sector *net cash requirement*). In January 1999, it was expanded further to include monthly estimates of net public sector debt. The release still shows the cash measures, which remain of interest for measuring financing requirements for the purpose of debt management.

In February 1999, the Office for National Statistics (ONS) began publication of a new quarterly First Release *Provisional Public Sector Accounts*. This gives quarterly information on the public sector in national accounts, such as the surplus on current budget, some three or four weeks before the publication of the main quarterly national accounts.

Development work is being undertaken by ONS to produce monthly estimates of the current budget surplus. Subject to feasibility, publication will begin in Autumn 1999.

Monthly Statistics on Public Sector Finances – A methodological guide was published in January 1999 as No. 12 in the GSS Methodology Series. This describes in detail the derivation of the monthly estimates of net borrowing, net debt and net cash requirement that now appear in the ONS's monthly Public Sector Finances First Release.

PUBLIC SECTOR CURRENT RECEIPTS

Net taxes and social security contributions in Tables B9 and B10 are measured on a cash basis, rather than a national accounts (accruals) basis, and, as far as possible, relate to actual cash flows. Income tax credits are netted off. VAT is net of refunds to the public sector. Social security contributions are scored gross of amounts netted off by employers as reimbursement in respect of statutory sick pay and statutory maternity pay. (These payments count as expenditure rather than negative receipts.) "Good causes" receipts from the National Lottery are included.

The accounting adjustments put these cash figures on to a national accounts (accruals) basis. Tax credits which score as expenditure in the national accounts are added back. VAT refunded within the public sector is added back. Those elements of the UK contribution to the EC budget which relate to the UK tax base are deducted as, under ESA95, they are treated for national accounts as taxes imposed directly by the EU.

Certain income tax reliefs are payable regardless of an individual's liability to income tax; thus some payments are made to non-taxpayers. Examples are mortgage interest relief paid under the MIRAS (mortgage interest relief at source) scheme, life assurance premium relief on pre-1984 policies and private medical insurance premium relief for over-60s. The Working Families' Tax Credit will also fall into this category. Total tax relief paid under these schemes is shown as income tax credits in Tables B9 and B10. Income tax receipts in these tables are shown gross of these tax credits. All such tax credits are shown in the national accounts as expenditure.

From 2001–02, income tax credits (Table B9) include the new Children's Tax Credit.

TOTAL MANAGED EXPENDITURE (TME)

Box B3: New public expenditure control regime

The last Economic and Fiscal Strategy Report (EFSR) in June 1998 also reformed the planning and control regime for public spending.

- **Overall plans are based on sound economic principles, with a new distinction between current and capital spending;**

- **Firm 3-year plans (Departmental Expenditure Limits – DEL) will provide certainty and flexibility for long-term planning and management;**

- **Spending outside DEL – Annually Managed Expenditure (AME) – which cannot reasonably be subject to firm multi-year limits commitments, will be reviewed annually as part of the Budget process. This review is to ensure that spending within AME remains consistent with the fiscal rules;**

- **Large public corporations, not dependent on government grants, will have more flexibility.**

Detailed plans under this regime were given in the Comprehensive Spending Review in July 1998 for the years 1999–00 to 2001–02.

Public sector **capital expenditure** is shown in Table B15. It includes:

(i)   gross domestic fixed capital formation (ie expenditure on fixed assets – schools, hospitals, roads, computers, plant and machinery, intangible assets etc) net of receipts from sales of fixed assets (eg council houses and surplus land);

(ii)   grants in support of capital spending by the private sector; and

(iii)   the value of the physical increase in stocks (for central government, primarily agricultural commodity stocks).

Net investment in Tables B5 and B6 nets off depreciation of the public sector's stock of fixed assets.

Departmental Expenditure Limits (DEL) have distinct current and capital budgets, shown in Table B20. The departmental groupings used in this table are defined at the end of the Annex. The numbers are on present definitions, there have been a number of classification changes since the PBR. The main changes are: pensions paid by the Department for International Development have been moved out of DEL and into AME; the product of Northern Ireland regional rates is now treated as part of AME and reduces DEL; and the redundancy payments scheme has been moved from DEL to AME. Total classification changes reduce DEL by £0·2 billion, £0·3 billion and £0·4 billion for the three forward years. Tables B12 and B19 show the old public expenditure **Control Total**, including changes from the PBR, for 1998–99, its final year of operation.

Annually Managed Expenditure (AME) components are shown in Table B13. These include all of social security benefit spending, housing revenue account subsidies, the Common Agricultural Policy, export credits, net payments to EC institutions, spending by self financing public corporations, public service pensions net of contributions, spending financed by the national lottery and central government gross debt interest.

Total Managed Expenditure (TME), the sum of DEL and AME, is shown in Table B13.

The **Export Credits Guarantee Department** programme includes a classification change since the CSR. The activities of the Guaranteed Export Finance Corporation (GEFCO), whose sole business is to refinance export loans guaranteed by ECGD, thus reducing the cost to Government, have been reclassified to central government and are now included. GEFCO's past activities are now regarded as agency transactions undertaken for the government, as is the funding raised by GEFCO. Its future activities will be funded through ECGD. However, although the refinancing activities are financial transactions affecting only the net cash requirement and so are netted out in the accounting adjustments, they do affect the Control Total as a classification change.

Locally financed expenditure comprises local authority self-financed expenditure (LASFE) and Scottish spending financed by local taxation (non-domestic rates and, if and when levied, the Scottish variable rate of income tax). LASFE is the difference between total local authority expenditure, including most gross debt interest but net of capital receipts, and central government support to local authorities (ie Aggregate External Finance (AEF), specific grants and credit approvals).

Central government debt interest is shown gross. Only interest paid within central government is netted off; all other receipts of interest and dividends are included in current receipts. The capital uplift on index-linked gilts is scored as interest at the time it accrues, whereas the cash tables record the actual payments of capital uplift on index-linked gilts, and includes the amortisation of discounts on gilts at issue. Following the GEFCO reclassification, interest is included on the net funds raised by that body (£114 million in 1997–98)

The **accounting adjustments** include various items within TME but outside DEL which are not shown separately in Table B13. These details are shown in Table B14. The definition of each line is as follows:

- *Line one* adds the value of general government non-trading capital consumption.

- *Line two* adds back VAT refunded to central government departments and local government. Departmental Expenditure Limits and Annually Managed Expenditure programme expenditure are measured net of these refunds, while Total Managed Expenditure is recorded including the VAT paid. Adds VAT refunded to NHS trusts, BBC and ITN in respect of contracted out services for non-business purposes, and adds VAT refunds to DIY housebuilders.

- *Line three* deducts traditional own resources (ie payments of Customs duties and agricultural and sugar levies) and VAT contributions to the European Community, which are included in the net payments to EC institutions line in AME, but excluded from TME.

- *Line four* adds income tax credits which score as public expenditure under national accounting conventions. These tax credits include Mortgage Interest Relief, Life Assurance Premium Relief, and (from 1999–2000) Working Families' Tax Credit and Disabled Persons' Tax Credit. They do not include the Childrens' Tax Credit announced in this Budget, which will not score as public expenditure in the national accounts.

- *Line five* includes the Valuation Office, Financial Services Authority and Redundancy Payments Scheme.

- *Line six* shows adjustments to move to a national accounts basis for scoring public corporations' current and capital spending; adds capital expenditure and debt interest payments outside the public sector; and removes capital grants from general government.

- *Line seven* deducts public sector capital transfer receipts from the private sector, which are netted off in Total Managed Expenditure.

- *Line eight* removes intra-public sector debt interest and dividend payments and receipts which are included elsewhere in Departmental Expenditure Limits and Annually Managed Expenditure.

- *Line nine* deducts those financial transactions which are scored in Departmental Expenditure Limits and Annually Managed Expenditure.

- *Line ten* shows other adjustments and include, amongst others, the deduction of grants paid to local authorities by non-departmental public bodies classified to the central government sector and the inclusion of utilities levies netted off in Departmental Expenditure Limits.

DEBT AND WEALTH

Public sector net debt is approximately the stock analogue of the net cash requirement. It measures the public sector's financial liabilities to the private sector and abroad, net of short-term financial assets such as bank deposits and foreign exchange reserves.

General government gross debt is the measure of debt used in the European Union's excessive deficits procedure. As a general government measure, it excludes the debt of public corporations. It measures general government's total financial liabilities before netting off short-term financial assets.

Public sector net wealth represents the public sector's overall net balance sheet position. It is equal to the sum of the public sector's tangible and financial assets less its financial liabilities at market value. The estimates of tangible assets are subject to wide margins of error, because they depend on broad assumptions, for example about asset lives, which may not be appropriate in all cases. The introduction of resource accounting for central government departments will lead to an improvement in data quality, as audited information compiled from detailed asset registers becomes available.

Departmental Groupings

Title	Departments included	Title	Departments included
Defence	Ministry of Defence	DETR – Local Government and Regional Policy	Department of the Environment, Transport and the Regions – mainly block and transitional grants to English local authorities
Foreign Office	Foreign and Commonwealth Office	Home Office	Home Office Charity Commission
Department for International Development	Department for International Development	Lord Chancellor's and Law Officers' Departments	Lord Chancellor's Department Crown Prosecution, Service Northern Ireland Court Service Public Record Office Serious Fraud Office Treasury Solicitor's Department HM Land Registry
Agriculture, Fisheries and Food	Ministry of Agriculture, Fisheries and Food. The Intervention Board	Education and Employment	Department for Education and Employment Office for Standards in Education
Trade and Industry – Programmes	Department of Trade and Industry Office of Electricity Regulation Office of Fair Trading Office of Gas Supply Office of Telecommunications	Department for Culture, Media and Sport	Department for Culture, Media and Sport Office of the National Lottery
Trade and Industry – Nationalised Industries	British Coal British Shipbuilders British Energy (privatised '96) Magnox Electric Nuclear Electric Post Office British Nuclear Fuels Limited	Health	Department of Health
Export Credits Guarantee Department	Export Credits Guarantee Department	Social Security	Department of Social Security
DETR	Department of the Environment, Transport and the Regions – Transport	Scotland	Scottish Office Forestry Commission General Register Office

	Office of Passenger Rail Franchising Office of the Rail Regulator Department of the Environment, Transport and the Regions – Housing Department of the Environment, Transport and the Regions – Other Environmental Services Office of Water Services Ordnance Survey PSA Services Health and Safety Commission		(Scotland) Scottish Courts Administration Scottish Records Office Registers of Scotland Crown Office, Scotland and Lord Advocate's Department
Wales	Welsh Office Office of Her Majesty's Chief Inspector of Schools in Wales	Northern Ireland	Northern Ireland Office and departments
Chancellor's Departments	HM Treasury Office for National Statistics Crown Estate Office National Savings Government Actuary's Department HM Customs and Excise Inland Revenue National Investment and Loans Office Registry of Friendly Societies Royal Mint Paymaster General's Office	Cabinet Office	Office of Public Service Central Office of Information Cabinet Office House of Commons House of Lords National Audit Office The Office of the Parliamentary Commissioner for Administration and Health Service Commissioners Privy Council Office Property Advisors to the Civil Estate
European Communities	Net payments to European Union institutions		

LIST OF ABBREVIATIONS

ACT	Advance Corporation Tax
AEF	Aggregate External Finance
AME	Annually Managed Expenditure
APAs	Advanced Pricing Arrangements
BEAT	Business Education Action Team
CAT	Charges Access Terms
CBI	Confederation of British industry
CED	Consumers' Expenditure Deflator
CFCs	Controlled Foreign Companies
CGT	Capital Gains Tax
CO2	Carbon Dioxide
CSR	Comprehensive Spending Review
DEL	Departmental Expenditure Limits
DETR	Department of the Environment, Transport and Regions
DfEE	Department for Education and Environment
DPTC	Disabled Person's Tax Credit
DTI	Department of Trade and Industry
EFSR	Economic and Fiscal Strategy Report
EIS	Enterprise Investment scheme
EMU	European Monetary Union
EU	European Union
FSA	Financial Services Authority
FSBR	Financial Statement and Budget Report
G5	Major five industrial countries comprising: France, Germany, Japan, UK and US
G7	Major seven industrial countries comprising: Canada, France, Germany, Italy, Japan, UK and US
GDP	Gross Domestic Product
GEFCO	Guaranteed Export Finance Corporation
GSI	Government Secure Intranet
HICP	Harmonised Index of Consumer Prices
ILA	Individual Learning Account
ILO	International Labour Organisation
IMF	International Monetary Fund

IS	Income Support
ISA	Individual Savings Account
IT	Information Technology
LASFE	Local Authority Self-Financed Expenditure
LFS	Labour Force Survey
LNCs	Learning Network Centres
MAPA	Members' Agent's Pooling Arrangements
MCA	Married Couple's Allowance
MIPs	Mortgage Interest Payments
MPC	Monetary Policy Committee
MtC	Million Tonnes of Carbon
NAIRU	Non-Accelerating Inflation Rate of Unemployment
NAO	National Audit Office
NAQS	National Air Quality Strategy
NFCs	Non- Financial Corporations
NHS	National Health Service
NICs	National Insurance Contributions
NIESR	National Institute of Social and Economic Research
NMW	National Minimum Wage
NOx	Nitrogen Oxides
OECD	Organisation for Economic Cooperation and Development
OEICs	Open-Ended Investment Companies
ONS	Office for National Statistics
PAYE	Pay As You Earn
PBR	Pre-Budget Report
PFI	Private Finance Initiative
PPI	Pooled Pension Investment
PRP	Profit Related Pay
PRT	Petroleum Revenue Tax
PSAs	Public Service Agreements
PSNB	Public Sector Net Borrowing
RAB	Resource Accounting and Budgeting
R&D	Research and Development
RDAs	Regional Development Agencies
RPI	Retail Prices Index
RPIX	Retail Prices Index excluding mortgage interest payments
SBS	Small Business Service

SDDS	Special Data Dissemination Standard
SDRT	Stamp Duty Rates and Threshold
SERPs	State Earnings Related Pensions
SME	Small and medium-sized enterprise
SSP	State Second Pension
TFP	Total Factor Productivity
TME	Total Managed Expenditure
ULSD	Ultra-Low Sulphur Diesel
UfI	University for Industry
VAT	Value Added Tax
VCT	Venture Capital Trust
VED	Vehicle Excise Duty
WFTC	Working Families Tax Credit
WTAS	Windfall Tax and Associated Spending

LIST OF TABLES

LIST OF CHARTS

Printed in the UK by the Stationery Office Limited
on behalf of the Controller of Her Majesty's Stationery Office
3/99 19585 Job No. 414672